Niccolò Machiavelli

Niccolò Machiavelli

AN INTELLECTUAL BIOGRAPHY

Corrado Vivanti

Translated by Simon MacMichael

PRINCETON UNIVERSITY PRESS

Princeton & Oxford

LIBRARY OF CONGRESS CATALOGING-IN-PUBLICATION DATA
Vivanti, Corrado.
  [Niccolò Machiavelli. English]
  Niccolo Machiavelli : an intellectual biography / Corrado Vivanti ;
translated by Simon MacMichael.
      pages cm
  Includes bibliographical references and index.
  ISBN 978-0-691-15101-4 (hardcover : acid-free paper) 1. Machiavelli,
Niccolò, 1469-1527. 2. Intellectuals—Italy—Florence—Biography.
3. Statesmen—Italy—Florence—Biography. 4. Florence (Italy)—
Intellectual life—16th century. 5. Florence (Italy)—Politics and
government—1421-1737. I. Title.
  DG738.14.M2V3813 2013   320.1092—dc23   [B]   2012047891

British Library Cataloging-in-Publication Data is available

The translation of this book has been funded by SEPS—Segretariato Europeo
  per le Pubblicazioni Scientifiche, Via Val d'Aposa 7, 40123 Bologna, Italy.
  seps@seps.it www.seps.it

S E P S
COMITATO EUROPEO PER LE PUBBLICAZIONI SCIENTIFICHE

This book has been composed in Garamond Pro

Printed on acid-free paper.∞

Printed in the United States of America

10 9 8 7 6 5 4 3 2 1

CONTENTS

PREFACE

The span of years encompassing Machiavelli's life—1469 to 1527—comes across as a time of profound change, overturning the very vision of the world that had dominated until then. The great navigations and voyages of discovery during that period opened up unknown horizons on oceans never before plied, and new lands and new peoples entered the common consciousness. Moreover, the period bridging the fifteenth and sixteenth centuries saw Italy and Europe undergo events that changed the borders and organizations of their states, altering the international balance of power. France, having survived the Hundred Years' War with the English, reestablished its power; the Spanish kings were united under a single crown, which, thanks to the empires conquered on the other side of the Atlantic and the treasures they brought, was able to impose its hegemony on Europe; the Italian states, devastated by the expeditions of the French king Charles VIII, were overwhelmed by wars that threatened almost all of them with the loss of their autonomy. In 1517 the Protestant religious reformation was ignited in Germany and soon spread to other countries, bringing changes in popular beliefs and feelings, but its most dramatic consequences—the Wars of Religion and the offensive of the Catholic Counter-Reformation—would happen only in the years following the third decade of the sixteenth century.

Machiavelli was aware of the transformations that were changing the world and warned of the need to adapt the institutions and rules of political life to them. His duties in the Florentine chancery made him aware of the problems and mechanisms of one Italian state, Florence, and at the same time introduced him to the great issues of European life. Accordingly, the functions he performed in the political life and administration of the republic helped him develop his thoughts and gave them substance and precision. Similarly, his diplomatic activities with the powers on the other side of the Alps allowed him to understand the new relationships between states and the necessity of introducing to Italian life principles and laws conforming to the new reality. Thus, the aim of this book is to gather together the nexus between these activities and Machiavelli's works, which quickly became fundamental to understanding the fortunes of men grouped in political societies. Here I seek to examine the ups and downs of Machiavelli's life and to offer information on his most famous writings, from *The Prince* to *The Mandrake*, from the *Discourses on the First Decade of Titus Livius* to *The Art of War* and *The History of Florence*. As Machiavelli himself stated, his works, which are based on the lessons drawn from ancient events and his experience of modern ones, proposed "doing... the things that I believe will bring benefit common to everyone,"[1] namely a better understanding of the times and the world.

As he himself wrote, Machiavelli was conscious of the risks to which his writings exposed him. In the preface to book 1 of the *Discourses*, he used an analogy in keeping with the times in which he lived, which were rich with accounts of navigations and voyages of discovery: "The envious nature of men" makes it "no less dangerous to find ways and methods that are new," which lead to the search for "seas and lands unknown." But adventures of the spirit attracted him overwhelmingly, and he felt that confronting the problems of political life posed by the changing fortunes and upheavals of the time responded to a moral need of the Italian crisis, which he lived through with an intense, sorrowful passion. Accordingly, even his research fits into that "discovery of the outward world and of man" that Jacob Burckhardt, studying Renaissance civilization, would define as the essential characteristic of the culture of that age.[2] These were years in which religious and political institutions and the very habits of daily existence, as well as the ways of life and thought, changed. The age of the great geographic discoveries was also the age of research directed toward ever-broadening horizons in all fields.

The barriers that were believed to have been placed between nature and human wisdom had been breached, and man followed "virtue and knowledge," as the Ulysses of Dante, a poet very dear to Machiavelli (*Inferno*, canto 26), had urged. The barrier of the Pillars of Hercules fell, as another poet he valued, Luigi Pulci, had foretold; Pulci had declared the existence of peoples and cities in the Antipodes at least a decade and a half before Columbus and Vasco de Gama embarked on their transoceanic expeditions.[3] The great navigations shattered the vision of a terrestrial sphere that prevented voyages and trade due to a torrid heat that impeded not only living in but also crossing the central band of the globe, as an ingrained doctrine had asserted.[4] Ariosto, a friend of Machiavelli, had sung of "new Argonauts, new Tiphyses," who would ply "routes unknown to this day."[5] The opening up of new lands and new skies thanks to new geographic knowledge was a phenomenon that increasingly came to overturn deep-rooted doctrines, and the presence of peoples on continents just discovered on the other side of the ocean put into doubt faith in the universality of the message of Christ and the apostles that, with the Pentecost, would have been spread throughout all inhabited lands, according to the testimony of the Letter to the Romans (10.18): "Their voice has gone out into all the earth." Guicciardini, with subtle irony, recalled this in his *History of Italy*.[6] If for a new conception of the universe, as well as the terrestrial sphere and the *œcumene*—that is, the known inhabited parts of the world—it was necessary to wait until the 1543 publication of Copernicus's *De revolutionibus orbium cælestium* (*On the Revolutions of the Celestial Spheres*), we can nevertheless note the fascination in the comments that the same author made in the preface to the work, revealing that he had "kept [this] hidden" inside him "not merely for nine years" but "for almost four times nine years";[7] even the heliocentric conception of the cosmos, destined to overthrow Ptolemaic theory despite the opposition of the Christian churches, would already have been outlined at the start of the sixteenth century, which, at least in metaphorical terms, could appear to us, according to the prophecies of the previous century, to be the age of "great conjunctions."

Thus, during the years in which a new vision of the world was being outlined and opening up to the consciousness of Europeans, destroying outdated theoretical models, Machiavelli developed an innovative form of political thought.[8] He was impelled to do so by the imposition of the great monarchies that prevailed on the old territorial fragments and that put Italy, then perhaps the most developed country in Europe albeit one governed by potentates incapable of seeing beyond their petty interests, into a succession of crises: The potentates were similar, said King Ferdinand of Naples, to "some small birds of prey, who so strongly desire to catch their victims, as Nature urges them to do, that they do not see above them another larger bird that will kill them."[9]

The Florentine secretary's work finds its space in the exhaustion of the ideas and assumptions that until then had regulated the life of the Christian republic, ideally contemplated as the earthly projection of the Celestial City, where religious, political, and economic ethics became jumbled in a single dominating law. But his writings often contrast with humanistic thought, whose references to obligation, more or less manneristic, were still Christian doctrines and Platonic or Aristotelian principles. Machiavelli considers only reality, and in his writings we never find "authorities" evoked; so, when Vettori quotes him Aristotle's *Politics* to support his view that the Swiss, thanks to their confederate government, cannot become a conquering power, he replies ironically of having no knowledge of "what Aristotle says about states made up of detached pieces," but recalls the difference between the reality of the present time and the period in which the ancient philosopher was writing.[10] The contingent episodes, or, in his own words, "human affairs," always in motion—since they "cannot remain fixed, they must by needs rise or fall"[11]—imposed themselves on his attention and pushed him to examine questions of politics in the light of harsh reality, without any doctrinal screen.[12]

The sole principle governing his judgment, which combined his experience as Florentine secretary with his later thoughts in *The Prince* and the *Discourses*, was the necessity to adapt to the times, according to the needs and the diverse behaviors of people.

That is why his experiences constantly mix with the formulation of his thought, and to understand this it is necessary to be aware of the events of his life. "From the mind of Machiavelli," wrote the great nineteenth-century historian Francesco

De Sanctis, "flows the modern world of the state,"[13] and his writings, considered in the light of the profound upheavals that took place in the corpus of knowledge characterizing his era, configure themselves not only as propositions dictated by the Italian reality of the period but in general as an open teaching for the future.

An author who was highly controversial for his naked realism was naturally destined to come into conflict with the defenders of the doctrines that he himself put up for discussion. After the great period of innovations and discoveries that had opened unknown perspectives to thinkers, the religious reaction of the Counter-Reformation would strike hard against works that, in a variety of fields, had threatened what until then had been considered inescapable values of faith.

The innovation of humanist wisdom, like the achievements of the scientific revolution, was also hit with strong condemnation, including furious attacks on its supporters if they were still alive. Thus the *Index of Prohibited Books*, starting from the first edition under Pope Paul IV, can be read as a list of texts that had contributed to the opening up of thought in a Europe on the threshold of the modern era.[14] Significantly, the first rumblings arrived from Venice, the greatest center of publishing in Italy at the time. Giovambattista Busini, in a letter to the historian Benedetto Varchi, wrote in 1549: "Here it has been forbidden and prohibited to sell any of the works of our Machiavelli, and they want to excommunicate anyone who keeps them in their house." And with foresight, he added: "God help Boccaccio, Dante, and Morgante and Burchiello."[15] If the work of Lucretius risked a similar fate, Erasmus was struck right away, and in 1557 the works of Ariosto, Boiardo, and Folengo were barely saved.

As for Machiavelli's works, in the entire history of political thought we cannot find another example of a flow of ideas so defined by hostility toward an author as is anti-Machiavellianism, which for more than two centuries had followers throughout Europe; nor can we find an example of an author whose work was adulterated to the point of becoming a system of principles at odds, in many aspects, with his true intentions.[16] Suffice it to recall that in the Age of Enlightenment the laborious exegetic work done to overcome the prevailing hostility toward him led to the formulation of an interpretation of *The Prince* as a "snare" intended to commit the Medici to an undertaking so ambitious as to portend their ruin, or else as a knowing denunciation of the rivers of tears and blood that dripped from the sovereigns' scepters.[17] On the other hand we can also view, as a heritage of intentions aimed at dignifying the Florentine secretary's thoughts, recent historiographic interpretations that end up subjecting Machiavelli's writings to a somewhat forced reading. Attempts have often been made to place his thoughts within a particular interpretive mold; in other words, to frame them within an ideology. In one notably prestigious critical school of our times, which is characterized by the work of Pocock,[18] the Florentine secretary was highlighted as the forefather of a flow of thought that expresses convictions and reflections inspired by a republican model, capable of imposing itself across the centuries in countries on both sides of the Atlantic.[19]

On the subject of such an interpretation, we can note how this reading of Machiavelli may have influenced the critical construction formulated from 1928 on by Hans Baron,[20] who defined the Florentine movement of ideas formed toward the end of the fourteenth century during the fight against Gian Galeazzo Visconti and developed in the following century as "civic humanism," precisely for the defense of the *libertas* of the *comune* against the Duke of Milan's tyranny. Disregarding the polemical comments that the author of *The History of*

Florence made on Leonardo Bruni, the politician and thinker whom Baron judged as one of the greatest exponents of that intellectual tendency, and especially the declared aversion expressed toward the oligarchic regime installed in Florence and dominated by the Àlbizzi, the republican idea has often become an interpretive key for Machiavelli's work.

Nowadays, the fact that republican feelings were very much alive in him is not in doubt, and this comes across clearly in various passages in his writings. Suffice it to remember the assertion that "a republic, being able to adapt herself, by means of diversity among her body of citizens, to a diversity of temporal conditions better than a prince can, is of greater duration than a princedom and has good fortune longer" (*Discourses* 3.9). By forcing the meaning of this somewhat, one can interpret "republic" as "*vivere libero*" (living free) and see it therefore extolled with impassioned tones when Machiavelli states that "all cities and provinces that live in freedom anywhere in the world, make very great gains" (ibid. 2.2). However, he expresses his preference in empirical terms, without ever proposing in absolute terms that the republic is the preferred form of government. His realistic mind, his aversion to abstract models, and his sense of the difference "between how men live and how they should live" (*The Prince*, chapter 15) led him to view the world in which he operated with detachment and to understand the variety of needs of human beings and societies. He was well aware of the "great difficulty a people accustomed to living under a prince has later in preserving its liberty, if by any accident it gains it," just as "a corrupt people, if it attains freedom, has the greatest difficulty in keeping itself free" (*Discourses* 1.16 and 17). It would be wrong, however, to propose a single type of government for every occasion. That is why he explained (*Discourses* 1.55) how in provinces where there were "gentlemen" who "command castles and have subjects who obey them," "a kingly hand" was necessary to keep them in order.

In short, someone who maintained that in politics "I must concern myself with the truth of the matter as facts show it rather than with any fanciful notion" and scorned those who had "fancied for themselves republics and principalities that have never been seen or known to exist in reality" (*The Prince*, chapter 15) was certainly not disposed to prefer in an abstract manner one political regime over another. Moreover, this "perfect" state would naturally be in conflict with continuous changes and the political necessity of modifying and adapting to changing times and circumstances. These are principles illustrated in *The Prince* and the *Discourses*, so much so that attempts have been made to explain the composition of *The Prince* with the growing conviction that in a "corrupt society," as was the case with the Italy of his time, a strong power was indispensable to restore its health. But from 1506, in the *Ghiribizzi al Soderino*, Machiavelli observed that "steering along a variety of routes can bring about the same thing and that acting in different ways can bring about the same ends," concluding: "Because times change and the pattern of events differs," even "one man's hopes may turn out as he prayed they would. The man who matches his way of doing things with the conditions of the times is successful."[21] This is a mother idea of his thought, which is repeated and discussed in the great works of his mature years. So in *The Prince* (chapter 25) we read that different outcomes can be observed from the same action, which "results from nothing else than the nature of the times, which is harmonious or not with their procedure," and in the *Discourses* (3.8) he warns that "men in their conduct, and so much the more in their great actions, ought to think of the times and adapt themselves to them."

In the conflict that can happen between the actions of men and the changing times, a space opens within which fortune can act with all its power, overthrowing kings and republics and turning everything upside down like "one of our destructive rivers which, when it is angry, turns the plains into lakes, throws down the trees and the buildings, takes earth from one spot, puts it in another; everyone flees before the flood; everyone yields to its fury and nowhere can repel it." But if men are capable of preparing for the weather "with both embankments and dykes," that is if they are possessed of "strength and wisdom," their "free will" can prevail (*The Prince*, chapter 25). Italy was lacking in this because its princes had thought they could behave as they had done throughout the fifteenth century, when the transalpine states were preoccupied with their own affairs and did not intervene in those of the Italian peninsula; these potentates had not understood the change that the fall of Charles VIII had wrought, which upset the entire situation in the peninsula precisely because of the inadequacy of its systems and the insipience of its rulers. But the "fifteen years while I have been studying the art of the state," as Machiavelli wrote to Vettori on 10 December 1513, had driven him to meditate on the possibility of overcoming this crisis. No longer in a position of acting in political life, from which he had been ousted, he forced himself to show a way out through his thoughts, nourished by the fruit of his experience together with his knowledge of the past.

Machiavelli never lost the hope of finding a remedy for the ills that afflicted Italy; it could be the advent of an exceptional person, such as the one he yearned for in *The Prince*, or a long educational work, which, drawing lessons from Rome in its early centuries, would attempt to create a "virtuoso" people.[22] He illustrated this to his young friends of the Orti Oricellari, and they urged him to write down "all I have learned in the course of my long experience and steady reading in the affairs of the world." In both *The Prince* and the *Discourses*, the elements that compose "all the states, all the dominions" are carefully pondered, but, as we note especially in the *Discourses* (1.18), the comments furnished impose themselves precisely because of their relativism; in political life, an absolute norm cannot be in force because of continuous changes, which need to be evaluated to establish a government capable of keeping the state apparatus secure. This absence of reference to superior and intangible values deeply wounded dogmatic minds, who were ready to condemn Machiavelli's work.

On the other hand, the tenacity with which he pursued the idea that must prevail over everything else, the one for which he was willing to sacrifice everything—namely, to restore Italian corruption to health with a deeply reforming work capable of ensuring the good of the country—seems to us the most dramatic aspect of his personality. His intelligence led him to understand how hopeless was the objective that he proposed; his ironic spirit made him laugh at the material at his disposal, and yet the impassioned empathy that moved him to implore Guicciardini right until the end to "free Italy from long anxiety" continued to torment him; he hoped to find some "gleams . . . for her redemption," to the point of adopting the traits of a civil religion.

I would like to thank Chantal Desjonquères for suggesting that I elaborate upon and expand for her publishing house the introductions to the volumes of *Opere di Machiavelli*, published by Pléiade Einaudi, thereby encouraging me to compose this volume. This book is now published in Italy through the initiative of a longstanding friend who was my pupil in Turin, Carmine Donzelli. I express my thanks to him.

TURIN, JULY 2008

PART I

The Florentine Secretary

A Shadowy Period

THE FIRST HALF OF HIS LIFE

It may seem curious that we are ignorant of almost everything about Machiavelli until 15 June 1498, when, at the age of twenty-nine, he became secretary of the Florentine chancery. It is almost as though his life began only when he entered the service of the city of his birth. He was so deeply linked to Florence that in a letter written in the final months of his life he declared: "I love my native city more than my soul."[1]

The scant information that we do have regarding his youth has reached us thanks to the *Libro di ricordi (Diary)* of his father, Bernardo.[2] The latter was a doctor of law and belonged to a family counted, in previous centuries, among the "middle class, noted families"; they were called upon on a number of occasions to occupy important positions as magistrates of the comune, but then the family fell into decline, especially following the ascent to power of the Medici.[3] From Bernardo's diary we understand that his financial situation was not robust, and the environment in which his son grew up was very modest. Machiavelli himself declared: "I was born poor and I learnt earlier to stint myself rather than to prosper."[4]

At the age of seven, he began to study the basic elements of Latin and at twelve to write in that language. Although he may not have received a refined humanist education,[5] we should not take literally the statements of the historian Paolo Giovio, who wrote that Machiavelli had "no knowledge of Latin, or at least very little."[6] It is scarcely believable that—in the most glorious period of Florentine humanism—an almost unknown young man who was ignorant of the language then used in public affairs and international relations would have been called to fulfill the role of secretary of the second chancery, which was concerned not only with internal matters but also with war and therefore relationships with other states.[7] Instead, Giovio's statements should be interpreted to mean that he considered Machiavelli's knowledge insufficient for composing works in that language, and we should also bear in mind that his encounter with Machiavelli happened when the latter was writing *The History of Florence*. Machiavelli's decision to write the work in Italian, during the years when a lively debate had begun on the vernacular language, may have given rise to a certain disdain on the part of Giovio, who professed he was a historian who always wrote his works in Latin.

It appears, however, that Machiavelli had not learned the Greek language, even though in those times Florence was the chief center in Europe of the new Hellenistic culture, where Guillaume Budé, for example—the humanist who can be said to have introduced the new wisdom to France—perfected his teachings. One can quibble at length on Machiavelli's ignorance of Greek only to be confronted by the fact that he was able to draw on the sixth book of Polybius, which did not yet have a published translation into Latin, when he used it in the *Discourses on the First Decade of Titus Livius*.[8]

In the *Libro di ricordi* we note that Bernardo Machiavelli was an inquisitive reader both of recent works, such as the *Italia illustrata* and the *Decades of History from the Deterioration of the Roman Empire* by Flavio Biondo, and ancient texts, from Cicero to Pliny to Ptolemy.⁹ Thus, on 22 September 1475 he noted having negotiated with the printer Niccolò Alamanno the editing of the index of geographic names contained in Livy's *Decades* and on 5 July 1476 of having kept "as a reward for my efforts" the printed pages of the work.¹⁰ The young Machiavelli therefore had the opportunity to read Livy at an early age, and besides we know from his father that, at seventeen years of age, he had the book rebound in half leather. Perhaps some discussions and hypotheses regarding the *Discourses* would have been clarified if this book had come down to us, or if at least we knew which edition was in Bernardo's possession.

Of the third decade of Machiavelli's life, a period that was decisive for his intellectual development, we have only a few glimmers.¹¹ A codex, transcribed in Machiavelli's hand apparently in this period, was found in the Vatican Library of the *De rerum natura* (*On the Nature of Things*) by Lucretius, the work that had been rediscovered at the start of the fifteenth century in a monastery at San Gallo.¹² It is reasonable to suppose that Machiavelli would not have undertaken such a demanding work without a real interest in this text of the highest poetry; at the same time this text is essential for the knowledge of a branch of Greek philosophy, which he no doubt found congenial, as we are aware from the numerous echoes of Lucretius that we find in his works.

In any event, the studies of his youth must have concentrated principally on the historians and political thinkers of the classical era that recur in his works: Livy himself, Tacitus, Sallust, and, among the Greeks, Plutarch, Polybius, and Xenophon. These are the writers to whom it is permissible to suppose he referred when in 1513 he wrote the famous letter to his friend Francesco Vettori, telling him that he had written *The Prince*:

On the coming of evening, I return to my house and enter my study; and at the door I take off the day's clothing, covered with mud and dust, and put on garments regal and courtly; and reclothed appropriately, I enter the ancient courts of men, where, received by them with affection, I feed on that food which only is mine and which I was born for, where I am not ashamed to speak with them and to ask them the reason for their actions; and they in their kindness answer me; and for four hours of time I do not feel boredom, I forget every trouble, I do not dread poverty, I am not frightened by death; entirely I give myself over to them.[13]

However, the legal texts his father owned were certainly not extraneous to his thoughts; a careful reading of his writings reveals echoes of them on some pages.[14] Although notarial studies were no longer required at that time to be nominated to the Florentine chancery, a juridical training was part of Machiavelli's education.

The Relationship with Savonarola

When Machiavelli entered the chancery of the Republic, Florentine political life was going through a period of agitated transition. Just four years had passed since Piero, the son of Lorenzo the Magnificent, had been ousted in 1494 due to his "tyrannical" behavior and for having handed over some fortresses to France, with republican government restored after sixty years of Medici rule. In the immediate aftermath, the austere Dominican friar Girolamo Savonarola imposed himself, who with his religious and moral rigor seemed to embody the severity of the *florentina libertas*, reestablished after years of concealed seigniorial regime. But the excesses of a strict moral discipline and the conflict with papal Rome, with which the finances of Florence were linked through so many channels, led to the fall of the friar. Condemned to death, on 23 May 1498, in accordance with the excommunication issued by Pope Alexander VI, he was hung and burned in Piazza della Signoria. For the time being, the aristoctratic party appeared to have prevailed, but the "governo largo" (a broad-based government), instituted by Savonarola, was not changed and the Great Council, its principal organ, remained in power.

Machiavelli's entry to the chancery a few days after Savonarola's execution raises some questions. His previous attempt
to accede to that office in February of that year had been unsuccessful, but at that time, although weakened, Savonarola's
supporters had still been dominant. The behavior of Machiavelli toward the Dominican friar is generally seen as decidedly
hostile, and in the nineteenth century the two personalities
were counterposed as emblematic of, on one hand, the persis-
tence of the Middle Ages and, on the other, the new era of the
Renaissance, or, as would also be said, the age of faith and the
age of science.

This judgment is based mostly on the letter that, a few
months before Savonarola's fall, Machiavelli wrote to Ricciardo Becchi, the Florentine ambassador in Rome, who had
asked him for news of "matters here concerning the friar." The
picture Machiavelli drew is a firmly negative one, and at the
end, after having described the latest preachings held in the
church of San Marco, he concluded: "Thus, according to my
judgment, he keeps on working with the times and making his
lies plausible."[1]

Undoubtedly, at that moment, when Savonarola still held
power, Machiavelli's opinion of him was clearly unfavorable;
it would be wrong, however, to judge his view in absolute
terms. It is true that the friar, with a vision that was alien and
contrary to Machiavelli's ideas, conceived of civil society and
the republic itself as being in the service of religion, but his
support of the creation of a "governo largo," in other words a
government extended to a number of fairly elevated citizens,
was viewed favorably by Machiavelli, and in the *Discourses* he
states that Savonarola's writings "show his learning, his prudence, and his mental power."[2]

However, in the summer of 1497, Machiavelli aligned himself against the work of Savonarola, since the latter had vio-

lated a law granting a right of appeal—which the friar himself had supported—in order to prevent five citizens accused of conspiracy from escaping capital punishment. The episode is mentioned in the *First Decennale* (v. 153), the chronicle in verse form of events in Italy between 1494 and 1504; it is also recorded in the *Discourses*, following the passage showing a general appreciation of the friar's writings. Evidently, even after many years, it remained in Machiavelli's memory as a grave political blow from Savonarola; in fact, he wrote that "among other enactments to give the citizens security, he got a law passed permitting appeal to the people from the sentences of the Eight and the Signory in political cases . . . but when, a short time after its confirmation, five citizens condemned to death by the Signory on behalf of the government attempted to appeal, they were not permitted to do so; thus the law was not observed."[3] The deliberate breaking of a law for the benefit of party interests disgusted Machiavelli, who moreover disapproved of the religious fervor that had led the friar to practice a policy of dividing the citizens. As he explained in his letter to Becchi, Savonarola in his preachings "indicated two companies: one which serves under God, namely himself and his followers; the other under the Devil, namely, his opponents."[4] We do not know whether Machiavelli had already fully formulated the idea, subsequently developed in the *Discourses*, that the internal struggles of a city could be advantageous to political life if in the end they resulted in the creation of new statutes and new laws. However, his inclination to pursue a union among citizens manifests itself starting in the early years of his political activity, for example in the attempt—which failed at the time—to bring Alamanno Salviati, the most influential member of the group of optimates, closer to the gonfalonier Pier Soderini. All these reasons explain how, after the execution of Savonarola, the men of the Florentine government were able to consider Machiavelli's opinions as being far removed from those of the Piagnoni, the followers of Savonarola, and therefore choose him as secretary of the second chancery in preference to other, more politically distinguished, candidates.

The Activity in the Chancery

The immediate problem for Florence at the time Machiavelli entered the chancery was the war with Pisa. The ancient maritime republic, conquered by the Florentines in 1406, had declared its liberty in 1494 when Charles VIII entered the city and the French sovereign granted its freedom.[1] Florence had unsuccessfully attempted to take the city back from the king, and then had tried to occupy it again by force; Pisa, however, had resisted and found protection in Venice, which, having sent a garrison, declared war on Florence, managing to penetrate its territory. The threat to Florence was a serious one, all the more so because among the Venetian army there was Piero de' Medici, who could still count on his supporters in Florence, which he had ruled. Thus Florence, which to combat the Pisans had already engaged a renowned condottiere, Paolo Vitelli, sent him to oppose the Venetians, and he managed to halt their progress. The war threatened to exhaust the forces in the field, and the Venetians, who had also made an alliance with Louis XII, the new king of France, who wished to possess the Duchy of Milan, accepted in 1499 the Duke of Ferrara's offer to mediate between the two republics and withdrew their troops. Now Florence could concentrate its forces on Pisa, but the resolution of the conflict with that city would be anything but rapid: the war would last ten more years, contributing greatly to the weakening of the republic, both internally and in its international ambition. In August 1499 Vitelli launched an attack against the rebellious city, which failed disastrously; even when the Florentine militia had opened a large breach in the walls of the city, the mercenary did not manage, or did not wish, to take advantage of the confusion that had overtaken the enemy's defenses, and he withdrew his soldiers. As a result, the Pisans were able reorganize themselves and repulse the Florentines, who, suspecting a betrayal on Vitelli's part, arrested him and cut off his head. Not by chance is the first political writing of Machiavelli concerned with Pisa itself and the necessity to "use force" to bring it back under Florentine control; one of his earliest letters is a tough reply addressed to a Lucchese chancellor, who had accused the Florentines of having killed their mercenary to avoid having to pay him.[2]

Machiavelli's duties were not well defined, or perhaps it would be better to say that the division of work between the first and second chancery had not been well defined. In general terms, it can be said that while the first chancery occupied itself with foreign affairs, the second was principally tasked with internal affairs and the conduct of the war.[3] We know, however, that Machiavelli very soon undertook diplomatic missions as well. Certainly, Marcello Virgilio di Adriano Berti, holder of the post of the first chancery, took precedence, holding the title of chancellor, and alongside that he taught at the Studio Fiorentino. But Machiavelli, the man who would become known as the Florentine secretary, had wide-ranging freedom of action precisely because of the indeterminate nature of his responsibilities, so much so that he was immediately also named secretary of the magistracy responsible for foreign affairs, the Ten of Liberty and Peace.

If the chancellors were no longer the prestigious scholars and men of letters whom they had succeeded to that office, such as Coluccio Salutati, Leonardo Bruni, and Poggio Bracciolini,[4] in that working environment the humanist tradition was still alive and well, so much so that we can establish that Machiavelli had drawn from it cultural influences comparable to those he obtained later in the company of young friends at the Rucellai Palace.[5] It is certain that his activity in the chancery contributed, in some measure that is not easy to define adequately, to his intellectual maturity. The Florentine secretary in fact had the opportunity to express not only his political intelligence but also his talents and his literary tastes in general. The study of the ancients evidently was not an activity he began during the solitude in which he was compelled to live after the fall of the republic in 1512; we have evidence of this in a letter dated 21 October 1502, in which his closest colleague, Biagio Buonaccorsi, communicated to him the difficulty of finding in Florence a copy Machiavelli had requested of Plutarch's *Lives*, and the impatient tone with which he expressed himself leads one to suppose that it was not the first time he had been charged with procuring books that were difficult to find.[6] On the other hand, if the loss of the play *Le Maschere*, written by Machiavelli in those years at the request, it appears, of the same Marcello Virgilio, does not permit us to value the precociousness of his *vis comica*, the assiduous work of his office and the various missions that took him away from Florence did not prevent him from writing the *First Decennale* and the *Capitoli*, which have been likened to Ariosto's *Satires* as a genre of poetry in the Horation mold.

Besides, the very fact that the first work Machiavelli published should be the *First Decennale* and that his earliest thoughts on political and moral character found their expression in the *Capitoli* leads one to think that even in those years he doubted being able to tackle in a piece of vernacular prose matters such as those laid out in verse. Moreover, when in the sonnet written while in prison, "Io ho, Giuliano in gamba un paio di geti" ("I Have, Giuliano, on My Legs a Set of Fetters"), he protested "so the poets are treated!" his greatest known intellectual production was precisely in verse, and undoubtedly he was convinced that it was to that work that he should entrust his fame; he still thought of it in 1517, when he wrote to Lodovico Alamanni to lament that Ariosto had not included him in "the choir of Muses" that joyously welcomed the reciter of *Orlando Furioso* at the end of the poem. It should, however, be noted how we can attribute a maieutic function to the daily activity in the chancery in relation to Machiavelli as a writer of prose: in the exercise of his office he was in fact developing the habit of dealing with the current problems of the Florentine Republic through governmental letters, diplomatic correspondence, and various opportunistic political writings, in which he frequently discussed general issues, formulating ideas and lines of argument that we later find in his great political works. Certainly, for all its intellectual dress, a far-reaching thought was judged possible only if written in a style capable of standing up to a comparison with the classics. "When I consider, then, how much respect is given to antiquity," he observed at the beginning of the *Discourses*, it must have seemed inadequate to him in the early years to write in the common vernacular texts which would be incapable of speaking of the present reality with the depth of argument and perspective that he demanded of himself. Today we can point to the appearance of political judgment in some annotations of the news and diaries of the time,[7] but the true and proper models are rare. Alberti and Palmieri, in their thoughts on family and civil life, had recourse to dialogue in the vernacular, subsequently adopted by Machiavelli in *The Art of War*, but for Poggio and Pontano, "discussing republics" and "to discourse" upon principalities had still been the heritage of the Latin language. Later on, Machiavelli would have Fabrizio Colonna say that "no man without inventiveness was ever great in his profession,"[8] and Machiavelli also became a "great man" by inventing his own stylistic forms that took as their example those used by the authors of the past. But in his early years the conceptual ideation and its translation into a text written in prose were difficult to achieve, whereas poetry offered an expressive form of vast and decorous tradition. If it is true that the comparisons with lyric poems and other compositions in rhyme, adopted, for example, for the *First Decennale*, had been open to question, we should recognize that a language for narration in verse "of a popular nature"—as Ridolfi suggested[9]—did exist, whereas that for a political "discourse" did not. In the private letters that have come down to us, the cordial and jocular tone is striking and prevails in the relationships with his assistants Biagio Buonaccorsi, Agostino Vespucci, cousin of the great explorer, and Andrea di Romolo. Right from the early days of Machiavelli's post as secretary, these men showed their affection for him, which demonstrates that he had organized their work in a manner that transformed his subordinates into friends: they joked freely with him, and when he was far away from Florence sent him missives in which, together with news and matters concerning the chancery—often cloaked in heavy and sometimes scurrilous witticisms—there always resounds the request to receive their letters and the exhortation to return as soon as possible. Thus, Biagio Buonaccorsi, lamenting on 22 August 1500 the prolonged silence of his superior, who was traveling in France, reveals his warm affection, bursting out with "My Machiavelli, a thousand poxes upon you, for you keep us in great anxiety."[10] And at the end of October of that year, Agostino Vespucci, signing off with "Yours very truly . . . in the chancellery,"[11] wrote how welcome Machiavelli's letters were when they arrived, but that he hoped to be able to see him again soon in Florence, since it seemed that the signory had so decided. Everyone in the chancery, he added, had fond memories of the "amusing, witty, and pleasant conversation"[12] with which he lightened their work and cheered them up, and as a result deplored "where that spirit of yours, so eager for riding, wandering and roaming about, has gotten us."[13] Evidently the tasks that led Machiavelli to hasten along the roads of Italy and the countries on the other side of the Alps must have attracted him, for he wanted to discover new horizons, new customs and men from all over the world. In short, what also becomes clear from this correspondence is his cordial and open nature, which we know, for example, from the famous letter to Francesco Vettori dated 10 December 1513, in which he writes of his relationship with the woodcutter, of talking with passersby in front of the hostelry to get "news of their villages," curious to learn "the various tastes and different fancies of men," or of the afternoons when "I sink into vulgarity for the whole day, playing at cricca and at trich-tach" with the host, the butcher, the miller, and two furnace tenders.[14]

The friendly trivialities of this correspondence reveal a climate of intimate complicity and familiar cheerfulness, which must have been a feature of Machiavelli's lively secretariat. "Your letters," another of the secretary's assistants wrote on 23 October 1502, "are most welcome to all, and the jokes and witticisms you write in them make everyone split their sides laughing and give great pleasure."[15] No less joyous must have been the welcome of his friends when Machiavelli returned from his diplomatic missions. From Blois, France, Roberto

Acciaiuoli, who had replaced Machiavelli as ambassador to France, speaks enviously of the friends who would have welcomed him back to Florence: "I seem to see Casa [Filippo Casavecchia] and Francesco [Del Nero] and Luigi [Guicciardini]," he wrote on 7 October 1510, "coming to drag you from your house after your arrival and taking you to a sunny place or to Santa Maria del Fiore to consecrate you and to hear about everything over here."[16]

It certainly seems important to understand better what united this circle of functionaries, around which Machiavelli intended to form—according to a line whose traces we find in the Florentine chancery starting in the previous century—an ensemble of people motivated to support the new structures of the Florentine Republic. This concerned citizens who must have been united through not only their political orientation but also their economic and cultural interests, able to replace the vast client base that the Medici had created.[17]

It is permissible, moreover, to observe that it was not because of his personality that Machiavelli could behave familiarly with his colleagues but because, as a good politician, he warned of the need to gather in the palazzo a group of people who agreed to promote a consensus around the gonfalonier. The solidarity that his assistants expressed toward Machiavelli, the apprehensions and alarms that from time to time resonated in their missives due to the partisan hostility created by the activities of those who had become Soderini's close collaborators, should certainly be considered as sure signs of the cohesion in that group of functionaries. These are pages, therefore, that should be read as evidence of the difficult political maneuver that was being attempted around the gonfalonier. Unfortunately, most of the private letters Machiavelli wrote in these years have been lost; otherwise we might have been able to grasp his intentions from these too.

As regards the nature and therefore the tone of such correspondence, however, it is permissible to suppose that it would not have differed much from his correspondence later on with Vettori, to whom Machiavelli wrote in January 1515:

> Anybody who saw our letters . . . and saw their diversity, would wonder greatly, because he would suppose now that we were grave men, wholly concerned with important matters. . . . But then, turning the page, he would judge that we, the very same persons, were light-minded, inconstant, lascivious, concerned with empty things.[18]

And he concluded with a passage typical of his thought: "This way of proceeding, if to some it may appear censurable, to me seems praise-worthy, because we are imitating Nature, who is variable; and he who imitates her cannot be rebuked."

These are characteristics of Machiavelli that we constantly find in the whole body of his correspondence. If in a letter to Luigi Guicciardini dated 8 December 1509 his account of an ugly erotic adventure has the tone of a novella,[19] even in the letters Machiavelli exchanged a decade or so later with Guicciardini's brother Francesco we note, alongside the serious reflections, the vivaciousness of scenes that elicit a comparison with his most famous play, *The Mandrake*. And something of this humor remains even in the official correspondence.

The Correspondence with Functionaries

of the Domain

Of necessity, the "public" letters have a character and style that are different from those of the private ones, although even in these we find personal tones, demonstrating that many official communications are not just the simple transmission of orders and dispositions of the government. The range of this material (consider that in the first four years alone, 1498–1501, 2,500 signatures by Machiavelli were preserved) has meant that, in contrast to the diplomatic correspondence, the government letters have been published only recently and then only in part.[1] Their interest lies in allowing us to follow his daily activities in the chancery and to observe the close relationship with the functionaries who filled different roles; moreover, they provide detailed knowledge of the various localities under Florentine control and of the needs of their inhabitants. These facts help us understand the way in which Machiavelli tackled the issues arising in the daily life of the republic; thus, when he had to act to put into effect the ordinance that provided for the enlistment of the territory's subjects, he was able to act with expertise and an understanding of diverse individual circumstances.

Right from the earliest missives, the ability to find a solution to disparate issues is evident, and the authority of his tone is striking. "You should have received the letter that commands these crossbowmen to obey," he wrote to the commissar of Pescia, " . . . or rather to have obeyed; if you have not done so, make them do so."[2] But he also saw to their sustenance and arranged that the hosts of the place provide the necessary bread and wine, as well as guaranteeing payment.

When disorder caused by troops who had been stood down broke out in a small *borgo* not far from the area where the war with Pisa was then being waged, he recommended acting fairly, reminding the local commissar "that they are soldiers, and since all soldiers are more liable to do harm than to do some other good deed, it is necessary to use . . . very great prudence." If it was opportune in "many things to dissemble," it was equally necessary to "punish most harshly," behaving "as the time, the manner and the place require";[3] some years later he would write that it was necessary to match one's "way of doing things with the conditions of the times,"[4] a principle—as we will see—that runs through his political works. He also resorts to mannerisms, for example when he delivers to the mayor of Empoli, who for personal reasons had left his position, a harsh "reprimand" in the name of "all those who as good citizens place the good of the homeland above their own comfort, and of those who do not look after it, to save the republic, submit themselves to any danger, even a very grave one."[5] But the imperiousness of the command to the mayor to immediately return to his office reveals the vigor of someone who, in his greatest works, would repeatedly indicate the need to know how to act without prevaricating. This behavior is almost theorized in a letter to the vicar of Pescia, who did not have the courage to punish without having obtained prior authorization a few landowners who had defied the ban on exporting grain, thus contributing to the risk that the besieged Pisa might be replenished. "There are many things that one would always rather see done than to give advice or seek counsel," he reproached him. How could the vicar have had doubts "about being impeded by us, who have written to you several times and so strongly?" Now he had to act quickly "without any respect . . . disregarding any characteristic of the offender."[6]

But in other cases he revealed his teasing spirit to his correspondent, as in May 1501, when the Valentino (Cesare Borgia) was passing through the Florentine domain, and Machiavelli replied to the vicar of Scarperia, a borgo in the Apennines, that the letters the vicar had sent him had exaggerated the situation, making it sound as though the army were encircling the place and threatening it. He explained the situation to him and reassured him ironically: "It is a good thing that this ordered camp and field artillery and other instruments have not come to conquer a land such as this. And even if they had come to you, artillery does not fly, it has to pass the mountains and for certain we must understand, and we will see to its being understood, that it is not necessary to frighten our subjects in that way."[7]

More examples can be given, but what is important is how, through his daily practice in his first months in the Florentine chancery, Machiavelli completed an apprenticeship that enabled him to understand the mechanisms of the republic. Moreover, he said so himself when he wrote of the "fifteen years while I have been studying the art of the state."[8] This expression could bring to mind Burckhardt, who in his *Civilization of the Renaissance in Italy,* about the tyrants of that period, observed that they built their states as works of art. In reality, the meaning of Machiavelli's phrase is entirely different. In a letter to Vettori dated 9 April 1513, he wrote: "Fortune has determined that since I don't know how to talk about the silk business or the wool business or about profits or losses, I must talk about the government; I must either make a vow of silence or discuss that."[9] It is clear, however, that the term "art" has nothing to do with an individual creation corresponding in some way to aesthetic criteria, as in the pages of Burckhardt, but signifies craftsmanship and artisanal activity, which are the arts of wool and silk; in short it is an ongoing activity, carried out day in and day out, such as those we can follow in the documents of the chancery. These documents show us a man of government who can escape our notice if we concentrated solely on political theory or on the envoy to princes and popes. Also his experience in the chancery resulted in his practical realism, which led him to deride in chapter 15 of *The Prince* those who "fancied for themselves republics and principalities that have never been seen or known to exist in reality."[10]

A study of this correspondence demonstrates the vivid reality and complexity of the Florentine territory, and we can catch sight of how a heterogeneous collection of cities, *borghi,* and villages, subject to a great comune with often diverse statutes, was governed. We can also learn how that administration was transforming itself at the start of the modern era. At the same time, we can understand how the Florentine secretary managed to learn at firsthand the mood of the inhabitants and to unravel the relationships that were formed in various places. Precisely because his duties had let him to visit and inspect the various places, he would avail himself of this experience to establish the Florentine ordinance, evaluating the different possibilities of enlisting the inhabitants. Thus, in the report written to illustrate *La cagione dell'Ordinanza* (*The Reason for the Militia*), he explains that he chose to begin with the inhabitants of the countryside near Florence, and not to enlist the inhabitants of the "distretto," or the territory of the domain, judging that such a decision would be imprudent, especially because it concerned places where there were "nidi grossi," or urban centers such as Arezzo, Cortona, Volterra, Pistoia, and so on.[11] In the *Discourses* (2.2) he would write that "of all hard slaveries, the hardest is that subjecting you to a republic; first, because it is more lasting and there is less hope of escape from it; second, because the purpose of a republic is to enfeeble and weaken, in order to increase its own body, all other bodies."[12] In fact, if in general terms the most important subject communities retained the right to administer themselves, the dominant power, Florence, succeeded in controlling their fiscal organization, rules surrounding rationing, the right to hold markets, regulations regarding traffic and highways, and above all that which was the prerogative par excellence of sovereignty, the administration of justice.[13]

Thus the various districts of the domain were often champing at the bit, and right at the beginning of his secretaryship, after Pisa, Machiavelli had seen Pistoia and especially Arezzo and the whole region surrounding Val di Chiana rise in revolt. Not by chance, the writing from these years that most clearly heralds the manner of reasoning of the mature Machiavelli is *On the Method of Dealing with the Rebellious Peoples of Valdichiana*, which also seems to presage the *Discourses* in the way it proceeds from a quotation from Livy to propose to Florence, regarding its domain, a behavior capable of "imitating those who had been masters of the world."[14]

Diplomatic Activity

The missives sent in the course of diplomatic missions also often evince an expressiveness that allows comparisons with Machiavelli's private correspondence or his later works. This is of value in general for the clearly outlined arguments regarding various situations and for the hypotheses aired, but most of all for a vivid reconstruction of the characters he met.

One example worth examining is the portrait Machiavelli drew of Cesare Borgia in his letter of 26 June 1502.[1] At that time, Borgia, the son of Pope Alexander VI, had taken control of the cities of Romagna, occupying them nominally under the authority of the church, and on June 21 he had also taken the Duchy of Urbino, casting out Guidobaldo da Montefeltro. The Florentine signory, concerned about the presence on its borders of this ambitious potentate, who counted among his mercenaries that Vitellozzo Vitelli who had been blamed for the revolt of Arezzo and Val di Chiana, sent to him as ambassador Francesco Soderini, then bishop of Volterra, accompanied by Machiavelli. The first meeting with Cesare Borgia turned out to be a very stormy affair, since the latter demanded nothing less than a change of government in Florence. Machiavelli reported the dramatic encounter, quoting the very words of Borgia, who, "without mincing his words," declared: "I do not like this government [of Florence] and I cannot place my trust in it; it needs to be changed." Then, at the end of the letter, he traced a detached portrait of his character, without hiding his personality:

> This Lord is very splendid and magnificent, and is so spirited at arms that it is no great matter that he seems small; and for the glory and to acquire states he never rests, nor does he know tiredness or danger. He reaches places first so that he can understand the game where it is played out; he endears himself to his soldiers, he has [paid] captains, he is the best man in Italy: all of which makes him victorious and formidable, to which is added perpetual luck.

One characteristic of Machiavelli's writing that gives particular vitality to the letters sent from his diplomatic missions is his use of direct speech in reporting meetings between important people. It is no doubt this peculiarity of his style, capable of describing situations with immediacy, that reveals his political acumen. At the same time we should note how, at the conclusion of his missions, he resorted to a method of communication that Venice would establish as obligatory for its ambassadors: the final report, in which, the task completed, the envoy describes the state of the country, its major institutions, its economic resources, and so on. Machiavelli, for his part, understood the usefulness of writing reports of this type on the affairs of France and Germany. It would also be interesting to read his writings in parallel with those written in the same years by Venetian ambassadors, which are an inexhaustible and valuable resource for learning about the countries and situations of that period, naturally taking into account the differences between the tasks and the opportunities of a special envoy and those of resident representatives. These were the years, let us remember, in which diplomatic relations between European states were undergoing great innovations: the organization and the very concept of the state were at the time being articulated in ever more complex forms and procedures,[2] and precisely because of this the ambassadors needed to know how to perceive with suitable methods the reality of countries to which they had been sent. Thus, the traditional embassies, charged with special missions at specific moments and with clearly defined duties, began to be replaced by permanent ambassadors with much wider long-term duties.[3]

That the first clear signs of these new functions should have come from those in the service of two great trading centers such as Venice and Florence, in an era in which new forms of mercantile capitalism were being developed, reminds us that businessmen always looked for news of their markets and for information on the regions from which the products they traded came and on agents who looked after their interests in far-flung posts. Those ancient customs may have been linked with the duties now assigned to the envoys of political powers, and we find confirmation of this in the painting that Hans Holbein created in 1533, *The Ambassadors*, now hanging in the National Gallery in London. The painting shows objects that may symbolize the activities, now in full development, of diplomatic representatives; these take on increasing importance when the relationships between states and the very idea of politics assumed new aspects, new contents, and new dimensions.[4] Thus we note instruments that may seem extraneous to the daily lives of the two people portrayed, a knight of the order of Saint Michael and a prelate: we see in a prominent position a large celestial globe, a terrestrial globe, a solar quadrant, an astrolabe, a pair of compasses, not to mention a book of calculations for merchants. These objects were essential for those who traveled around the world and lived in foreign lands and who, to carry out their tasks, had to know the nature of those places, the territory, its resources, and the economy of the country. If in the *Discourses* Machiavelli warned that "among the things necessary to a general is the understanding of positions" and cited, for example, Cyrus, who, according to Xenophon, went on hunting expeditions specifically to learn about countries,[5] it is all the more true for an ambassador, in the age of the great voyages and geographic discoveries, to have a broad and up-to-date vision of the world. In line with these requirements is without doubt the counsel Machiavelli provides to Raffaello Girolami in *Advice to Raffaello Girolami*,[6] sent to Spain in 1522, but his missives also show how his information is always precise and given in minute detail; often, as the treatises of the time suggest,[7] they highlight to the signory even unwelcome truths, giving a picture that is as broad and complete as possible of what he has learned.

The Experience of the Early Missions

The first important diplomatic mission—for the opportunity it offered him to gain direct knowledge of a great European power—was entrusted to Machiavelli very early on: in July 1500, together with Francesco della Casa, he was sent to the French court "for the purpose of explaining to his Majesty all that has occurred in the camp before Pisa." The secretary had already been on some secondary missions, to Iacopo d'Appiano, the Lord of Piombino; and Caterina Sforza Riario, Lady of Forlì, to secure troops so that Florence could proceed against the rebellious cities. Now he was sent to Louis XII because he had personally been in the Florentine camp when the assault on Pisa, attempted in that year with the help of French forces, had failed because of the mutinous troops, who had been inadequately resupplied by Florence. He had to give an explanation of what had happened and persuade the king to continue to help without his demanding, however, immediate payment for the expenses already incurred. The mission was anything but easy. Nevertheless, in the letters Machiavelli sent we note his diplomatic abilities and his boldness in matching the powerful minister Georges d'Amboise, archbishop of Rouen. He writes in *The Prince*: "When the Cardinal of Rouen said to me that the Italians know nothing of war, I answered that the French know nothing of politics, because if they knew anything, they would not let the Church attain such strength."[1]

At the root of the dispute was the enterprise of the Valentino, who, under the papal banner, was imposing his own rule on a substantial part of central Italy; even if we do not consider the disaster that in 1512 the church, under Julius II, had caused for Louis XII (and, by extension, Florence), when the Holy League drove the French out of Italy, Machiavelli's biting response was no doubt widely aimed, since in those years the church was becoming particularly powerful in Italy.[2] Thus, in *The Prince* he would point out which of Louis XII's mistakes had "destroyed the lesser powers" and had "increased in Italy the might of one already powerful," in other words, the pope.[3]

Yet the value of this mission in Machiavelli's training lies especially in the first contact he made with France and the conclusion he immediately drew from it: France's strength due to its cohesion and organization. This principle would remain solidly rooted in his political orientation and would induce him always to point toward the French alliance. He sought this in the years of the republic and, later on when in December 1514, with Vettori acting as a go-between, Pope Leo X himself would consult him on the possibility of France's attempting a military enterprise in Italy, which in fact happened the following year with Francis I, and again in the final phase of Machiavelli's life when, by now despairing of the liberty of Italy, he feared Spanish superiority and sought to avert it in any way he could.

Even before the writings specifically dedicated to that kingdom, starting from the *De natura gallorum*, we have evidence of his conviction in the *Discursus de pace inter imperatorem et regem* of 1501,[4] where for the first time he discussed the great issues of international politics. Although he expressed his admiration for Germany and its cities, appreciating their liberty and rectitude, his judgment of the imperial power is from that point onward a negative one, where he notes its weakness and internal divisions, which were made chronic especially by its princes. On the contrary, anyone wishing to profit from the internal disorders, thinking that "the provinces and the barons of France might make a rebellion," "would be greatly deceived." Rather, the king appeared to him "insuperable due to the arrangements of his kingdom." Later, after further missions that had taken him to those countries, in the *Ritracto di cose di Francia* and *the Ritracto delle cose della Magna,*[5] he developed these lines of reasoning and outlined with greater precision the reasons that led him to these judgments. "The crown and the king of France are today stronger, richer, and more powerful than ever before," he observed resolutely at the beginning of the *Ritracto di cose di Francia,* and he highlighted the supremacy that the sovereign had by now obtained over the "barons," who unlike in times past were no longer capable of opposing his policies or of reaching agreements with foreign potentates. Besides, the organization of the kingdom, whether in terms of its armed forces, the country's wealth, the administration of its finances, or the laws in general that governed the monarchy (a subject that he would return to in *The Prince* and the *Discourses*), appeared so stable to him as to lead him to overlook the personality of the sovereign, in contrast to the analysis reserved for Germany. The French political structure was actually not subject to variable circumstances, to the changing nature of ruling princes. However, the weakness of the Holy Roman Empire, notwithstanding the abundance "of men, of riches, and of arms," appeared obvious to him because of its internal divisions, the egotism and arrogance of the princes, the will of the cities to keep their liberty, and the hostility between princes and cities. However, everything was rendered more critical by the nature of Maximilian, whose mercurial character was highlighted by a member of his court:

> The Emperor asks counsel of no one, but all the world advises him; he wants to do everything himself, but does nothing in his own way. And notwithstanding that he never communicates to anyone, of his own accord, the secret designs which he has formed, yet, as their execution makes them known, he is dissuaded from them by the persons he has about him, who draw him off from his original plans. And those two qualities which many persons praise in him, the liberality and facility of his character, are the very qualities that ruin him.[6]

In summary, the internal divisions and therefore the political weakness of Germany seem to be its chief factor for Machiavelli; they are so deeply rooted that even the 1519 election of a sovereign such as Charles V as Holy Roman emperor, with the domains extending through such a large part of the world, did not appear to change his opinion.

Shortly after the legation to France, another opportunity to develop his political thought arose for Machiavelli, as previously mentioned, by his meeting with the Valentino, the son of Pope Alexander VI. Right from the first mission in June 1502, however brief it may have been, Machiavelli had been vividly impressed by the Valentino's personality and had not hidden his admiration in the portrait he drew of him in a letter to the signory.

On another occasion, he had the chance to get to know him better, staying with him from October 1502 until January 1503; he was therefore present during the dramatic episodes of the encounters with the Valentino's disloyal mercenaries.

Machiavelli—who had already had the opportunity to criticize Florence's policy, its continual playing for time and seeking the "middle way"—remained attracted to this resolute and energetic personality. When he traced the Valentino's career in *The Prince* to offer a model of the "new prince," he mentioned how his quick action had brought him success; at the same time he noted the good government that led to the Valentino's appreciation by his subjects in Romagna. On the other hand, the Valentino's action against his rebellious lieutenants had ensured the stability of his power, and on this episode Machiavelli wrote a report to the signory that, in its dramatic curtness, heralded a new piece of writing, *A Description of the Method Used by Duke Valentino in Killing Vitellozzo Vitelli, Oliverotto da Fermo, and Others.*[7]

The "virtù," consisting of the manly gifts of energy and shrewdness, appeared to him to be the chief qualities of this extraordinary personality, and again in 1515 he would write to Francesco Vettori that if he were a new prince, he would always take him as an example of how to operate.[8] The precariousness of human affairs must push those who wish to succeed in political life to seize opportunities, but they also had to know how to create such opportunities, if need be. And this is what Cesare Borgia had done when his mercenaries had plotted against him. The various petty tyrants of central Italy in his pay—Giampaolo Baglioni of Perugia, Vitellozzo Vitelli of Città di Castello, Oliverotto da Fermo, and the Orsini—who felt personally threatened in their possessions after the Valentino had taken control of Romagna and the duchy of Urbino, had met between late September and early October 1502 in the Castello della Magione, near Perugia, with the representatives of the Sienese Pandolfo Petrucci and the Bolognese Giovanni Bentivoglio, and had reached agreement "for the salvation of all and to not be devoured by the dragon one by one."[9]

Thus wrote Baglioni to the chief magistrate of Florence, hoping to attract that city too to the enterprise against the Valentino. Florence, however, refused to unite with the conspirators and sent Machiavelli to the Valentino to confirm the friendship of the republic and to examine the situation.

In his final report, Machiavelli would write of having found Cesare Borgia "full of fear in Imola," but that "his spirits had lifted up with the offer of the Florentines." In truth, the letters sent after that first meeting did not give that impression; yet it is also true that the Florentine envoy, contrary to custom, was received as soon as he arrived, so swiftly that he had to present himself "in my traveling costume."[10] Machiavelli stayed among the duke's retinue for almost three months, and despite the rumors spread to appease the conspirators, guessed at the plan to divide them and to destroy their plot. Nevertheless, even on the night of December 26 he wrote to the signory that it was not clear what Cesare Borgia proposed to do. Five days later, in a few hurriedly written lines, he told the signory:

> At an early hour this morning his Excellency the Duke started with his entire army and came here to Sinigaglia, where all the Orsini and Vitellozzo are. . . . They met his Excellency on his arrival, and escorted him; but so soon as he had entered the place with them at his side, he suddenly turned to his guard and ordered them to seize these men; and having thus made them all prisoners, the place was given up to pillage.[11]

The following day he told of having been called in the late evening to the Valentino, who "and with the most serene air in the world, expressed to me his delight at his success."

In chapter 7 of *The Prince* the events of Sinigaglia come back into the general picture of Cesare Borgia's policy, and

Machiavelli speaks of them in a detached tone, but the report to the signory and *A Description of the Method Used by Duke Valentino in Killing Vitellozzo Vitelli, Oliverotto da Fermo, and Others*, written later, dramatically reveal not only the "virtù" of Valentino but also the inadequacy of the conspirators. He actually paints a squalid picture of them in the letter to the signory:

> They did not all come together, but one after the other; from which one presumes that they were going, not to hold a discussion together, but to their homes, forced to do so by necessity and shame, or rather the good luck of the others and their own bad fortune. Vitellozo [*sic*] came on a mule, unarmed, with a threadbare black coat, worn tightly, and above a black cloak lined with green, one would never have guessed that it was he who twice this year had sent the king of France packing from Italy. His face was pallid and astonished.[12]

Of those men, one can say—as of Giampaolo Baglioni, who was involved in the same plot but escaped the massacre at the time only to fall under the justice of Pope Leo X in 1520 — that they did not know how to be "splendidly wicked" (*Discourses* 1.27).

On the other hand, Machiavelli demonstrated his admiration for Cesare Borgia's ability to create a state and wrote in *The Prince*:

> Having wiped out these leaders, then, and changed their partisans into his friends, the Duke had laid very good foundations for his power, holding all the Romagna along with the Dukedom of Urbino, especially since he believed he had made the Romagna his friend and

gained the support of all those people, through their getting a taste of well-being.[13]

In fact he had managed to transform that "whole province . . . full of thefts, brawls and every sort of excess" into an orderly country. A few months later, however, when it seemed that the Valentino would become master of a large part of Italy, his fortunes plummeted: his father, the pope, died unexpectedly, and he himself fell gravely ill and was unable to control the situation. He could not even profit from the very brief pontificate of Pius III, and the accession to the papal throne of Julius II signified his political end. Kept prisoner in the Vatican, he saw all of his lands occupied. Nor was this the only sudden change in Italy; another reversal of fortune struck the French, who, defeated by the Spanish on the Garigliano, lost the Kingdom of Naples. The entire political structure of the peninsula changed in a few weeks. The man who now asserted himself was the new pope, with his impetuous ways of doing things, which helped him to reconquer the lands owned by the Papal States.

Changes of Fortune and the
Ghiribizzi al Soderino

In this ever-changing rush of events, Machiavelli's writings elaborated a more complex relationship between fate and "virtù." In September 1506 he was sent by the signory "to see his Holiness the Pope," in Rome "or wherever else you may learn that he is to be found."[1] Julius II had gone on an expedition against Giampaolo Baglioni in Perugia and planned one against the Bentivoglio family of Bologna; the secretary joined his retinue. Rather than wearing his pontifical vestments, in these days the pope dressed in the armor with which he would erupt through a breach opened by a cannon in Mirandola. Erasmus, who in November would watch him advance solemnly and in triumph into Bologna, deplored the spectacle offered by this Julius who seemed to him to be "another Julius [Caesar]"—not a vicar of Christ, but a knight's squire. For his part, Machiavelli was amazed by these successes, the result of the rash impetuosness that enabled the pope to conquer Perugia almost unarmed. He was also disgusted, however, by the "cowardice of Giovampagolo," who, certainly not "through goodness or through [a] conscience that held him back"—on account of his criminal nature—"could not or, to put it better, did not dare, when he had a perfect opportunity for it, do a deed for which everybody would have admired his courage," namely, taking his enemy prisoner.[2]

Events in mid-September 1506 prompted Machiavelli to write the *Ghiribizzi al Soderino*; of this letter, only the draft remains to us. In 1969 the rediscovery of Machiavelli's signature allowed this piece of writing to be given a precise date. Whether due to an incorrect reading of the addressee or because of the maturity of the concepts , scholars believed it was written at the time of *The Prince*; in fact it had been written seven years earlier, during his trip in the company of Julius II.[3]

What is clear, in any event, is the consonance between this text, which "outlines the most complete theorization" formulated by Machiavelli during his secretaryship,[4] and his major political works. The crux of this thought is made up of the contrast between the actions of men and the fluctuations of time. Fortune imposes herself as the mistress of worldly events, and changes in terrestrial affairs do not always permit a successful outcome.

But the will, or better still the wisdom, of men is able to bend, if not fortune, then perhaps the influence that the stars exert on destiny; previously, Ptolemy had asserted: "Sapiens dominabitur astris" (The wise man will rule the stars).[5] We can wonder at this hypothesis of a supernatural nature, analogous, moreover, to the one we find in the *Discourses*, where Machiavelli supposes that "it could be that since, as some philosophers hold, the air about us is full of intelligences—and . . . having compassion on men—these spirits warn men with such signs, so they can prepare for resistance."[6] As Lucien Febvre has observed, in the view of men of the sixteenth century the relationship between the natural and the supernatural is a continuous one, and their world is populated by invisible powers, by forces and influences that surround them on all sides and govern their fates.[7] Opinions of this kind rarely appear in Machiavelli's texts; nevertheless, in 1504 he had written to Bartolomeo Vespucci, the son of a notary of the Florentine chancery, who was studying astrology at the University of Padua during the years in which Nicolaus Copernicus was attending that seat of learning, to ask him for confirmation of Ptolemy's opinion: the wise man will command the stars. Vespucci had replied that his opinion was "absolutely correct" and that in fact the ancients maintained "that the wise man himself is able to alter the influences of the stars." Yet, by way of clarification, he added that it was not the case that the stars changed their influence, "[since] no change can happen throughout eternity," but that the wise man, thanks to his learning and his experience, understood when it was necessary to change his own behavior and actions, thereby making the variations of celestial influences secondary.[8]

The events that had taken place in recent times clearly showed the rapid changes in human fortunes, and those who did not know how to protect themselves from them had been overwhelmed. Machiavelli wrote in the *Ghiribizzi* that given "that steering along a variety of routes can bring about the same thing and that acting in different ways can bring about the same end," it was necessary to understand "the reason why different actions are sometimes equally useful and sometimes equally detrimental." And he explained: "I believe that just as Nature has created men with different faces, so she has created them with different intellects and imaginations." However, "Times change and the pattern of events differs," so that "one man's hopes may turn out as he prayed they would. The man who matches his way of doing things with the conditions of the times is successful." As a consequence, "because times and affairs often change—both in general and in particular—and because men change neither their imaginations nor their way of doing things accordingly, it turns out that a man has good fortune at one time and bad fortune at another." In conclusion, "Anyone wise enough to adapt to and understand the times and pattern of events would always have good fortune or would always keep himself from bad fortune," and then it would be true that "the wise man could control the stars and the Fates." But "such wise men do not exist"; therefore "Fortune is fickle, controlling men and keeping them under her yoke."[9] The observation is repeated in almost the same words in *The Prince* (chapter 25): "I believe also that a prince succeeds who adapts his way of proceeding to the nature of the times"; and in the *Discourses* (3.9) we read: "Many times I have observed that the cause of the bad and of the good fortune of men is the way in which their method of working fits the times." The ability to protect oneself from changes in fortune was the most precious attribute of the wise man; Machiavelli formulated this conviction at that time, and all of his political thought would remain rooted in this premise.

Fortune can be conditioned by ability, which can operate according to the times: men's ability to protect themselves depends on their nature . Nevertheless, fortune is the determining force. "Her natural power for all men is too strong," Machiavelli wrote in a chapter in verse, "Tercets on Fortune," once again dedicated to Giovan Battista Soderini, which reprises and develops the opinions in the *Ghiribizzi*. And when in *The Art of War* he criticized the Italian princes, he observed that "since there is little vigor here . . . Fortune rules everything."[10] But in the *Ghiribizzi* he noted in the margin: "To try fortune, who is the friend of youth." He would take up this observation again more fully in chapter 25 of *The Prince:*

As for me, I believe this: it is better to be impetuous than cautious, because Fortune is a woman and it is necessary, in order to keep her under, to cuff and maul her. She more often lets herself be overcome by men using such methods than by those who proceed coldly; therefore always, like a woman, she is the friend of young men, because they are less cautious, more spirited, and with more boldness master her.

The new prince, therefore, to succeed as a liberator, must act like a young man. It was thought that Machiavelli may have made this suggestion because he himself was animated by this spirit, which sustained him in his darkest moments and encouraged him not to resign himself to his fate, not to give in, and to fight against fortune. His nature or, if we like, his optimism, led him to force matters to achieve positive effects in any way possible. The first goal was to provide a remedy for the weakness of the Republic of Florence, which was hardly conducting itself with distinction because of its inability to subdue the revolt in Pisa.

The Florentine Ordinance

The war against Pisa continued to drag on, and the mutiny of the paid captains certainly did not favor a resolution. In 1504 the gonfalonier embarked on a huge project, one in which perhaps even Leonardo da Vinci collaborated: to create a deviation in the course of the Arno to prevent Pisa from obtaining supplies by sea. The enterprise, which was set in motion and swallowed up seven thousand ducats, turned out to be too arduous and had to be abandoned. Amid this state of affairs, Machiavelli had for some time been meditating on the necessity of reintroducing a military organization, similar to one in the early period of the comune, which had subsequently been suppressed as a result of a variety of events. The issue was about arming the republic with its "own arms," that is organizing enlisted militias within its domains. The idea had already been aired during the years of Savonarola, and it was probably taken up again by Machiavelli in the days of the legation to Rome at the end of 1503, when Florence, occupied on the Pisan front, had been unable to counter the advance of Venice into Romagna, in the lands previously subject to the Valentino. The latter had armed his subjects in Romagna, and it is probable that the memory of this experiment suggested the

appointment of Don Micheletto Corella, a notorious lieutenant of Cesare Borgia, as captain of the new Florentine militia.[1]
In the course of the mission to Rome, Machiavelli must have
spoken of it to the brother of the gonfalonier, Cardinal Francesco Soderini, who was the godparent of one of his children;
this is attested to by the letter of 29 May 1504 addressed to him
by this prelate, who encouraged the ordinance to promote the
arrangements that would permit the establishment of a Florentine militia. This project, however, was immediately opposed
by the optimates, who feared that the gonfalonier would use
the city's own arms to seize power, and Machiavelli must have
feared that Soderini might have "cooled off" to the idea until
the cardinal, at the end of October, gave him renewed courage, suggesting that his brother had given that impression only
"to take away the opportunity from those who want to speak
and do ill."[2]

Machiavelli threw himself passionately into this undertaking. Not only did he work on it in the chancery, but he also
dedicated his literary efforts to it. His first piece of writing
destined to be published was from this period: *The First Decennale*, a poem in *terza rima* (three-line stanzas), which narrates the events in Italy from 1494 to 1504. Coming from a
government employee, it is decidedly out of the ordinary; an
astute critic has noted that "if through some absurd hypothesis a Venetian secretary had divulged something similar, he
would certainly not have had time or means to give any further news of himself to the world."[3] In fact, the poem is a history of Italy that is sharply critical not only of the country's
incompetent princes but also of Florence, whose weaknesses
and mistakes are not covered up, and so it performs a precise
political function. The opening reference to "Italian hardships
during those two lustrums that are now just over" shows the
seriousness of the Italian situation and the necessity for Flor-

ence to resort to a remedy capable of putting right the most serious of the "mortal wounds" that afflicted it, the war with Pisa. And the ordinance had to serve this purpose, as he indicates to the Florentines at the end: "The voyage would be easy and short if you would reopen the temple of Mars," that is if they decided to arm themselves. At the same time the reference to "mortal wounds" allowed Machiavelli to insert a warm eulogy to the head of the optimates, Alamanno Salviati, who for the most part had found a remedy for them. In fact, he credited him with having pacified Pistoia and put down the revolt of Arezzo and the Val di Chiana, and especially of having laid the foundations for the constitutional reform that had strengthened the government of the republic, placing at its head a gonfalonier for life in the footsteps of the doge in Venice. In the project of Salviati and the other optimates there was also a proposal to establish a senate made up of aristocrats, which like the Venetian one would have the function of deciding on the most important matters. Pier Soderini, once elected gonfalonier, realized that such a body would remove a large part of his power; therefore not only was he very wary of setting one up but relied on popular assemblies, breaking with the nobles' group. Machiavelli had actually wanted to dedicate the poem to Alamanno Salviati with the intention of bringing him closer to Soderini's policies, but the attempt failed; Salviati refused the homage and proudly opposed the ordinance, which he considered a threat to Florentine liberty. Thus the *Decennale* was published only in 1506, with a generic dedication to the citizens of Florence.

Nevertheless, Machiavelli's military reform was successfully carried out. The secretary dedicated himself actively to its realization, and Giovan Battista Soderini, who knew him well, in the letter to which the *Ghiribizzi* was a reply, wrote that on his return from the mission to Julius II, "we shall see your flash

and hear your thunder at the same time," so sure was he that
his friend would be able speed up the decisions. As Guicciardini wrote in his *History of Florence*, there was a trial of the
new militias, "with the authority of the Signoria, he [Machia-
velli] had our officials in the county districts, and in the Romagna, Casentino, Mugello and in all the most warlike
districts, register the names of those men who seemed most
suited for this service. These men were then given leaders and
made to undergo training on holidays."⁴ The trial went well
and met with public favor; we read in the diary of a Florentine
of that period that on 15 February 1506, "this was thought the
finest thing that had ever been arranged for Florence," the first
review of the new militia.⁵ The success led to the approval of
the provisions of the ordinance, and as Cardinal Soderini
wrote to Machiavelli on 15 December 1506:

> It really seems to us that this militia is a *God-given thing*,
> because it grows every day, notwithstanding malice,
> etc.... We do not see that the city has done anything for
> a long time so honorable and certain as this, if it is used
> properly. The good people must put all their efforts to
> this and not let themselves be led by those who, for other
> purposes, do not love the welfare of that city as much as
> is fitting in this new freedom of hers.⁶

The cutting remark against those who did not wish for the
well-being of the city was directed at the optimates, who continued to oppose the new institution, fearing it to the point
where Bernardo Rucellai deemed it prudent to leave Florence
with his two sons, concerned that Soderini would declare
himself prince. Machiavelli, however, was triumphant, and in
January he was nominated chancellor of the magistracy that
oversaw the militia's affairs, the nine officials of the ordinance.

The new arrangement certainly strengthened the republic, which had been one of the aims of the man who had conceived it. In explaining *La cagione dell'Ordinanza*,[7] Machiavelli had evoked the two essential elements of sovereignty that, according to the constitution of His Imperial Majesty Justinian, should be "armis decorata" and "legibus armata"—endowed with arms and armed with laws. He had in fact begun his writings with the following observation: "Everyone knows that whoever speaks of empire, kingdom, principality, or republic and whoever speaks of men who command, starting from the highest rank and descending to the captain of a brigantine, speaks of justice and arms."

These prerogatives were so little present and operational in the Italian reality as to push him to highlight their indispensability both in *The Prince* (chapter 12) and in the *Discourses* (3.31). The warning he addressed with surprising frankness in *cagione dell'Ordinanza* to those who governed Florence— "You have little justice, and no arms at all"—can be extended to all the Italian states of the period, if that weakness had caused—as he would later observe in *The Art of War*—"great terrors, sudden flights, and astonishing losses."[8] But the relationship between the organization of the states and their defense or, as he would also say, between good laws and good arms, must be especially borne in mind for a republic that had sprung up from the base of the urban *comune*, where there was a deep disparity between the inhabitants. In a state of this type the circle of fully entitled citizens, with the right to participate in official duties and in the government, was very restricted; in those years, which saw the institution of the "widest" government that Florence had witnessed, their numbers did not reach four thousand. All the others, who lived in the same city or in the country surrounding it, were excluded from active political life. Even worse was the condition of the subject cities, which, together with their liberty, had lost the right to govern themselves; from their fiscal management to rationing laws, from norms on traffic and goods to the administration of justice, the dominant power was in a position to impose rules that were often disadvantageous to them.

Precisely in consideration of this state of affairs Machiavelli, as mentioned, made a distinction in the *Ordinance* between three different areas of militia recruitment: city, countryside, and district. The city was for the time being excluded from recruitment, because in an army there are "men who command and men who obey," and there are "men who fight on foot and men who fight on horseback"; Florence had to preserve its supremacy, and to "start from the easiest point," it needed to enroll especially those who would obey and who fought on foot; hence, not the citizens. Also to be excluded were the inhabitants of the "distretto," in other words the subject cities; to arm them would have placed the republic's security in danger, "because the mood of Tuscany is such that once people experience being able to live alone, they no longer want a master." For now the choice was a sensible one, but if the republic had lasted longer, there would have been the contradiction of an army formed of subjects who are not citizens. In *The History of Florence*, Guicciardini, with good reason, observed that it would have been necessary "that some reward be given to those enrolled, so that they would train willingly and serve faithfully."[9] Moreover, if Machiavelli had taken as a model for Florence's "own militia" the army of ancient Rome, which was made up of armed citizens placed under the command of the supreme magistrates of the republic, namely the consuls, then one can believe—as some signs lead us to suppose—that he may have been thinking of "rewarding them," conferring to members of these militia some form of citizenship.

In Machiavelli's governmental letters and missions to the various localities of the domain, we see the Florentine secretary dedicate himself intensively to this activity, and the results are notable, not only for the favorable response it elicited among the population, but also for the success that these soldiers experienced in the final phase of the war against Pisa. The letters that Machiavelli sent to the Dieci also testify to this success, such as the one dated 7 March 1509, in which he writes of the attachment of the infantry to "this enterprise against Pisa"; "they count upon gaining some reputation," and he recommends keeping that group under arms, "for it is a good and handsome company."[10] If in 1512 the clash at Prato and the sack of that city ended with the darkening of this militia's reputation, one must take into account the fact that on that occasion, they found themselves confronted by the Spanish army, which, together with the Swiss, constituted the fiercest army of the time. Meanwhile the most obstinate adversary that the architect of the Florentine militia and naturally Pier Soderini faced was the optimate faction. At the time the latter was seeking diverse ways to provoke a crisis that might undermine the power of the gonfalonier, even at the cost of serious fractures, and the opportunity appears to have presented itself to them in 1507. News arrived that Maximilian I of Hapsburg had decided to come to Italy to have himself crowned emperor by the pope, and to this end he had obtained financial subsidies from the diet meeting at Constance. After the defeat on the Garigliano and the loss of the Kingdom of Naples, France appeared to be less powerful than had been believed, and in Florence, in circles opposed to Soderini, it was thought that aligning the city with the empire would have placed it in conflict with its old ally, weakening the gonfalonier and perhaps leading to his downfall.

Since in the event of Maximilian's arrival in Italy, Florence would have to make a large contribution to him, an ambassador was sent to find out the emperor's intentions and options. Soderini's candidate would have been Machiavelli, but the optimates succeeded in having his nomination rejected. The secretary was embittered by the humiliation he suffered; we have evidence of his resentment both in the letters of consolation addressed to him by friends[11] and in the opening verses of the *Tercets on Ingratitude*, which mention "that sorrow for my afflictions that madly pursues my soul."[12]

Nevertheless, even an embassy composed of Alamanno Salviati and Piero Guicciardini was hampered while waiting for the international situation to become clearer and to see what attitude France would adopt toward Maximilian. The departure of Francesco Vettori, however, was decided upon: the Florentine noble, then aged thirty-three, needed to find out for himself what the emperor's demands were regarding the Florentine contribution; at the same time he had to ascertain the makeup of the imperial army so as to understand its potential for arriving in Italy. It was in fact known that the diet of Constance had been inclined to provide large military forces, but the emperor, wrote Guicciardini, "wanted to wage the campaign himself, so that all the gain would be his. Confident that he would need the aid of the diet because the pope, the Venetians, and the Swiss would surely follow him, he strongly opposed their proposal."[13]

Vettori sent dispatches to Florence that left no doubt about Maximilian's preparations. At first he spoke of fifty thousand men being ready to descend on Italy; then that number was reduced to thirty thousand. In any event, he left no room for doubt over the expedition, and as a result negotiations were set in motion for the payment of the requested contribution. The amount to be advanced, however, caused serious hesitation even in proimperial circles in Florence, and they decided to send a representative who could bring detailed instructions to the ambassador. For this mission, which should have been no more than a transmission of orders, the task was entrusted to Machiavelli, and on 21 December 1507 Vettori was informed that the secretary had left "by way of Geneva," bringing him the new instructions. One might have expected a negative response from the ambassador, since the new representative did not limit himself to giving him the instructions of the signory but stayed with him, almost as if he meant to check up on him. However, Vettori accepted this collaboration with good humor, and soon the relationship between the pair turned into a friendship that would last for the rest of their lives. Nor did Machiavelli hide his opinion of the emperor, which was quite the opposite of that expressed by the ambassador up to that point. Besides, the latter cannot be accused of naïveté; even the Venetian ambassador, Vincenzo Quirini, gave credence to Maximilian's proposals. By contrast, there was the sagacity of Machiavelli, who arrived to evaluate the obstacles facing an expedition in Italy.

First of all, he understood that the military forces were flimsy; due to the meager imperial finances, as many soldiers left the camp as arrived. Machiavelli warned, without sarcasm, that Maximilian's only chance lay in the Italian states' poor condition: "That which raises the most hope in him are two conditions that exist in Italy, which have provided infinite honor to anyone who has invaded it, which are: being completely exposed to rebellions and changes and having inadequate arms; whence are born the miraculous gains and the miraculous losses."[14]

In fact, the imperial expedition was shipwrecked. Machiavelli's view had been correct, as it also was when in the report he drew up at the end of the mission, he described an empire divided by hatred and arguments, which nullified its potential power. He wrote his report in time for delivery the day after his return to Florence, on 17 June 1508, furnishing the Florentine optimates with food for thought.[15]

It would have been difficult for the optimates to convey the suspicion that the observations of someone to whom they had been so opposed might not correspond to reality: the hard lesson of the facts was proof enough. Maximilian, who had counted on the support of the Venetians for his expedition, faced their refusal to let him travel through their territory, and when he had sought to force his way through, had been repulsed by force of arms in a humiliating manner. Some days before the arrival of Machiavelli in Florence, he had been compelled to sign a truce with Venice and France, renouncing for the moment any vain notion of a venture in Italy.

The Venetian Defeat and the Reconquest of Pisa

Imperial weakness would manifest itself again shortly after Maximilian's failed expedition. The end of 1508 saw the formation of the League of Cambrai: the pope, Louis XII, Maximilian, and the king of Spain allied themselves against Venice, the only Italian state to expand its territory in those troubled years. On 14 May 1509 a disastrous maneuver by the Venetian forces had led to their defeat at Agnadello, not far from Cremona,[1] at the hands of the army commanded by the king of France. This was immediately followed by the total loss of the Venetian domains on the mainland. It is unsurprising to find the Republic of Saint Mark overcome by the great powers of Europe; rather, the surprise comes from the sudden disintegration of its domain. Machiavelli would meditate at length on the poor organization of Venice, especially its military arrangements, which were entrusted exclusively to mercenary troops. Agnadello appeared to be proof of the need for the Florentine Ordinance.

Confirmation of this need arrived a few days after the Venetian defeat, with the long yearned-for fall of Pisa. During operations preceding this event, Machiavelli was particularly busy, acting freely on several occasions, to the point of generating complaints from the commissar general, Niccolò Capponi. He also took the initiative to go to Lucca to protest that aid was allowed to pass through on its way to the besieged city, but in this case the government of Florence approved his undertaking. "Your going to Lucca," the Ten wrote to him, "pleased us, and more so the terms used by you: we believe it may have helped something."[2] When the Pisans then sought to negotiate, proposing as an intermediary the lord of Piombino, Machiavelli was sent and, having reached the place, refused any negotiation. With this rebuke, he sought to divide the delegation composed of representatives of city and countryside, and apparently he succeeded. After having given assurances regarding the lives and possessions of the Pisans, because the Florentine government wished only to have "Pisa unrestricted, with all her territory and jurisdiction, the same as before the rebellion," he turned to the representatives of the peasants and derided them for their "simplicity." He warned them that when the Pisan citizens had obtained a certain level of comfort, "they would not want the country people any longer as their companions, but as slaves, and would send them back to their ploughs."[3]

In the final weeks of the siege he continually inspected the battalions created by the ordinance, dispersed through three different camps, so much so that the soldiers ended up acknowledging his authority more than that of the commissars, prompting angry reactions from the latter. Perhaps also because of this, the Ten asked Machiavelli not to tire himself out by running between the various camps but to base himself in one place, Càscina, not far from Pisa. But the secretary refused; he was aware that "that post would expose me to less danger and fatigue, but if I wanted to avoid danger and fatigue, I should not have left Florence." He therefore wished to "remain in the camps to co-operate with the commissaries." If he did not do this, he concluded, "I should not be good for anything, and should die of sheer desperation."[4]

Finally, on May 20 a Pisan delegation asked to negotiate a surrender. The talks, in Florence and Pisa, went on for some days, and Machiavelli was present at all of them. Thus on the final document, the *Submissio Civitatis Pisarum*, signed on June 4, his name appeared immediately after that of Marcello Virgilio, the Florentine chancellor. After fifteen years of war, the rebellious city opened its gates, and the militias of the ordinance entered it in victory. Agostino Vespucci described to Machiavelli the Florentines' rejoicing and paraphrased Ennius's famous verse on Fabius Maximus the Cunctator: "If I did not think that it would make you too proud, I should dare say that you with your battalions accomplished so much good work, in such a way that, not by delaying but by speeding up, you restored the affairs of Florence."[5]

The lengthy military operations laid waste to the Pisan countryside, which would recover with great difficulty. Machiavelli found the lands seized from Venice by the French and imperial forces in an even more wretched condition. The victors met with hostility from the local population, which rose up against the occupiers almost everywhere. Maximilian, after occupying Padua and Treviso, was immediately driven out by their insurgent populations and was even compelled to abandon the siege of Padua. The straitened financial circumstances he found himself in were putting his army at risk, and he even asked Florence for help, with the city unable to refuse him the sum of forty thousand ducats, negotiated two years earlier. Machiavelli was charged with the task of negotiating.

In November 1509, he left for Mantua, where he met Isabella d'Este, who ruled the marquessate in place of her husband, Gian Francesco Gonzaga, prisoner of the Venetians. From there he went to the emperor's camp at Verona, from

where he sent to the signory dramatic news of the destruction
of the countryside, for which he held responsible "these Germans . . . and saw and heard innumerable wretched things."[6]
This too made the emperor's situation highly critical, and he
did not seem capable of overcoming the resistance. It is astonishing that because of his dislike of Venice, Machiavelli was
not induced to reflect on the significance of the attachment of
the local populations to the Republic of Saint Mark, even
though he himself informs us of the revolts that were unleashed in its behalf.

"The minds of the country people," he wrote from Verona on 26 November 1509,

are filled with a desire for death and vengeance, and they
have become more obstinate against the enemies of the
Venetians than ever the Jews were against the Romans;
and it happens almost daily that some one of them that
is taken prisoner, allows himself to be killed rather than
disown the name of Venetian. . . . Thus, all things considered, it would seem impossible that these sovereigns
[Maximilian and Louis XII] should be able to hold this
country as long as these peasants live.[7]

All around him, Machiavelli saw nothing but desolation, in
which—as he wrote in the *Tercets on Ambition* at the end of
1509, while he was on a mission to Maximilian—Italy "now . . .
lives, if it is life to live in tears," and there one saw only "people
thunderstruck and bewildered" who lamented their "wealth
ravaged and scattered."[8] A new element was added to his
thought: "discipline," in its broadest sense, such as the civil
and military training of a people who "in times gone by made
Italy flourish and [conquer] the world from end to end"; but

"Sloth" had brought it to ruin. The sight of lands fallen prey to foreign armies led him to meditate on the governing forces in political life: the fluctuations in fortunes over time could also arise from the fact that human nature, because of ambition, was incapable of safeguarding against itself. And ambition was so much more dangerous if it resulted from the egotistical goals of private individuals. Thus his concerns for the fate of Florence crept into his thoughts on the Venetian crisis, and the optimates still presented a threat to the life of the republic.

As a result he strove to mend his relationship with their most influential representative. In the concluding months of the war against Pisa, sent on a mission to the camp of the Florentine forces, he had managed to get closer to Alamanno Salviati, one of three commissars of the army. He had also profited from the fellowship that arose during that dramatic experience to renew a cordial relationship, and the ensuing correspondence between the two shows their lasting friendly rapport. At the end of September Machiavelli wrote a letter to the optimates' representative where he told him of the imperial siege of Padua, and dwelled at length on an original analysis of the situation, stating in conclusion that there was nothing to fear from the emperor. His respectful tone did not hide a tacit invitation to Salviati not to delude himself that the league's victory over Venice might lead to an imperial triumph that could change the international picture. Rather, he seemed to suggest, in a situation in flux such as the one where the relationships between the victors over Venice had become critical, even the optimates should cooperate to strengthen the Florentine Republic. In his reply of October 4, Salviati showed his appreciation of the letter he had received, which he proposed to show "to Their Lordships the Condottieri and the Consuls . . . and it was very highly praised by all." He stated that he was unable to express an opinion regarding what Machiavelli had written to him, since he was too poorly informed of the episodes; nevertheless, demonstrating his faith in the action that the secretary would take, he seemed to adapt himself to his advice. He closed the letter in jocular terms: he declared himself "monkish," in other words a supporter of Savonarola, and as a result thought to "look to God" for the fate of Florence, but made fun of his correspondent, who he imagined would not be very satisfied with his behavior, "not because I believe you are lacking in faith, but I am sure that you do not have much [faith] left."[9] This joke also reveals the cordial relationship that had been reestablished between the two, and the opportunity for the gonfalonier's government not to have to continue to clash with this powerful person. Unfortunately, in March 1510 Salviati was struck by malarial fevers and died, not yet aged fifty, in Pisa, where he had been appointed captain. None of the other optimates had his authority or intelligence. The verses with which Machiavelli—having recalled the disasters of the wars in the lands the Venetians had lost—concludes the *Tercets on Ambition* are therefore justified:

> Alas! For while with another's affliction I am
>   keeping my thought engaged and my speech, I
>   am weighed down with greater fear.
> I see Ambition, with that swarm which Heaven at
>   the world's beginning allotted her, flying over
>   the Tuscan mountains;
> and already she has scattered so many sparks
>   among those people swollen with envy that she
>   will burn their towns and their farmsteads if
>   grace or better government does not bring her to
>   nought.[10]

This final verse of the poem seems to adhere more to a formula of manners than to be a real conviction. Until 1512, those "so many sparks," rather than being extinguished, would be reignited and scattered widely by the rapid changes in the international situation.

The End of the Republic and the Return
of the Medici

Machiavelli had realized that, in the prolongation of the war
in the Veneto, the relationship between the emperor and the
king of France was deteriorating. Regardless of Maximilian's
policy never to let information leak out, the secretary's concerns are transparent in both his official missives and in his
private correspondence. In Verona people had begun "to talk
very disparagingly about the French; say that the Emperor will
make terms with the Venetians, and drive the French out of
Italy."[1]

If for now events had not reached that point, there was nevertheless the radical change of position on the part of Julius II,
who, with Venice having yielded, turned on France with his
usual impetuousness. He was also seeking an alliance between
the king of Spain and the emperor and launched his campaign
of war with the cry "Out with the barbarians!" The power of
the French now seemed to him to present an obstacle to any
expansion of the Papal States: with the possession of the
Duchy of Milan, the domain of Genoa, and the solid alliance
with the Duchy of Ferrara and with Florence, Louis XII had

no one to oppose him in northern Italy, since Maximilian's weakness had become evident in the difficulties he had encountered in his attempt to occupy Venice's subject cities on the mainland. Julius II, "fatal instrument of the misfortunes of Italy," as Guicciardini would write,[2] did not hesitate to make peace with Venice and, to obtain the aid of Ferdinand of Aragon, recognized his conquest of the Kingdom of Naples, conceding it to him in fief. Moreover, he succeeded in tying himself to the Swiss with a five-year alliance, obtaining from them the provision of an army of six thousand men and the guarantee that they would not permit other powers to enlist soldiers in the confederation. France thus found itself deprived of what until then had been its greatest infantry force.

Florence appreciated the danger that threatened it due to the breaking of the treaty between France and the pope. As a result, in June 1510 Soderini sent Machiavelli to Louis XII with the aim to persuade him that, to secure the situation in Italy, two conditions would take precedence: "The one to preserve friendly relations with the Emperor, and the other to continue to harass and enfeeble the Venetians." Next it was important "to make every effort not to break with the Pope, for," as the gonfalonier observed with much good sense, "even if a Pope's friendship is of no great value, yet his enmity may do great harm."[3] For Florence, a break with France was unthinkable due to the many interests that linked it to that kingdom, but a clash with the pope would prove to be just as dangerous, if not more so. Despite raising many objections and protesting to the Florentine envoy, Louis XII seemed willing to negotiate and proposed that Florence mediate an accord with the pope. But Julius II proved intractable. He wished to conquer Ferrara, taking it away from the Este, who were allied with France, and wanted to break the French domination of Genoa.

Most of all Julius II was furious at Louis XII's plans to convene an assembly;[4] as for the peace proposals that the Florentine ambassadors presented, the pope lashed out with threats against their city. When an envoy from the Duke of Savoy arrived in Rome with similar peace proposals, the pontiff—as the Ten told Machiavelli on September 2—"had him put in prison and gave him rope." The situation appeared very serious to Machiavelli because while the pope was heading resolutely toward a clash, Louis XII seemed indecisive and neglectful of affairs of state. The death of the cardinal of Rouen, an energetic minister who had an offensive thrust on French policy, had opened a void that no councillor appeared ready to fill. If anything, a strange game was being played out between the parties: while the king dedicated himself to the Gallic Council of Tours, which that general, the archbishop of Rouen, was to have prepared and even went so far as to hold forth on matters of theology, Julius II rearmed and readied for acts of war against Ferrara and, by sea, Genoa. Placing himself at the head of his army, he conquered Modena and attacked Mirandola, which he entered while wearing armor through a breach that a cannon shot had opened in the walls.

Machiavelli, having returned from France, actively dedicated himself to Florence's military preparations. To this end he sought to organize the cavalry and, at the end of 1510, went to Val di Chiana to prepare for the first enlistments of light cavalry. The signory also tasked him with supervising the construction of the citadel of Pisa, entrusted to the architect Giuliano da Sangallo, who had specialized in fortifications after following Charles VIII to France. But most of all, Machiavelli was preoccupied with rearming Florence and in those months wrote a discourse on horseback militia, which he had started to organize; on 27 April 1511 he succeeded in carrying out the first review of one hundred cavalry in Florence.

For a time it seemed as though Julius II's adventure had taken a turn for the worse. The French intervention in aid of the Duke of Ferrara was crowned with success: Bologna was seized from the pope, and Louis XII's army, under the command of Gian Jacopo Trivulzio, was able to invade the Papal States. But inexplicably the king ordered his captain to return to Milan, showing respect for the pope with the declaration that he did not want to invade his states; at the same time, however, he did not dismiss a proposal to convene a council and in January 1511 requested that Florence make available the city of Pisa so that he could bring together the ecclesiastical council there in September, with even Maximilian apparently wishing to participate. Julius II replied on July 18, calling the convocation of a council at the Lateran for Easter 1512 (April 11).

While in France this agitation over plans to convene gave rise to debates and thoughts of religious reform animated by a Christian humanism rich in innovative ferments,[5] in the city of Savonarola and in Italy in general there was no particular interest in these plans, which could also involve important innovations in the church. The Florentine government sought, as far as it could, to avoid having the council take place in Pisa because of the difficult situation of the city after long years of war with Florence. It hoped that the emperor's interests would prevail in convening it in a city where he could participate in person (Trento and Verona had been mentioned), but the French did not deviate from the idea of holding it in the Tuscan city.

In August the news that Julius II had fallen seriously ill led Cardinal Soderini, brother of the Florentine gonfalonier, to feel certain of the victory of the "French party"; he therefore sent to Milan his own representative to communicate to the prelates convened for the council the Florentine decision to concede Pisa. But unexpectedly, in early September, the pope got better and railed furiously against Florence, threatening it with an interdict and reprisals against the large Florentine colony in Rome. Machiavelli, who until then had been on minor missions, received a new order: to intercept those prelates who were rebelling against the pope and who had started their journey from Milan to Pisa, to stop them on their way, and to dissuade them from continuing with their journey; then he was told to head to Milan to explain to the French governor the difficult situation Florence found itself in as a result of the pope's threats, made more serious by the king of Spain, Ferdinand the Catholic, who was willing to lend his support. Finally, he had to go to the French court, then at Blois, to negotiate with Louis XII. According to the instructions he received, the most desirable outcome would have been "to make the king deviate from this idea of the council and make him disposed toward peace"; otherwise he needed to seek to have the council held elsewhere, but if even this were not possible, at least to have it deferred for several months to allow Florence to reinforce its defenses, in the hope that "in this way something good may happen." In fact this would be the sole concession that Machiavelli would obtain from Louis XII: the council would meet in November. But on October 22 Julius II interdicted Florence.

On his return from this mission, Machiavelli had hardly set foot in Florence on November 2 when the signory immediately sent him to Pisa, to persuade the clergy gathered there to transfer their meeting elsewhere. The council turned out to be a total failure; only twelve prelates, among them archbishops and bishops, were present, and four of those, who had enjoyed the title of cardinal, had been demoted by the pope. The regular clergy were not represented except for eight abbots, and otherwise there were a dozen theologians and canon lawyers.

At Pisa the local clergy proved themselves loyal to Rome and held hostage, to the extent that they could, what would be pejoratively called a "conciliabolo," that is, secret meeting. As a result too of the evident hostility of the population, Machiavelli succeeded in obtaining the transfer of the council, which—after having held an opening session on November 5 and another on the seventh—moved to Milan.

Now, however, nothing could calm down Julius II, who from October on was in league with Spain and Venice against France and was determined to overthrow its ally in Italy, Florence. Here, confusion was as great as it could have been, fed by fear and the internal divisions caused by the noble families who were ever more hostile to Soderini's government. The choice between fidelity to the old alliance and acquiescence to the demands of the league, which was asking the Florentines to join and become part of it, remained perpetually in suspense, and from many quarters neutrality was highlighted as the best solution: some because they hoped to avoid the risks of a conflict between such powerful states, others because not holding for France meant a renunciation of the gonfalonier. Precisely these behaviors may have dictated to Machiavelli the bitter observations in the *Discourses*: "Not less injurious than hesitating decisions are slow and late ones, especially those that have to be made in favor of some friend."[6] The two factions that were active in Florence in those months from 1511 into 1512, while referred to in the text in other circumstances, were undoubtedly pertinent to that situation and were branded in contemptuous terms: similar decisions "come either from weakness in courage and in forces or from the wickedness of those who decide, for, moved by selfish passion to attempt to ruin the state or to carry out some other desire of theirs, they do not allow the decision to be made but impede it and oppose it."

Not even the French victory at Ravenna on 11 April 1512 swayed those who hesitated, all the more so because this success was not followed through by the army of Louis XII, partly due to the ineptitude of the commanders succeeding Gaston of Foix, who had fallen in that battle. Now the Swiss and the Germans too joined the league commanded by the pope; the very soldiers of the confederation would conquer the Duchy of Milan the following year after the battle of Novara (6 June 1513). In the meantime, however, the Florentine Republic had already fallen.

A diet of the league, held in June at Mantua, decided to restore the Sforza in Milan and the Medici in Florence. The viceroy of Naples, Ramón de Cardona, was tasked with leading the army, which needed to move against Tuscany. In the first six months of 1512, Machiavelli dedicated himself almost exclusively to the organization of the militia, especially the light cavalry, but his battalions could do very little against the fierce enemy forces, and besides, they moved against them only once they had entered Florentine territory. Machiavelli himself narrated the fall of the republic in a "letter to a lady" who is not named, but who is thought to have been the marchesa of Mantua, Isabella d'Este.[7]

"The hostile soldiers being already only a day's journey from our boundaries, all the city was at once disturbed by this sudden and almost unexpected attack," Machiavelli wrote to her. In an effort to distract Cardona from the assault on Florence, troops were sent from the Florentine part of Romagna, to threaten him from behind. "But the Viceroy, whose intention was not to attack the towns but to come to Florence to change the government, hoping with the aid of the party to do it easily," continued his advance. Before assaulting the city of Prato, the viceroy sent ambassadors to Florence to declare to the signory that "they did not come into this province as enemies and did not intend to make any change in the liberty of the city"; he wished only that the republic should join the league against France, but knowing that Soderini was "a partisan of the French," he asked that he should be removed from the position of gonfalonier and that "the people of Florence would choose another gonfalonier as they wished." The proposal was rejected, but Cardona, after meeting with strong resistance before Prato, sent another ambassador, asking Florence for a large sum of money and, for the reentry of the Medici, "he would turn over their case to His Catholic Majesty." As was its habit, Florence, instead of replying, began to prevaricate, and at that point the Spanish moved ahead with the assault on Prato, took the city, and sacked it ferociously.

"This news caused a great disturbance in Florence," Machiavelli wrote to the lady. Nevertheless Soderini, in exchange for a large amount of money, sought Cardona's retreat without the Spanish demanding the return of the Medici. This proposal was rejected. "Everybody feared that the city would be sacked, on account of the cowardice of our soldiers in Prato. This fear was increased by all the nobility who wished to change the government." In this atmosphere of discomfort and confusion, the palace remained "without guards," and the signory was compelled to release many supporters of the Medici who had been "held . . . many days in the palace." On August 31, they, "along with many others of the most noble citizens," "came armed to the palace, and having seized all the places in order to force the gonfalonier to leave, were persuaded by some citizens not to use violence but to let him go by agreement." Thus Soderini abandoned the city, and the Medici, in agreement with the Spanish viceroy, entered it. The government that was formed, strongly influenced by the optimates, did not satisfy Cardona, who declared that "it was necessary to put the government in the form it had during the lifetime of the Magnificent Lorenzo." While the Florentine leaders were discussing the new regime to be emplaced, the supporters of the Medici, with the help of the soldiers who had entered the city, incited a revolt, took control of the palazzo, and imposed a *governo di balìa*, that is, a government endowed with exceptional powers, which having liquidated what was left of the republic and starting with the Grand Council, issued a law reinstating "the magnificent Medici . . . in all the honors and ranks of their ancestors."

In the new situation, we see Machiavelli remaining faithful, to the extent that he could, to his ideals. Thus, he addressed a letter to the supporters of the Medici, asking them to accept the cooperation of those who had supported Soderini, with the aim of opposing the nobles. It appears that the text was written in early November, when for several days the Florentine situation appeared uncertain due to Julius II's hostility toward Cardinal Giovanni de' Medici, who was the true master of the city. The pope accused him of having allied himself with Ferdinand the Catholic instead of carrying out the orders he had given him and, with the Spanish army now far away, believed that he could promote a government of the optimates. The cardinal succeeded, however, in smoothing over the dispute and certainly took no heed of Machiavelli's advice. The intent of Machiavelli's writing was to show how the Medici should not trust the optimates, who had opposed Soderini and who now launched accusations against him not "to do good to this State, but to enhance their own reputation" and "to pursue their own ends." The interests of the Medici, however, would lie in aligning themselves with those of the people and therefore pit themselves against those who now "prostitute themselves between the people and the Medici" and who viewed Soderini as an enemy and wanted to take from him the position he had with the people; in other words, Machiavelli was accusing the optimates of having deprived the people of their liberty.[8] This reasoning brings to mind pages in *The Prince* and the *Discourses* where Machiavelli states that only a government founded on the people is solid. In this case, however, the government remained ineffectual, also because Cardinal de' Medici used only those optimates whom he could trust. So when in March 1513 he was elected pope, it opened to the Florentines new ways of making a name for themselves via appointments within the papal court and ecclesiastical benefices. In this way, Florence became a kind of Roman protectorate.

PART II

Exile in His Homeland

The Confinement at Sant'Andrea

On 7 November 1512 the new signory created by the Medici removed Machiavelli from the office of secretary, barring him from access to the palace. Between this sad end to the year and the spring of 1513, Machiavelli did not experience just humiliation, bitterness, and worry but also prison and torture as a result of his suspected participation in an anti-Medici conspiracy. At the beginning of March, having "got out of prison amid the universal rejoicing" of the Florentines because of the election to the papacy of Giovanni de' Medici, who took the name of Leo X,[1] he was confined to Sant'Andrea di Percussina, a village in the Florentine countryside, where he had a small family property.

By writing his letters to Francesco Vettori, he managed to pull through the loneliness and the sadness of those days, when his body, and not just his spirit, still felt the effects of his imprisonment. The Florentine patrician, then ambassador to the papal court, had the merit of remembering the old friendship even at that moment. Despite an affectation of protection, he did not manage to procure any real benefit for Machiavelli; he himself admitted: "I am not a man who knows how to help his friends."[2] Although he managed to encourage him with his assiduous correspondence, it was not easy to place the former secretary in a state of good relations with the Medici.

His friend's words comforted Machiavelli, who hastened to reply to him: "Your very friendly letter has made me forget all my past troubles, and though I was more than certain of the love you have for me, this letter has been most pleasing to me."[3]

But to the exhortation to "take heart against this persecution," Machiavelli replied with great dignity: "As to turning my face to resist Fortune, I want you to get this pleasure from my distresses, namely that I have borne them so bravely that I love myself for it and feel that I am stronger than you believed."

He added that he would be very happy to take up his work again, though he was aware of the difficulties: "And if these masters of mine [the Medici] decide not to let me lie on the earth, I shall be glad of it, and believe I shall conduct myself in such a way that they too will have reason to approve. If they decide differently, I'll get on as when I came here, for I was born poor and I learned earlier to stint than prosper."

In reality he hoped to find a way—as he had written to Vettori the day after his liberation—for Leo X to "employ me."[4] Thus, on April 9, he asked Vettori if it might be possible to ask Cardinal Soderini, apparently on good terms again with the Medici, to recommend him to the pope, even if it was not Vettori himself who might interest the Florentine prelate in his case. It was probably in those days, to demonstrate his own willingness, that he composed the *canto carnascialesco*, or carnival song, titled "By the Blessed Spirits," in line with the expectations of the election of the new pontiff. The event had been marked in Florence with celebrations of the peace, which Leo X had favored, in contrast with the warlike feats of his predecessor. And Machiavelli also opened his composition with this theme: "Blessed spirits are we, who from the celestial benches come here to present ourselves on earth," to show men "that our Lord is greatly pleased when arms are laid down and continue unused." There is also the customary reminder of the Turk, of whom it is necessary to be wary because he "grinds his weapons and seems to be all burning with desire to overrun your pleasant fields."[5]

Machiavelli's effort proved fruitless, even though again on April 16, in another letter, he may have revealed that he was suffering from delusions regarding his own opportunities when he asked if "my affair" might be "handled with some skill"; this was precisely what Vettori did not manage to do, as he was hesitating whether to influence Cardinal Soderini and whether the cardinal himself might want to influence the pope. Thus, with the intention perhaps of distracting him, Vettori began to write to him of the relationship between Spain and France, and Machiavelli, realizing the difficulties, played along.

The very tone of their correspondence reveals how much he needed to open up and unburden himself to his friends to break the monotony of the cloistered life that was imposed on him and to return to his true interests. He therefore seized the opportunity to "talk about the government" and tackled the issue of the truce signed by Ferdinand the Catholic with the king of France. It is difficult to understate the fascination of this correspondence, especially when hearing ideas resonate on some pages of *The Prince*.[6]

Vettori wrote to him that the king of Spain, having reached an agreement with Louis XII, had not demonstrated, at the height of his fame, that he was an astute and wise man, "or else ... there is a snake in the grass"; in other words, he thought that there were hidden reasons behind the agreement "and that the king of Spain, the king of France and the emperor are planning to divide this poor Italy up among themselves."

In a subsequent letter, he more fully explained his perplexity at the behavior of Ferdinand, who, having signed the truce, had opened up again to France the possibility of intervening in Italy. If this was his intention, he would have done better, then, to reach an agreement directly with the Duchy of Milan. "France would have received it from him as a favor" and would have an obligation to him. Thus, after putting forward other hypotheses, he repeated that he was convinced "that there must be something else beneath this that is not understood."

Machiavelli did not agree. Though he protested that he did not know what was going on and therefore had to discuss it "in the dark," he did not believe that the truce "hides some great thing which now neither you nor anybody understands." Today one would say that he was refusing to take part in conspiracy theories. In fact, despite being "in the dark," he gave an explanation. To begin with, he described Ferdinando as "more crafty and fortunate than wise" and, after reexamining the episodes of the previous two years, observed how until then that king "without necessity . . . put into danger all his territories, which is a very rash thing in a prince." He recalled the actions of the anti-French league up to the time of the battle of Ravenna, when the Catholic king also risked losing the Kingdom of Naples, "and the kingdom of Castile was tottering under him"; nor could he foresee the decisive help that would come to him from the Swiss and repeated: "So if you will consider that whole action and the handling of those things, you will see in the King of Spain craft and good fortune rather than wisdom or prudence. And when I see a man making a mistake, I suppose he will make a thousand of them."

He highlighted Spain's financial weakness owing to the backwardness of its state apparatus compared with that of

France. Thus, in all of this analysis of Spanish policy, he proceeded with a method analogous to that which he would follow in the third chapter of *The Prince*, in which he criticized the actions of Louis XII, adding some comments on the "new prince" that give us advance notice of his future work.

"I have composed a little work *On Princedoms*"

Machiavelli returned to these matters of European high politics through the duration of the exchange of letters he had with Vettori until August, probing and passionately debating the issues.

At that time various operations were under way: Venice, which had united with Louis XII, was once again having difficulties, and the French, in an attempt to take back Milan and its territory, were defeated at Novara by the Swiss and were attacked on their own soil by the English, victors at the battle of Guinegate. Nevertheless, in the Italian peninsula there was almost a stalemate, and anything could happen.

The panorama that Machiavelli depicted in his letter of August 26, before a three-month interruption in his correspondence with Vettori, provides a picture of the situation in that moment:

> And as to the state of things in the world, I draw this conclusion about them: we are ruled by princes of such a sort that they have, either by nature or by accident, these qualities: we have a Pope who is wise, and therefore serious and cautious; an Emperor [who is] unstable and fickle; a King of France inclined to anger and timid; a King of Spain stingy and avaricious; a King of England

rich, fiery, eager for glory; the Swiss brutal, victorious, and arrogant; we in Italy poor, ambitious, cowardly. (*Works*, 2:922)

Thus he saw a situation that was amenable to various outcomes, but he feared that the defeat of France and the Swiss dominance over the Duchy of Milan placed the entire Italian peninsula at risk. As a result, he concluded that "Italy will owe that to Pope Julius and to those who do not protect us, if protection can be found."

It brings to mind chapter 12 of the first book of the *Discourses*, in which he attributed the division of Italy to the policy of the church. But in that climate of uncertainty the former secretary, accustomed to reflecting on the problems of political life and to taking action, may have felt forced to reorder his thoughts and immediately to write a work concerning the Italian reality. The experience of "present things," based on the "lessons of past things," which he usually pondered in his evening readings, suggested to him "a small work"; with this, he was confident that he would manage to return to his former activities. On 10 December 1513, he wrote to Vettori announcing that he had written *The Prince* and wished to make it available to Giuliano de' Medici, "because I am using up my money, and I cannot remain as I am a long time without becoming despised through poverty" (*Works*, 2:930). Then, to show Vettori how much he felt the necessity to return to work, he added: "There is my wish that our present Medici lords will make use of me, even if they begin by making me roll a stone." Regarding the possibility of returning to political action, he thought, therefore, of Giuliano, the member of the ruling family with whom he had a rapport, as witnessed by two sonnets he wrote when he was still in prison[1] and by the correspondence with Vettori;[2] but also probably because, evoking the experience of the Valentino, creator of a vast state thanks to the support of the pope, he thought that those "gleams . . . for her [Italy's] redemption,"[3] which had flashed a decade or so earlier, could now shine again with new vigor thanks to the support of the only power remaining in Italy, the Holy See. Just as Cesare Borgia had enjoyed freedom of action and was able to count on the support of Pope Alexander VI, now with Leo X sitting on the papal throne, a member of the House of Medici would have similar possibilities. And we know that with the support of Giuliano, the pope, his brother, would have wanted to endow him with a state in Italy.

This was apparently the opportunity; but *The Prince* is certainly not a work of opportunism. Its author appears well aware of the vast body of political literature produced by humanist culture—to some extent the continuation, albeit with other ideal principles, of the literary genre opened by the medieval *Specula principis.*[4] This body of work, however, appeared to him to be a long way from the reality, and in the opening of chapter 15 he underlined the difference between the "many who have written about this" and his intention of focusing on "the truth of the matter as facts show it," rather than "any fanciful notion." And to be clear, he added sarcastically, "Many have fancied for themselves republics and principalities that have never been seen or known to exist in reality," to the point of discussing not "how men live" but "how men should live." As a result, the search for antecedents and precursors of *The Prince* risks being merely a scholarly exercise, precisely because the work's innovative strength is its ability to blend the political experience of his time with reflections on classical texts, often adopted in an implicit way.[5] Even the textual comparisons that often recur in the annotations serve to identify Machiavelli's readings, rather than showing sources and "authority." In his letter of 29 April 1513 we find a phrase that, even if taken out of its specific context, can help us understand the author's way of thinking: "I do not think the moon is made of green cheese and in these matters I do not want to be prompted by any authority but reason."[6]

Some questions have been raised regarding Machiavelli's cultural education, but in my opinion they are not very convincing. Often, the obstacles preventing the circulation of books were not taken into consideration; books were still rare and precious, inaccessible to those of meager means. Even this can explain various inaccuracies encountered in the passages cited, perhaps due to references from memory or from annotations written hurriedly and inaccurately or, as has been said, drawn from anthologies, which were widespread because they served as a substitute for costly publications.[7] On the other hand, the distinction—on which some have insisted in order to indicate his literary production's presumed breaking up into pieces—between his period in the secretariat and when he was out of favor after 1512 is based on the difference between the literature from the Florentine tradition of a popular character, which Machiavelli undoubtedly appreciated, and that which had been introduced by the Medici patronage, through the refined works of Ficino and Poliziano, the philosophy of Plato, and the most original contributions of philology; now, such diversity does not necessarily mean that by proposing one of them one is ignorant of the other. In fact, one cannot overlook the fact that those experiences had by now become out of date and in some measure had been surpassed by the new feeling that had spread after the restoration of the republic in 1494.[8] Certainly, if Machiavelli "was not," as Dionisotti observed, "a humanist in the proper sense of the word," he was, "as he demonstrates in his role in the Segretaria . . . a man who had a humanistic education in the Florence of Poliziano and his school."[9] In fact, previously in the

Ghiribizzi al Soderino he had demonstrated his knowledge of classical texts and shared certain concerns of humanistic thought, as suggested by the science of Ptolemy. We should not ignore the fact that two scholars, Roberto Ridolfi and Gennaro Sasso, judged the work of the Florentine secretary to be grounded in a thorough knowledge of classical culture, albeit one that he at times absorbed through the literary output of the fifteenth century.[10] Certainly, the presence of the ancients was not always clearly declared. We do not find in his writings comments such as those in Vettori's letter of 23 November 1513, in which Vettori, describing a typical day in Rome, tells of his readings:

> At nightfall I return home; and I have arranged to get quite a few histories, especially of the Romans; for instance, Livy with the epitome of Lucius Florus, Sallust, Plutarch, Appianus Alexandrinus, Cornelius Tacitus, Suetonius, Lampridius, and Spartianus, and those others who wrote about the emperors—Herodian, Ammianus Marcellinus, and Procopius. And with them I pass the time.[11]

The roll of authors that the Florentine noble had at his disposition is undoubtedly notable. But it is not that Vettori wants to show off his wisdom; knowing his friend's interests, he thus adds an incentive with the following affectionate phrase: "Nicolò [*sic*] my friend, this is the life I invite you to."

Machiavelli would reply with his famous letter of 10 December 1513,[12] in which he in turn recounts his day "in villa." During the day he dedicates himself to various tasks that put him in contact with local people, and, if he does read, he distracts himself with poetry: "Leaving the grove, I go to a spring, and thence to my aviary. I have a book in my pocket, either

Dante or Petrarch, or one of the lesser poets, such as Tibullus, Ovid, and the like. I read of their tender passions and their loves, remember mine, enjoy myself a while in that sort of dreaming."

From "dinner" to the remainder of the day, he adds, "I sink into vulgarity" with the patrons of the inn, and thus, "mixed up with these lice, I keep my brain from growing mouldy, and satisfy the malice of this fate of mine, being glad to have her drive me along this road, to see if she will be ashamed of it."

Only in the evening does he dedicate himself to higher readings:

> On the coming of evening, I return to my house and enter my study; and at the door I take off the day's clothing, covered with mud and dust, and put on garments regal and courtly; and reclothed appropriately, I enter the ancient courts of men, where, received by them with affection, I feed on that food which only is mine and which I was born for, where I am not ashamed to speak with them and to ask them the reason for their actions; and they in their kindness answer me; and for four hours of time I do not feel boredom, I forget every trouble, I do not dread poverty, I am not frightened by death; entirely I give myself over to them.

We may regret the fact that he does not declare who those ancients are, whose names, moreover, we must extract from a careful analysis of his works.

On the subject of his reading, it may be interesting to examine the differences that might exist between references to *The Prince* and those to the *Discourses*. To give just one example, we may note how in the "little work" there is no reference to the sixth book of Polybius, which was used in the *Discourses* and on which rivers of ink have flowed in an attempt to explain how Machiavelli could know it, despite being ignorant of Greek, at a time when only the first five books had been translated and published in Latin. Perhaps this silence may permit one to infer the period in which he drafted each of these works, but the terrain on which one generally proceeds on this topic is slippery and bristling with obstacles. We may only record that, according to one theory, Machiavelli would already have started the *Discourses* after his exit from prison and before writing *The Prince*, and in dealing with the subject matter of chapters 16, 17, and 18 of the first book of the *Discourses*, where he addresses the relationship between liberty and principality, would have had an inkling of the "little work." According to this theory, having put aside the work he started, he would have dedicated himself to the new book. The error in this hypothesis is not only that it correlates the relationship between these two works in a mechanical way; since Machiavelli had stated that to correct a corrupt people it was necessary to resort to a strong power, he had interrupted the *Discourses* and started *The Prince*. We should also note that in this way one would have to concede to the author a very limited lapse of time: in nine months he would have had to have written a complex and demanding set of chapters of the *Discourses*, not to mention *The Prince*.

According to another hypothesis, since the second chapter of this work began with "I shall omit discussing republics because elsewhere I have discussed them at length," Machiavelli had already composed a "trattato delle repubbliche" (treatise on republics), which would then be merged into the first part of the *Discourses*. That would call for previous knowledge of the sixth book of Polybius prior to his writing of *The Prince*, given that the cycle of the transformations of governments suggested by the Greek historian is the central theme of the second chapter of the first book of the *Discourses*. It seems strange that, when in chapter 9 of *The Prince* he points out three forms of government in cities, he limits himself to "princely rule or liberty or license," avoiding any reference to the variety of governments that Polybius included. Naturally this argument cannot exclude the fact that the *Discourses* may have been drafted first, but it is nevertheless a detail that should not be ignored.

The discussion on the writing of *The Prince* has generated very different texts that contradict each other. In 1927, in an essay that caused a stir, Federico Chabod, contesting the thesis of his teacher Friedrich Meinecke, maintained that the drafting of the "little work" had happened in one burst in the summer and autumn of 1513.[13] The latter had claimed that when Machiavelli had sent his letter of 10 December 1513 to Vettori, announcing that he had written *De principatibus*, he had in fact written—according to hints he gave in the letter—only the first eleven chapters. Recently, this theory has been taken up again by other scholars, but Gennaro Sasso has persuasively argued that, even if in December 1513 only the first eleven chapters had been finished, the remainder would have been completed within the arc of a few months, before the summer of 1514.[14] In fact, a work such as *The Prince* appears strictly applicable to a particular situation, and it seems scarcely credible that Machiavelli, in his realism, would have returned on various occasions to what he had written when the relationship between the forces that governed the Italian political panorama had profoundly changed.

In any event, without precise news and dates, it seems preferable to adhere to what we know for certain: in December 1513 Machiavelli communicated to Vettori that he had written "a little work *On Princedoms*"; from various sources we know that between 1517 and 1518, the *Discourses* was written in the version that has come down to us. Wisely, Ridolfi has defined as futile "going and fantasizing over lost works"; similarly, the inferences about the chronology of the works or part of them, not being based on exact documentation, often appear to be flimsily made.

The "Myth" of *The Prince*

"It is better to be impetuous than cautious," we read in chapter 25 of *The Prince*: words that could be taken as a motto of the work, which has become a milestone of political thought, despite being written on impulse for a specific moment. We can repeat the observation of Antonio Gramsci at the beginning of his "notebooks" on Machiavelli: "The basic thing about *The Prince* is that it is not a systematic treatment, but a 'live book, in which political ideology and political science are fused in the dramatic form of a 'myth.'"[1] The term *myth* seems to define the exemplary idealization of the person designated "to grasp Italy," to take action on Italy's behalf, and it seems more appropriate than the word *utopia*. With this, one runs the risk of attributing theoretical characters from outside history to the flight of fancy that the politician, like the artist, must carry out within the context of applying a rational procedure to find solutions for an inchoate and obscure reality.

Machiavelli's entire thought, however, is cloaked in history. It is a history that is typically humanist, because the examples he adopted to illustrate the arguments and personalities he evoked were either recent and in general terms contemporaries of Machiavelli or ancient, belonging to the eras of ancient Greece and Rome. The intervening centuries that made up what was then called the Media Ætas, or the medieval period, do not feature, unless exceptionally, as in the *Discourses* (1.12), with the call to action for the church to keep Italy divided. We know that Machiavelli was aware of Flavio Biondo's *Decades*, where Biondo narrated history "from the decline of the Roman Empire" on, yet such events did not suggest any example to him. He thus shared the thinking of contemporaneous scholars; the centuries dominated by the "barbarians" were not worth taking into consideration. Only later, when studying the history of Florence, would he pay attention to that period, because he saw in the trials and tribulations of that time the origin of the vicissitudes and ills destined to burden Italian life. He could find no positive legacy in the medieval period.

If the beginning of *The Prince* may give the impression of a review of a body of literature, in the third chapter, on "mixed princedoms," Machiavelli starts a coherent weaving of the very recent past, that is the events of the reign of Louis XII, and the behavior, taken as a model, of the Romans. The pitiless analysis of French policy was done with a coldness that—if the term were not annoyingly abused—one would call scientific, insofar as it succeeded in dampening the passion that animated the man who formulated it, who was aware of the tragic consequences of those errors for Italy and Florence.

Starting with these pages, we note European life bursting in on Machiavelli's thoughts on Italian issues. A new chapter in Italy's history had begun with the invasion of Charles VIII in 1494. During the entire fifteenth century the states of the peninsula had for the most part remained sheltered from interventions from beyond the Alps as a result of the ups and downs that were shaking the neighboring countries. The French monarchy had been engaged in the Hundred Years'

War with the English (1339–1453) and in internal struggles, such as those waged by Louis XI against the great feudal lords who had united themselves in the League of Public Good. The emperors of the House of Luxembourg and the first Hapsburgs had turned to eastern Europe with the aim of conquering the crowns of Bohemia, Hungary, and Poland. The Iberian kingdoms were absorbed in their internal clashes, and only the House of Aragon, which already possessed Sicily and Sardinia, had participated in the fight for the succession of the king of Naples, although it kept the two monarchies apart. The expansion of some Italian states was witnessed during that period, especially the Duchy of Milan, the Republic of Venice, and the Papal States, but the expansion of their dominions did not generally correspond to a more stable organization of power that could overcome feudal or civic local particularities.[2] The very precariousness of the central powers and their fears of their subjects' potential revolts had led those who governed them to resort, both in their own endeavors and in self-defense, to mercenary militias, whose inadequacies would become apparent during the wars in Italy.

We thus discern a close connection, implicit in Machiavelli's examination, between events in Italy and the actions of powers on the other side of the Alps, which to assert themselves were developing new instruments of power, based, however, on arrangements inherent in political and civil life. This already was an innovative element compared with previous humanist or medieval treatments, which generally referred to a Christian republic that was as yearned for as it was tenuous. Machiavelli, precisely because he wanted to show what made Italy weak compared with the countries that surrounded it, determined to point out the various peculiarities of the world in which he lived. If in chapter 4 he wrote of Darius and the Oriental empires, it was to establish the difference in background between those ancient monarchies and the new kingdoms that were forming in Europe; however, he immediately abandoned the distant past to outline a relationship with his own time. Thus, for the first time he formulated a distinction destined to develop in political debates for more than two centuries: that between "the Turk and the king of France," between the dominion of a despot over uniformly subservient subjects and a state divided into social classes and structures, endowed with institutions that turned its inhabitants, according to their situation, into people with rights and power.[3] In embryonic form, we gather here the first enunciation of that which gives strength and roots to a political formation; that which later, in the eighteenth century, would be defined as civil society.

Continuing with the analysis of the work, we find a discussion of different ways of dominating the "states that are conquered," according to the model of Sparta or Rome (chapter 5). Sparta was incapable of keeping the cities it had conquered loyal to itself; Rome, on the other hand, managed to create an empire. Machiavelli tackles the relationship to be established with peoples who are used to living free, as well as the measure of their vitality. Machiavelli had set out these thoughts in his writing of 1503 regarding the revolt of Val di Chiana, and he would later reprise and expand them in the *Discourses*, revealing the continuity of his thought. The tone of his writing rises again when he is dealing with "completely new princedoms" (chapter 6), where we note moving undertones that bring to mind the exhortation in the final chapter, allowing us to understand how close the issue is to the author's heart, with Machiavelli having set himself the task of writing precisely so that he could outline the extraordinary possibilities of a new prince.

To this end he cited the example of "those that through their own ability and not through Fortune have been transformed into princes,"[4] and he mentioned Moses, Cyrus, Romulus, and Theseus. If the first is put aside, "since he was a mere executor of things laid down for him by God," the process serves to show that the "actions and individual methods" of the other founders of states were not "different from those of Moses, who had so great a teacher." Their ability raises them up to the level of the prophet, and in this way the figure of Moses becomes desacralized and liable to a political analysis. The new prince must compare himself in virtue with these persons, so as to be, in turn, capable of seizing the opportunity, because, "without opportunity, . . . [his] strength of will would have been wasted, and without such strength the opportunity would have been wasted."

Together with the relationship between fortune and "virtù," previously dealt with in *Ghiribizzi al Soderino*, here Machiavelli poses the question of force, stated moreover as an essential right since his earliest political writings, the *Parole da dirle sopra la provisione del danaio* (*Words to Be Spoken on the Law for Appropriating Money*) and *La cagione dell'Ordinanza* (*The Reason for the Militia*). Now the issue is outlined dramatically when considering the "armed prophets" and "unarmed" ones: the former "gained long continued observance [from the people] for their constitutions," because they were endowed with force; the latter "have great difficulty as they go forward" and can fall like Savonarola; but whenever they succeed in overcoming the dangers thanks to their ability "and . . . are revered . . . they are powerful, firm, honored, prosperous." Thus we glimpse the strength of consensus, the most solid basis of any power, which will become clearer in *Discourses*.

This strength had permitted the Valentino to "[put] down the roots" of his new state. In chapter 7 Machiavelli analyzes his behavior, since "I for my part do not see what better precepts I can give a new prince than the example of Duke Valentino's actions." He therefore illustrates the policy that the Valentino followed to create a state in Romagna. Having become lord of Romagna and wanting to reinforce and extend his possessions, he took the initiative to create his own military force, which freed him from the shackles of French protection as well as from mercenary armies. He thus succeeded in taking away from the Orsini and the Colonna their allies and supporters and won the latter over to himself. Subsequently, reacting to the conspiracy hatched by his mercenaries, he succeeded in eliminating them in the massacre of Sinigaglia.

At this point "the Duke had laid very good foundations for his power, holding all the Romagna along with the dukedom of Urbino," particularly because he had "made the Romagna his friend and gained the support of all those people, through their getting a taste of well-being." Whereas until then they had been governed by "weak lords who had plundered their subjects rather than governed them," now they lived in peace and unity. Certainly, they had reached these through harsh measures; to eliminate "thefts, brawls and every sort of excess," the Valentino had placed as governor of Romagna a "man cruel and ready," who "in a short time rendered the province peaceful and united." Immediately afterward, however, "to purge such men's minds and win them over entirely," he unexpectedly had the powerful minister put to death, and "he set up a civil court in the midst of the province, with a distinguished presiding judge." He had conquered the affections of his subjects, as can be seen at the death of Alexander VI when, although the Valentino was far from Romagna and in increasing difficulties, his duchy, by and large, remained loyal to him. To his misfortune, however, the death of his father happened not only before he had ended his plan to become lord but also while he was seriously ill. "And he said to me himself, on Julius

II's accession-day, that he had imagined what could happen when his father died, and for everything he had found a solution, except he had never imagined that at the time of that death he too would be close to dying."

This eulogy to the most vilified of Italian princes could only provoke scandal. Almost as if to add to it, Machiavelli dedicated the following chapter to "men who gain a princedom through wicked deeds," as though to underline the "virtù" of the Valentino with a contrast. What is in fact abominable is the prince raising himself to the princedom by reducing the motherland, which has been freely entrusted to him, to servitude. Thus, in antiquity Agathocles, having taken command of the Syracusan army, "one morning . . . assembled the people and the Senate of Syracuse as if he were going to consider things relating to the state" and had his soldiers massacre "all the senators and the richest of the people," and then took control of the city. In recent times Liverotto had assumed power at Fermo, after having had killed, together with the local leading citizens, the uncle who had brought him up. This behavior is differentiated from that of the Valentino, because "it cannot be called . . . virtue to kill one's fellow-citizens, to betray friends, to be without fidelity, without mercy, without religion; such proceedings enable one to gain sovereignty, but not fame."

Certainly, cruelties were sometimes necessary, but there are cruelties that are "badly used or well used." And so he clarified the two:

> *Well used* we can call those (if of what is bad we can use the word *well*) that a conqueror carries out at a single stroke, as a result of his need to secure himself, and does not persist in, but transmutes into the greatest possible

benefits to his subjects. *Badly used* are those which, though few in the beginning, rather increase with time than disappear.[5]

In *Discourses* (1.27) he observed that there could also be grandeur in treachery: politics was dripping with tears and blood, and in *The History of Florence* (7.6) he would refer to the fact that Cosimo de' Medici was accustomed to saying "that states are not held by carrying rosaries."[6] Because of this, Machiavelli continued in *The Prince*, "On seizing a state a prudent conqueror makes a list of all the harmful deeds he must do, and does them all at once, so that he need not repeat them every day, because, not repeating them, he makes men feel secure, and gains their support by treating them well."

It is crucial to take into account these stratagems in order to attain a "civil princedom" (chapter 9); to this end it is not necessary to have "either ability altogether or Fortune altogether but rather a fortunate shrewdness."

One accedes to the principality "with the aid either of the people or of the rich." The antagonism between "these two opposing parties" is constant. And here the hostility toward the "rich," nourished by Machiavelli via his political action during the time of Soderini and his preference for taking the part of the people, which would be repeatedly displayed in *Discourses*, is explained in arguments that refer to the weaknesses of the power of the Italian states, undermined by party interests. In the *Ritracto di cose di Francia* he had observed that in that kingdom too "formerly . . . the powerful barons" had dared to rebel against the king, but "are now most submissive."[7] Italy, however, did not have a sufficiently authoritative sovereign, and the "rich" threatened the prince's actions, since they considered themselves his equals. As a result, it was more prudent to lean on the support of the people, among whom there was "either nobody or very few who are not prepared to obey." Above all it was easier to satisfy them, "because the people's object is more creditable than that of the rich: the latter wish to oppress and the former not to be oppressed." With regard to the rich, one may use consideration when they are loyal and not "rapacious"; this passage is to be noted because the same principle would in some way be repeated in 1520–22, in the piece composed in those years for the reform of the state of Florence.[8] The prince must distrust the other rich people, however, "as though they were open enemies, because always in adverse times they help ruin him" to satisfy their personal ambition. It was a lesson drawn from years of struggle between the optimates and Soderini, and it had been confirmed in 1512, the moment of the Spanish attack on the republic, when the Florentine aristocrats had played a part in overthrowing the gonfaloniers.

The well-balanced state, therefore, is supported by the people. "Let no one oppose this belief of mine," he added, "with that well-worn proverb: 'He who builds on the people builds on mud,'" because the examples that are usually given to support this saying refer to private citizens, who expect to be helped by the people when they find themselves in danger of being defeated in their political struggle.[9] Here, however, we are dealing with a prince endowed with power and authority, who "is a stout-hearted man who does not waver in adverse times," who should know how to govern honestly and "through his courage and his management keeps up the spirits of the masses": so "he is never deceived by them, but receives assurance that he has made his foundations strong."

The problem of defending against external enemies is addressed in chapter 10, where Machiavelli examines the strengths on which all principalities are founded. Those that can "repel attack through [their] own strength . . . through large resources in men or in money" and are capable of maintaining an army are secure. The others would do well to fortify the capital and be ready to abandon the rest of the country. The example comes from Machiavelli's experience of his mission to Germany:

> The cities of Germany are very free, have little farm land, and obey the Emperor when they feel like it; they do not fear him or any other potentate near them because they are so fortified that everybody reckons their capture as sure to be tedious and difficult. They all have adequate ditches and walls; they have plenty of artillery; and they always reserve in the public storehouses enough to eat and to drink and to burn for a year. Besides that, in order to keep the people fed without using up the public funds, they always have in store everything needed to provide work for a year at those trades that are the strength and the life of the city and of the industries by which the people earn their bread.[10]

However, the essential condition that enables a prince to behave in this way is having his subjects unite around him so that he can count on popular favor.

There are no concerns of defense, however, for the princes of the church (chapter 11), and although the latter are taken into consideration, it is certainly not for lessons that can be learned from their government: "The pope alone has states and does not defend them, subjects and does not keep them in order; yet his states, through being undefended, never are snatched away; and his subjects, through not being kept in order, never feel any concern, and do not imagine being alienated from him and cannot be" (*Works*, 1:44).

Ecclesiastical states, wrote Machiavelli, could claim to be the only "secure and prosperous" states, but his apparent homage to them was dripping in sarcasm, the writer declining to discuss them further, since they were "protected by superior causes, to which the human mind does not reach," that is to say, God (*Works*, 1:44).

What interested Machiavelli was to understand how this state of affairs had been reached, and he therefore recalled the situation of the Papal States prior to the arrival in Italy of Charles VIII, when the peninsula was still "ruled by the Pope, the Venetians, the King of Naples, the Duke of Milan, and the Florentines." The confusion caused by the coming of the French and the Italian Wars allowed Pope Alexander VI— "though [his] purpose was to strengthen not the church but the Duke [Valentino]"—to bring "strength for the Church," whose domains were expanded farther still by Julius II. In other writings these factors would be judged negatively, and in *Discourses* (1.12) Machiavelli would not hold back from making harsh accusations against the church, which "has kept and still keeps this region divided"; but here his reflections are different, all the more so because the work, under the reign of Leo X (mentioned at the end of chapter 11), was to be addressed to a Medici.

According to some scholars, when in December 1513 Machiavelli wrote to Vettori of having "composed a little work *On Princedoms*," he would have reached only this point. In fact, the end of his chapter 11 and the beginning of the following one can give the impression of, if not a true and proper interruption, at least a caesura, since the opening of chapter 12 takes the form of a reprise: "Having discussed in detail all the qualities of those princedoms, which in the beginning I set out to discuss, and observed in various respects . . . and shown the methods . . . it remains for me now to discuss. . . ." It therefore appears likely that the hypothesis advanced by Sasso, who, though admitting that *The Prince* could not have been completed by December 1513 and that the mention in the letter to Vettori refers only to the first eleven chapters, strongly rejects the idea of a much later development and conclusion of the work and supposes that Machiavelli completed it by late spring 1514.[11] Thus, in the subsequent chapters the organization of the work appears to have changed. The "good foundations" of a state are illustrated with the reminder that the principal ones are "good laws and good armies," the binomial that is at the foundation of any sovereignty, previously recorded in *La cagione dell'Ordinanza* of 1506. In chapter 12 he explains that "there cannot be good laws where armies are not good, and where there are good armies, there must be good laws."[12]

He therefore takes up again the hard polemic against mercenary armies, which are "disunited, ambitious, without discipline, disloyal; valiant among friends, among enemies cowardly." In fact, "when the foreigner came, they showed what they were, so that Charles the king of France was allowed to take Italy with chalk." This expression was used by Alexander VI and quoted by Commynes: "The French . . . came with wooden spurs, and chalk in their harbingers' hands to mark out their lodgings."[13] Every method of fighting the mercenary forces was contrary to every norm of the art of war, starting from the fact that mercenaries, "in order to give reputation to their own forces," had taken away "the reputation of the infantry" (*Works*, 1:51). Again in the following two chapters he insisted upon the necessity of arming a state, because without his own armed forces no prince is secure. Moreover, the prince must personally look after the army and put himself at its head. Thus Machiavelli declares the indissoluble connection between government action and military action—"laws and armies." This connection needs to be viewed as a cornerstone of Machiavelli's thought; his polemic against mercenary armies cannot be considered separately from his political thought. Rightly, it has been noted: "The mercenary became the symbol of fifteenth-century Italy, that is, of the general prevalence of the oligarchic powers or specifically feudal ones over the cohesive tendencies of the city-states, just as in the kingdom in the South: the symbol and expression of a political system doomed to ruin."[14]

From chapter 15 onward, it is the prince's behavior and qualities that are at the center of attention: not in the abstract, but, as I have noted, according to "the truth of the matter as facts show it." And precisely in these pages we find the most contested passages in which the autonomy of politics is clearly noted: "of politics," wrote Croce in a famous passage, "which is beyond moral good and evil, which has its own laws against which it is useless to rebel."[15]

Certainly, it is necessary to remember that Machiavelli's instructions were meant to be applied to a "corrupt" situation, and again Croce highlighted "the acrid bitterness with which Machiavelli accompanied these statements on politics and its intrinsic necessity." The prince is called upon to provide a remedy to a situation of crisis and general ruin, and for this he must refrain from any ethical considerations, exactly as the Valentino had done in Romagna. Undoubtedly, the Valentino's action, at the moment of conquest, had been ruthless, and as a result "Cesare Borgia was thought cruel: nevertheless that well-known cruelty of his re-organized the Romagna, united it, brought it to peace and loyalty."[16]

The new duchy had been ruled in a way—noted Guicciardini too, who had the reputation of being a skeptic but not of being treacherous or cruel—that benefited everyone who served united under that prince, instead of under the various minor lords that the Valentino had deposed.[17]

Thus Machiavelli wrote that "the new prince—above all other princes—cannot escape being called cruel, since new governments abound in dangers" (chapter 17). If anything, the prince has to make "himself feared in such a way that, if he does not gain love, he escapes hatred." And here we run into one of the observations that has most ignited indignation among God-fearing souls: Machiavelli in fact writes that the prince should even take it upon himself, if he must, "to take anyone's life," but "refrains from [taking] the property of others . . . because men forget more quickly the death of a father than the loss of a father's estate." Moreover, he had previously observed (chapter 15) that the prince "needs to be so prudent that he escapes ill repute for such vices as might take his position away from him, and that he protects himself from such as will not take it away," adding "if he can." However, "He does not even worry about incurring reproach for those vices without which he can hardly maintain his position."[18]

Since the prince needs to know how to fight with laws and with force (chapter 18)—the former a quality of men, the latter of animals—the example of the centaur is associated with him, "half animal and half man," which the ancients attributed to Achilles's tutor. To "play the animal well," the prince must imitate the fox and the lion, "because the lion does not defend himself from traps; the fox does not protect himself from the wolves." It is therefore necessary to "be a fox to recognize the traps and a lion to frighten the wolves." This is the reversal of a lesson by Cicero, who is not among the authors Machiavelli loved: these two animals were mentioned in *De officiis* (1.41) as symbols of the injustice incurred through violence and fraud. In fact, as Cicero explained, "Fraud [belongs] to the fox, [force] to the lion," and he clarified: "Neither to be congenial with man. Yet of the two, fraud is the more detestable." Certainly two princes such as the Valentino and Ferdinand the Catholic had not escaped the example of the "fox"; the latter in particular (Machiavelli avoided naming him openly) "never preaches anything except peace and truth, and to both of them he is utterly opposed. Either one, if he had practiced it, would many times have taken from him either his reputation or his power."[19] The art of dissembling is evidently not a creation of the Baroque era.

Machiavelli, however, agreed with Cicero when he stated that the conservation of the state was a norm essential to politics, according to the motto "Salus populi suprema lex esto" (Let the good of the people be the supreme law) (*De legibus* 3.8). In fact, he wrote: "So if a prince succeeds in conquering and holding his state, his means are always judged honorable and everywhere praised." Placing it in a more open and longer-term perspective, in *Discourses* he condemned the "very cruel methods, and enemies to all governments not merely Christian but human" (1.26), and yet he warned with profound passion: "When it is absolutely a question of the safety of one's country, there must be no consideration of just or unjust, of merciful or cruel, of praiseworthy or disgraceful; instead, setting aside every scruple, one must follow to the utmost any plan that will save her life and keep her liberty" (3.41).

In *The Prince*, written in response to a dramatically urgent situation, his focus was on the present, and he took into account the critical situation he aimed to remedy. The picture he outlined was a bleak one: "The mob is always fascinated with appearances and by the outcome of an affair," and, he concluded bitterly, "in the world the mob is everything." Even

Romulus, one of the models in *The Prince* who in *Discourses* is described as "a founder of a state (1.9), had to act without mercy; also, if Moses, "who had so great a teacher," was "to put his laws and regulations into effect, he [would be] forced to kill countless men" (3.30). As the moral of the story, in chapter 17 of *The Prince*, Machiavelli quotes the words that Virgil placed in the mouth of Dido at a time when she was establishing her new kingdom: "Res nova et regni novitas me talia cogunt moliri" (My hard condition and the newness of my sovereignty force me to do such things).[20]

A great historian has observed that these pages of Machiavelli "always dictate, in their cold political realism, scandalous words to those who have no experience of at least a broad and accurate reading around historical events and situations," and that "such scandal is made more irritating by the evocative and figurative powers of the writer."[21]

In addition, many pages from Erasmus, no less severe and just as provocative—at least for conformists—due to the polemic he turned against princes and prelates or against the religious norms and practices that were common in his time, were equally likely to give rise to scandal and condemnation. Thus, it is worth noting how the circles in which new ideas and the desire for a simpler and more direct religious feeling were strongly held were particularly receptive to the works of both Machiavelli and Erasmus, both of whom were capable of arousing interest as a result of their more innovative cultural thrusts.[22] And significantly, the works of the Flemish humanist, in common with Machiavelli's writings, were placed on the Index of Prohibited Books during the Counter-Reformation. The new spirit that was emerging in the early years of the sixteenth century was full of renewals and upheavals capable of unleashing forces and imposing solutions that until then had been unimaginable, rendering old conventions and conformities intolerable; these were imposed by a society that in many ways was turned in on itself and by a system of moral values that by now was devoid of meaning and opposed by those who should have respected it in the first place. On the other hand, for Machiavelli, the interpretation that the Christian message had offered of giving the world "as prey to wicked men" (*Discourses* 2.2) impeded, following these precepts, the creation of a vigorous and stable society.

At the time a new awareness of organized society was coming into being and a new religiousness was asserting itself. If Machiavelli mentions the religious crisis only fleetingly through hints at the scandal of indulgences, which had fueled Luther's protest,[23] his pages clearly express a new civil faith, which imbued his political vision with extraordinary vigor. His thoughts therefore appear to be animated by the highest tradition of humanism, precisely inasmuch as "it [humanism] consisted in a renewed confidence in man and his possibilities and in an appreciation of man's activities in every possible sense."[24] Machiavelli stated as an objective the creation of a state with institutions and laws that rule it with stability, free from corruption and the miseries into which Italian life had fallen; this vision of degradation triggered his scorn for inept rulers incapable of foreseeing developments in the political situation, and he reproached them severely in the *Second Decennale*, the contemporary of *The Prince*: "You, who hold the scepters and the crowns, and of the future do not know a single truth!"[25]

In *The Prince* he bitterly scorned dispossessed princes: "Therefore these princes of ours, who have been many years in their princedoms, and then have lost them, should not blame fortune but their own laziness."[26] His civic conscience had been fed by the communal and republican experience, which was still alive in the Florentine chancery, despite being almost exhausted in Florence. He was well aware of this when he criticized the weaknesses and defects of the Florentine arrangements and the internal divisions that had blocked the development of society and its potential for growth. In reality, the entire Italian political experience, founded principally on urban society, had reached its peak, and now the bird of Minerva had taken flight, pointing the way to a new horizon, to the study of the relationships of associated life of men. Against this background, it is unsurprising if the final chapter of *The Prince* has the style of a prophetic passage.

Frequenting the Orti Oricellari

One may think that the innovations in the previous chapter might have prevented the first readers of *The Prince* from understanding its magnitude. Thus, the offer of the work to Giuliano de' Medici did not take place, notwithstanding the attempts—which do not appear to have been very convincing—of Francesco Vettori. Worse still, every hope that the Medici may employ Machiavelli failed. Reading the correspondence with Vettori, we see disappointment heaped upon disappointment, until the following heartfelt sentence of 10 June 1514: "I shall continue, then, among my lousy doings, without finding a man who remembers my service or who believes that I can be good for anything."[1] Machiavelli was led to believe that his difficult situation obliged him to become a "tutor or a secretary to a constable, . . . or fix myself in some desert land to teach reading to boys." Even Paolo Vettori's attempts to entrust some position to him failed after the pope's secretary in Rome warned Giuliano himself "to not embarrass yourself on account of Niccolò."[2]

If we can admire the strength of spirit that Machiavelli displayed in his letters to Vettori, where he took heart and gave himself over to "empty things," we also know that in this period, as if to distract himself, he dedicated himself— whether motivated by revenge or by desperation—to the composition of a satirical poem in three-line stanzas, *The Ass*.[3] The bitterness of the time is reflected in the deeply pessimistic spirit that pervades these verses. The beginning may be interpreted as a veiled anti-Medici allusion because it talks of the presence in Florence of "a certain young fellow" struck by the strange ailment of always wanting to run.

The young fellow's father entrusts him to "a certain quack doctor," who guarantees his recovery, and the author comments: "And since those who promise benefit are always believed (from which it comes that men put such faith in doctors...)."[4] The profession, "medici" in Italian, also refers to the name of the ruling family in Florence, against whom an accusation would be made that "often, by believing them [the Medici], a man deprives himself of his property."

The autobiographical tone of the novella that opens the poem is clear enough: the mind of the author, eager to run around the world (as Agostino Vespucci accused him of wanting to do)—that is, his feverish activities from his time in the secretariat onward—manifested itself in the illness that afflicted the "young fellow" depicted in *The Ass*. But the anxiety of running can also allude, it has been said, to the wish to tease, to satirize, as Machiavelli himself declares: "So I, having early turned my thought to nipping this and that"; this wish had found expression, although we know little about it, in the play *Le Maschere*, in which Machiavelli had set about ripping into and abusing various still-living citizens in 1504.[5] Certainly his mocking spirit could lead him to rash acts, and in this sense there is a hint in the letter he wrote to Vettori the day after he was released from prison, where he promises to be more "careful" in the future.[6] "But the present age so grudging and evil" leads him to see bad rather than good; "hence if now I scatter a bit of poison," he is led to do so by this state of affairs, as he explains in the first chapter of *The Ass*.[7] The poem must have taken its inspiration from *The Ass*, the novel by the Latin writer Apuleius, who lived in the second century, in which a young man is magically transformed into in an ass. Nevertheless, in chapter 8 (Machiavelli did not progress beyond this chapter, leaving the work incomplete) the transformation into a donkey has not yet taken place. On the contrary, in addressing a "big fat porker," isolated from other animals, which once upon a time had been men, the hero tells of having received from the gods "such great grace" as to "take me from the afflictions you will suffer";[8] he therefore appeared to be safe from being changed into the ass that gives the poem its title. The fat porker, on the other hand, reveals his own thoughts to him, which celebrate the renunciation of the drama of human life, and one may suppose that Machiavelli might have thought that whatever the young man might have been able to say once he was transformed into a donkey had already been revealed by the character with whom he was conversing. The work had therefore reached a dead end, and, perhaps dissatisfied with it, he gave up writing it. He had all the more reason to do so because precisely at that time he was able to show in *The Mandrake*, the play written for the carnival of 1518, the bestiality of men within a specific reality: "Your Florence," as he wrote in the prologue.[9]

In his theatrical masterpiece, Machiavelli undoubtedly succeeded in expressing his own thoughts vigorously, resolving, in the roles of the play, the contradiction that had emerged in chapter 5 of the poem between the political deliberation whose profound pessimism demonstrated a sensitivity to the problems of organized society and the exasperated individualism expressed by the pig in his eulogy on animals.

From at least 1516 on Machiavelli had frequented a circle of young men who, resorting to a custom begun in the very first years of the century by Bernardo Rucellai, congregated, after the latter's death, around his nephew Cosimo, in the gardens of the palace, called the Orti Oricellari in Latin.[10] These gatherings harked back to a noble humanist tradition of literary and philosophical conversations and debates, but now, with Cosimo, political issues were becoming increasingly popular topics of discussion, animated by an antityrannical spirit and inspired by the memory of the ancient Roman republic, which had been handed down from the great historians of the past: Livy and Tacitus, Plutarch and Polybius. In this environment Machiavelli read or explained passages from his *Discourses on the First Decade of Titus Livius* and discussed themes he took up again in *The Art of War*.

In the dedications and in some pages of these two works, we can still discern the bonds of friendship that, notwithstanding the age difference, tied Machiavelli to these young men. He was much older, and because of his experience during the republic, he seemed a maestro to them; these young men persuaded him to express his thoughts in literary form. Thus, at the beginning of the *Discourses* he addressed "you, who have forced me to write what I of myself never would have written," and to express "all I have learned in the course of my long experience and steady reading in the affairs of the world." He dedicated the work to them, against "the common custom of those who write, who always address their works to some prince." He therefore chose "not those who are princes, but those who because of their countless good qualities deserve to be." These words sound as a self-criticism for the ill-fated dedication to Lorenzo de' Medici in *The Prince*.

Machiavelli felt connected by a strong sense of responsibility—fed by the anxiety he felt about the future—to the young men with whom he commentated on the ancient classics and discussed current problems in the gardens of the Rucellai Palace. He wrote: "For it is the duty of a good man to teach others anything of value that through the malice of the times and of Fortune you have been unable to put into effect, in order that since many will know of it, some of them more loved by Heaven may be able to put it into effect."[11]

Similar thoughts would be addressed by the former condottiere Fabrizio Colonna to the young people he was speaking to in *The Art of War*—the dialogue was always set in "the most secluded and shady part" of the Rucellai garden—who shared with them the thoughts he had developed through experience:

> And I repine at nature, who either should have made me such that I could not see this or should have given me the possibility for putting it into effect. Since I am an old man, I do not imagine today that I can have opportunity of it. Therefore I have been liberal of it with you who, being young and gifted, can at the right time, if the things I have said please you, aid and advise your princes to their advantage.[12]

In the troubles of the present day, the wealth of knowledge, which feeds hopes of renewal and freedom, must not become lost but should be invested in the last hope remaining, the future as represented by the younger generations.

An Original Comment on Livy

We do not know how far Machiavelli had progressed with the *Discourses* (or making a first draft) when he began visiting the Orti Oricellari. The hypotheses regarding the period of its composition have already been pointed out, and, besides the doubts surrounding the moment at which it was begun, we should also note that it did not perhaps proceed according to the order of the chapters known to us today. As mentioned, the initial quotation in the third chapter of the second book, which is repeated in the conclusion, leads one to think that this may be a rough precursor of that comment. We certainly cannot discount that for a long time Machiavelli may have been accumulating notes, thoughts, and perhaps even passages later inserted into the *Discourses*. We know that between 1516 and 1517 he toiled assiduously on the work, diligently reordering it and thoroughly revising its parts.

Beneath the hand-me-down gown of a commentary on Livy, set out in an apparently disorganized series of essays of various lengths, he was articulating a coherent vision of the world, which rejected any doctrinal arrangement deriving from philosophical or religious speculations. It has been observed that we can glimpse an antecedent of this process in the *Miscellanea*, the work by Poliziano published in 1489.[1] Breaking with the traditional gloss, subordinated, even typographically, to the original text, that innovative work, in an autonomous commentary, developed a historical-philological interpretation capable of clarifying issues of a general nature, and it is apparently the only possible known precedent of that unique literary creation that is the *Discourses*. Nevertheless, even if until the time of Poliziano this type of commentary had not been applied to literary texts, it appears to have been introduced in the works of lawyers and doctors, and it is legitimate to suppose that Machiavelli had access to some of these legal publications, since they passed through the hands of his father. In fact, in the preface to the first book of the *Discourses*, he evoked precisely the "opinions given by the ancient jurists," as well as the "experiments made by the ancient physicians," with the conviction that similar processes should be followed in political life when one had a "true understanding of books on history."[2]

It seems easy to pass from Poliziano's *Miscellanea* to Erasmus's *Adagia*, with their diverse thematic, but also historical and moral, philology; Machiavelli's *Discourses*, which moves off from a different cultural terrain, seems more distant from these works and does not apparently draw on what existed before—in whatever way it may have been mediated—other than through some formal suggestion. It then remains for us to ask whether with these diverse works, we are not instead witnessing the birth of a literary genre from new means of expression, better suited to reflecting on world affairs in that moment of crisis, of detachment, and of breaking away the new wisdom, as compared with the closed and systematic forms of traditional thought. Thus, the deliberately broken writing of the *Discourses* may be compared with that of the essays of Montaigne and Francis Bacon. In opening up new horizons, in expanding upon thoughts about the greatest problems of human existence, the ponderous treatises, the methodical *summae,* must have appeared to be inadequate instruments, by now obsolete. The brief essays present themselves as an encyclopedic keyboard that permits new interpretative concepts to be plainly discussed. Some speak in an improvident manner of fragmentation and incompleteness; it is much more appropriate to recall how Italo Calvino had tackled the category of multiplicity in his *Six Memos for the Next Millennium:*

> Medieval literature tended to produce works expressing the sum of human knowledge in an order and form of stable compactness, as in the *[Divina] Commedia,* where a multiform richness of language converges with the application of a systematic and unitary mode of thought. In contrast, the modern books that we love most are the outcome of a confluence and a clash of a multiplicity of interpretative methods, modes of thought, and styles of expression.[3]

In the *Discourses,* the relationship between nature and society is repeatedly discussed. History appears as a mediator between these two categories and, through the various actions of men, reveals the potential, the conditioning, the opportunities of the times. While being convinced of the immutability of the laws that govern nature and people, Machiavelli caught sight of, beneath the tempestuous rush of events, great historical phases; they are phenomena that over the millennia lead to changes in religion, they are the catastrophes capable of almost completely destroying the "mixed body of the human race" and to destroy memory (2.5), or "the circle in which all states revolve as they are governed and govern themselves" (1.2). If for the great natural disasters we remember the verses of Lucretius, which evoked the cataclysms in which entire populations were annihilated through the heat of fire or the fury of water (5.338–42), for a vision of universal history Polybius offers his theory of the cycles, which unfolded in a natural concatenation of events, where any eschatological conception turns out to be extraneous. We should note, however, how the risk of determinism, which a succession of different forms of government may bring, can be overcome with the correction that Machiavelli introduced in the irresistible return to the beginning of the cycle; this return is possible via changes arising from historical factors.

It is precisely to allow the intervention of the human will in the course of events that the politician, the legislator, the founder of republics, or—in the exceptional case of Rome— the "prudence" and "virtù" of its people must be capable of exploiting the natural tensions and the dynamic mechanisms of society. There are internal disorders and imbalances that open the way for the conscious actions of humans, once they know how to seize the opportunities offered by nature and the succession of various vicissitudes. Starting from the supposition that people tend to "act according to the wickedness of their spirits whenever they have free scope" (1.3), and knowing that "nature has made men able to crave everything but unable to attain everything" (1.37), it is possible to bend this natural need to the common good through political institutions and laws. It is those internal contradictions that gave rise to talk of Rome as a "disorderly republic" because it had not been understood that those struggles and disagreements had been the ground upon which laws and institutions that acted for the public good had been developed and that those revolts "as a first cause kept Rome free."[4]

Machiavelli's Rome, however, is not a static model of a single period, that is, taken as a whole, outside the flux of time, but it grows, it expands, civically and territorially, until the inexorable degeneration into the civil wars of the time of Marius and Sulla. Equally, the affairs of men of his time are seen, yes, according to the principle that the past repeats itself, but liable to profound changes, according to the circumstances and the actions taken. History as "life's teacher" (*magistra vitæ*) is, in short, history as the making, as the transformation, and, in the final analysis, as the perfection of human affairs. We must not seek in Machiavelli anything similar to the enlightening idea of progress; if from his way of seeing history we exclude any form of providentialism, then we note that a teleological conception is equally foreign to him. In the *Discourses* the word *civiltà* appears more than once, and there we find a picture of the origins of human society that implicitly contains the idea of civil development and growth: human beings, "in the beginning of the world," lived "in the fashion of beasts," and only over time, growing in number and gathering in communities, did they arrive at an "understanding of things honorable and good, as different from what is pernicious and evil," and therefore at an "understanding of justice."[5] As a result, they organized themselves by choosing a chief: to begin with, the strongest, then the wisest and most just, and their way of political life became a way of civil life.

However, this process is not irreversible. This is not only because human history proceeds via a succession of phases that, at the end of the cycle, can lead back to the previous cycle, but also because events may cause regressive changes. Thus, the example of the Samnites shows how a people, through the loss of their liberty, may decline to the extent that, after having been able to stand up to the Romans year after year, defeating entire consular armies, in the end "were scarcely able to defend themselves from one little Roman legion in Nola."[6]

But then, in addition to the people, the entire country was in ruins, and "where there were so many cities and so many men," all that remained was an "almost uninhabited" territory.[7] Therefore, alongside the contrast between civil and uncivil, there is the relationship between civilization and liberty, which Machiavelli praised in terms that are absolute: "All cities and provinces that live in freedom anywhere in the world . . . make very great gains." There we see that "their populations are larger, since marriages are freer and more attractive to men" because liberty leads to security, and "each man gladly begets those children he thinks he can bring up, without fear that his patrimony will be taken from him; he knows not merely that they are born free and not slaves but that by means of their abilities they can become prominent men."

Thus,

> Riches multiply in a free country to a greater extent, both those that come from agriculture and those that come from industry, for each man gladly increases such things and seeks to gain such goods as he believes, when gained, he can enjoy. Thence it comes that men in emulation give thought to private and public advantages; and both kinds keep increasing marvelously.

If liberty is the impulse to civilization, corruption—in the broad meaning that Machiavelli gave this word, as the degeneration not only of customs but also of institutions and laws—is the negation of liberty. "A corrupt city living under a prince," even if the latter dies and the dynasty is extinguished, "never can bring itself back to freedom" (1.17). Corruption is the principal element of decadence and regression. The nexus between the three words—*liberty, civilization,* and *corruption*—is indicated almost in the form of a paradox: "Anyone who at present wishes to build a state will find it easier among mountaineers, where there is no culture, than among those living in cities, where culture is corrupt."[8] Besides, "in a corrupt city" it is almost impossible not only to create but also "[to maintain] a government [there]." In fact, "things like good morals, if they are to be maintained, have need of the laws, so the laws, if they are to be observed, have need of good morals" (1.18). Dictatorships may be established for reasons of public order but not to remedy a corrupt situation, and the figure of the "good tyrant" is not to be discounted but is viewed with much skepticism:

> To reorganize a city for living under a good government assumes a good man, and to become prince of a state by violence assumes an evil man; therefore a good man will seldom attempt to become prince by evil methods, even though his purpose be good; on the other hand, a wicked man, when he has become prince, will seldom try to do what is right, for it never will come into his mind to use rightly the authority he has gained wickedly.[9]

In the historical contradiction between liberty and corruption, at the base of "political living" sits "civil equality," which, once violated, leads to the degradation and perversion of communal living and civilized society itself (1.2). If there is no clear explanation of what this equality between citizens consists of, undoubtedly there is a yearning for a republic of strict morals, based on the traditional historiographic interpretation that luxuries and "delights" were the cause of the decadence and ruin of Rome. By contrast, Germany is the country that still contains the ancient goodness, allowing "many republics to exist there in freedom and to observe their laws so well that nobody outside or inside the cities dares to try to master them."[10] One principle is established: "Well-ordered republics ought to keep their treasuries rich and their citizens poor."[11] But if equality may be desired in the economic sphere, it must also be secured in the political field. In fact, while repeating that "the most useful thing a free state can bring about is to keep its citizens poor,"[12] Machiavelli relates how in Rome there could have been contempt for or indifference toward wealth, inasmuch as "men went to seek ability whatever house she lived in." Livy's first decade allows Machiavelli to follow— through the struggles between patrician and plebeian in the name of civil and political rights, even more so than for economic reasons—the exemplary formation of a state that had taken place with instruments and arguments belonging to the political realm.

To ensure the simplicity of customs and public morality, the determining force is religion, here meant as a sentiment not limited to the Christian faith; rather, the religion of the ancient peoples was better suited than Christianity to teaching civil virtues: in Rome religion "caused good laws; good laws make good fortune; and from good fortune came the happy results of the city's endeavors" (*Discourses* 1.11). However, Christianity is judged to be the prime cause of the weakness in which men found themselves in the present day, because "our religion has glorified humble and contemplative men rather than active ones." Having "set up as the greatest good humility, abjectness and contempt of human things," it "made the world weak and turned it over as prey to wicked men" (2.2). However, the religion of the ancients placed its notion of the greatest good "in grandeur of mind, in strength of body, and in all the other things apt to make men exceedingly vigorous."[13] Moreover, the church, "through the [bad] examples of that [Roman] court," is accused of having made us "Italians . . . without religion and wicked" (1.12). Clearly the religion that Machiavelli sees as the foundation of a well-ordered state is not so much a doctrine as a feeling capable of causing solidarity between people and of creating a solid bond between them.[14]

Religion is therefore not intended as an individual feeling; its deepest essence consists of the ability to reflect on a world of values and relationships that find a way of expressing themselves through communal life. Therefore the distinction between politics and morality, which would be established in Machiavelli's teaching, should be seen not as a recourse to amoral practices but as an affirmation of a new, more coherent, and higher social morality.[15]

Equality, and therefore living freely, is thus entirely incompatible with the presence of "gentlemen" who "without working live in luxury on the returns from their landed possessions, without paying any attention either to agriculture or to any other occupation necessary for making a living," especially if "besides the aforesaid fortunes, [they] command castles and have subjects who obey them."[16] This involves "men of these types . . . altogether hostile to all free government" and in the countries where they dominate—in particular "the Kingdom of Naples, the City of Rome, the Romagna and Lombardy"— "where the matter is so corrupt that the laws are not restraint enough." We find again the complementary relationship between civility and liberty, contrasted with the corruption of political life. So much so that to reform a city afflicted with similar corruption "some greater force must of necessity be established, namely a kingly hand that with absolute and surpassing power puts a check on the over-great ambition and corruption of the powerful."

The arrangements should be adapted to specific situations, and it is necessary to adapt these to the possibilities and to the ebb and flow of human affairs. This foundation was already enunciated in the *Ghiribizzi al Soderino*: men must know how to react, comparing their way of reacting with the times. In line with this principle there is also the superiority of republics over monarchies. "A republic, being able to adapt herself, by means of the diversity among her body of citizens, to a diversity of temporal conditions better than a prince can, is of greater duration than a princedom and has good fortune longer."[17] The *Discourses*, however, does not express a preferential judgment on the best political regime in absolute terms other than to affirm the superiority of a free government over a tyrannical one; even the fact that Machiavelli does not point out abstract models is a way for him to concern himself "with the truth of the matter as facts show it."

The republic can have a longer life, but where there is corruption in political life, monarchy is the only means of escape. This is shown in *The Prince*, at a time that seemed to favor a quick and decisive solution to Italy's problems. In the *Discourses*, through the Roman model, Machiavelli proposes an objective that is more remote and harder to achieve: "living free," the "popular state." Yet it is not a remedy to the immediate situation, and Livy's account, which covers a wide span of time, can therefore offer an example that can be imitated.

If these thoughts developed at different periods, from the time Machiavelli had started to read Livy's *Decades* in the volume belonging to his father, the meetings in the Orti Oricellari must have borne particularly stimulating fruit, partly because they were with young men who perhaps had a better relationship with fortune in the future. After two key states in the peninsula, the Duchy of Milan and the Kingdom of Naples, had been taken over—one by France, the other by Spain—there no longer was any hope for "Italian might to defend . . . against foreigners," as he had written in chapter 26 of *The Prince*. A certain equilibrium appeared to have been created between the sovereigns who for a short time had ruled the two major European monarchies, the twenty-year-old Francis I and the sixteen-year-old Charles of Hapsburg; besides, after Maximilian of Austria had withdrawn from the Venetian mainland, the prospects for peace in Italy seemed greater. In short, the agitated final exhortation in *The Prince* certainly was not suited to the situation that was created after Machiavelli's meetings in the Orti Oricellari. The Italian crisis persisted and even worsened because it was deeply rooted in the life of the country, but if in 1515, before the Battle of Marignano, which Francis I won in mid-September, *The Prince* could still be dedicated to the young Lorenzo, by now the illusion that a descendant of the House of Medici might be able to resolve it had become outdated: one could no longer trust in the "virtù" and the fortune of an exceptional personality. It was necessary to think about a long-term operation, the formative process of a people becoming a state. Hence, a pedagogic function can be added to Machiavelli's work, which was no different from that which, with a different sentiment, Erasmus wrote in 1516: the *Institutio principis christiani*. We can in fact read the *Discourses* as an *institutio populi*, in the sense that it proposes the training of a new protagonist coming for the first time onto the stage of political thought, drawing strength from the experience of those Romans who had been a "people" in the full meaning—including the institutional one—of the term. More than once, the model Machiavelli invoked was opposed by the so-called realism of Guicciardini, who in the *Ricordi* (110) wrote: "What a mistake is theirs who cite on all occasions the example of the Romans!"[18] But if we move a little further on with the reading, we note that his observation is dictated by an awareness of the disproportion: it would be "to require of the ass the fleetness of the horse." Now, with a dramatic difference between the Italians of his time and the ancient Romans, it was certainly not Machiavelli who ignored it. His reading of ancient history also enabled him to understand, by contrasting the different periods, the ills of the present. Nor was he a cold observer of it; he wrote to clarify the present misfortunes, but also to examine potential remedies. Besides, the same circle of young friends who had urged him to write the *Discourses* had been moved by the desire to understand so as to find the strength and ability to act. Frequently Machiavelli has been the target of criticisms that have twisted his meaning. In particular, serious misunderstandings have occurred of the continuity that allegedly has been established between his thought and that of theoreticians of the reason of state, placing on the same plane two totally contradictory methods of engaging in politics. If instead of considering these theories in absolute terms to indicate their "essence"[19] we compare the texts of this original reaction of Catholicism with the "authentic thorn in the side of the church of the Counter-Reformation," as represented by Machiavelli's thought,[20] we can understand the profound differences between them. First, one of the major exponents of reason of state, Giovanni Botero, placed at its foundation the principle of the "preservation of the state."[21] Machiavelli, far from accepting and defending the status quo, was moved by a radical criticism of the situation into which Italy was being plunged and proposed a sweeping transformation of it: one might say the subversion of the "arrangements and laws" that were then in force. Regarding the relationship between politics and religion, Botero subjugated any "deliberation in the council of state" to the prior opinion of "doctors of theology and canon law"; at the same time he asked for the condemnation of "those who make new things out of divine matters," not only through obsequience to the true faith "but [also] because those who alter religion push hard for the alteration of things, where they hide plots, sedition, and cliques." In short, he wished to create a close link between the conservative action of the prince and the repression of the church that followed the Council of Trent. It is a vision that, on an ideological level, connects the policy of the Counter-Reformation to the counter-revolutionary theories of the age of the Restoration. It seems truly curious to insert the impious Machiavelli within such company!

The doctrine of the reason of state would show which favors religion could offer to those in power, thus reducing faith to its handmaiden, precisely because it could not accept the lay morality of Machiavelli. Recently, one scholar has observed:

> Machiavelli sketched out a religion based on virtue, capable of correcting the bad religious education of the Catholic church. . . . He chose to replace a religion that preached docility, and made men weak, with a religion that would teach a love for liberty and virtue. . . . He aspired to a religion that would teach men that their first duty to God, and the sole path to salvation, is to be strong citizens.[22]

The great lesson of the *Discourses*, in stark contrast to the theories of reason of state, was one of liberty; this went well beyond the traditional *libertas* and was certainly not meant to be distributed in the Florence dominated by the young descendant of the Medici family, the person to whom *The Prince* was dedicated, who is said to have preferred a gift of a pair of dogs to the "little work."[23] Perhaps Machiavelli was aware of this when, having completed the work, or nearly, he held well back from publicizing it, making it known only to trusted friends such as Francesco Guicciardini.

The Art of War

Machiavelli would publish another work born in the environment of the Rucellai Palace: *The Art of War*. This work, written between 1517 and 1520 and dedicated to the memory of his young friend Cosimo, who died in 1519, takes its cue from the visit the condottiere Fabrizio Colonna paid to Machiavelli in September 1516 and is set out in the form of a dialogue between the latter and visitors to the Orti Oricellari. The arrival of Charles VIII in Italy had highlighted the military weakness of the Italian states in the face of an army such as France's, which was superior in organization, armaments, tactics, and military technique. Of all this we have numerous eyewitness accounts by the writers of the time, but Machiavelli's originality lies in clarifying the tight nexus between such issues and political life in general. In political life, states are organisms to be studied in the same manner as the human body in order to understand their development and growth, even their corruption and decline; war is therefore a way for states to express themselves and demonstrate their vitality.

In *The Prince* and the *Discourses,* the question of arms is tackled as a complementary element of the political treatise; in *The Art of War* it is treated as the principal topic, the basis required to understand the necessity of an efficient military organization is politics. The principle is stated polemically right from the first lines of the preface, which take issue with what is said to be the opinion of many: "No two things are more out of harmony with one another or differ more from one another than civil life and military life."[1] In this sense *The Art of War* completes the trilogy of the great political works, examining beneath a particular glimpse the serious flaws of the Italian states as a whole. If this work, unique among Machiavelli's writings (other than those of a specifically literary nature), was published in 1521, it was probably because he had developed a topic more covertly political and therefore more palatable to the Medici and to those who governed Florence at that time, partly due to the competence ascribed to the author on the subject. This is demonstrated in a letter that Cardinal Giovanni Salviati, the pope's nephew, sent to him a month after the book's publication: "I . . . have looked diligently at your book, and the more I have considered it, the more I like it, for it seems to me that you have coupled to the most perfect manner of warfare in antiquity everything that is good in modern warfare and compounded an invincible army."[2]

In fact, Machiavelli had made his name as an expert in military affairs to such an extent that when in the Florence of the Medici the idea of reestablishing the ordinance was discussed, it was considered opportune to consult him. Some years after the book's publication he would be entrusted again with a government office as the chancellor of the magistracy that supervised the defense of Florence. He would subsequently enjoy such fame among both theorists and military leaders, and in France during the Wars of Religion, that François de La Noue and later Henri de Rohan, the defender of La Rochelle, would admire him as a military theorist, notwithstanding the notoriety of the Florentine secretary, who had been accused of being the secret inspiration of the Saint Bartholomew's Day Massacre in 1572.

His renown in the military field among his contemporaries allows us not to take too seriously criticisms of *The Art of War* on technical issues. Thus, regarding his renewed polemic against mercenary forces, critics have observed that other monarchies of the time had recourse to these, beginning with France; we should remember, however, that in Italy mercenaries enjoyed a freedom that was unknown anywhere else. Even Machiavelli's so-called underestimation of the value of artillery should be considered in relation to the specific conditions of the earliest years of the sixteenth century, when the use and manufacture of heavy arms were undergoing a difficult transition, and the development of such instruments of war would not happen until the 1530s.

In the seven books that comprise *The Art of War*, the central motive is governed by the necessity to "restore some of the forms of earlier excellence."[3] The issues are eminently technical: from the recruitment of soldiers to the armament of infantry and cavalry, from the order of battle to billeting, discipline, and fortifications. But the political problem continually rears its head and is in the background of Fabrizio Colonna's speech; right from the opening exchanges Colonna declares that "a well-ordered city will then decree that this practice of warfare shall be used in times of peace for exercise and in times of war for necessity and for glory, and will allow the public alone to practice it as a profession."[4] And in conclusion he states that "in Italy, then, to know how to manage an army already formed is not enough; a general must know first how to form it and then know how to command it." The mercenary armies that are found there are undisciplined, intolerant of hard work, insolent, and depraved. The Italians, "not having wise princes, ... have not adopted any good ... hence they are still the scorn of the world."⁵ We thus find the well-known reprimand directed against the Italian potentates in the years that preceded the Italian Wars: "The common belief of our Italian princes, before they felt the blows of Transalpine war, was that a prince needed only to think of a sharp reply in his study, to write a fine letter, to show quickness and cleverness in quotable sayings and replies, to know how to spin a fraud."

.These princes lived in luxury and dissoluteness, treated their subjects with arrogance, and granted favors to servient courtiers, even in the selection of captains for their armies: "It did not enter the minds of these wretches that they were preparing themselves to be the prey of whoever attacked them. From that came in 1494 great terrors, sudden flights and astonishing losses ... but what is worse is that those who are left continue in the same error and live by the same bad system."

Nevertheless, some glimmer of hope sparkles at the end of the condottiere's speech: "Of those who today have states in Italy, he, rather than anyone else, will be lord of this country who first sets out on this road [of military and political reform]." It will be as Philip of Macedonia, who organized an army capable of subjugating all of Greece, leaving to his son "such a foundation that he made himself ruler of all the world."⁶ From the same analysis of the dialogue a dramatic contradiction emerges between the possibility of organizing one's "own militia" and the impossibility of bringing into being a similar military force without a profound change in the Italian political order. Thus Fabrizio Colonna puts it to his young listeners that they would be able to see, in happier times, a situation more favorable for such profound reforms. "I do not wish you to be dismayed or terrified, because this land seems born to raise up dead things, as she has in poetry, in painting, and in sculpture."[7] The hope that had animated the final page of *The Prince* is still alive years later, enlivened—in this friend of Ariosto, of Leonardo, and of Michelangelo—by faith in the works of the Italian spirit.

PART III

"Niccolò Machiavelli, Historian, comic writer, and tragic writer"

A New Season in Machiavelli's Life

In the letters written in 1517 to his nephew Giovanni Vernacci, who was involved in commerce in Pera, a suburb of Istanbul where Europeans lived, Machiavelli had recalled the adversity and the "countless troubles" of the past few years and had used words of profound dejection, going so far as to write: "I have become useless to myself, to my relatives, and to my friends, because such has been the decision of my sad fate."[1] As early as the following year, however, a glimmer of hope for new possibilities opened up to him: a less hostile atmosphere was surrounding him in Florence given that, for the first time since he had been driven out of the palazzo, he had received a commission from a group of merchants to go to Genoa to recover at least part of the money lent by them to a bankrupt weaver. It certainly was not a prestigious mission, even if it involved Ottaviano Fregoso, the former doge of Genoa; nonetheless, as Ridolfi wrote, "to earn a few florins, especially to become active, 'to act alive,' the former secretary began to ride again."[2]

A sign of this improved state of affairs appears to be the fact that, having left off the composition of *The Ass*, he wrote, for the carnival of 1518, what is considered his theatrical masterpiece and undoubtedly one of the greatest comic creations of Italian literature, *The Mandrake*.[3] His calling for these expressive forms seems to date back to the years of his youth, when he dedicated himself, for example, to copying, along with Lucretius's *The Nature of Things*, Terence's *The Eunuch*, which the ancients judged the most successful work by the Latin playwright. We also know from his nephew Giuliano de' Ricci that in his years in the secretariat, he had written, with the encouragement of Chancellor Marcello Virgilio, a play in "imitation of *The Clouds* by Aristophanes," entitled *Le Maschere*, which was subsequently lost.[4] The relationship between "important matters" and "empty things," which, according to Machiavelli himself, characterized his correspondence with Vettori,[5] is equally intertwined in all of his multiform literary activities, and, further, an eminent critic has noted the stylistic affinity—in expressions, terms, syntactical and semantic forms—between those we call the "major works" and the playful writings or jocular letters.[6]

The earliest theatrical work remaining to us is the translation into the vernacular of another of Terence's plays, *Andria*, which survives in two editions: a more hurried version from 1517, written perhaps in response to requests for a performance, and another revised and notably modified version from 1520. This work is not devoid of originality in the choice of language and in some adjustments made to the script; yet Machiavelli reached the highest point of his comic genius in *The Mandrake*, which shows how much theater was an art form that he found congenial. The play is full of moral meaning and is broadly political through the representation of a simulation of humanity, in which deception is the driving force of the action. In the *Discourses* (1.30) Machiavelli had stated that "men cannot be wholly good or wholly bad"; the same ambiguity envelops the characters of the play, in parts that cast a sinister light on them. In fact, even the man who should be the hero, Callimaco, in order to succeed in winning the love of the beautiful wife of Messer Nicia, whom he had heard talked about when he still lived in Paris, puts himself in the hands of a ribald such as Ligurio and, in a moment of desperation, declares his readiness to "try any plan whatever, even if it's stupid, cruel, wicked" (1.3). But in the end the mandrake, the miraculous root that gives the play its title, has an ambiguous power; it encourages the woman's fertility but is also deadly for the first man who lies with her.[7] At least that was the widespread belief referred to by Callimaco, whom the rogue Ligurio introduces as a great doctor from Paris to Nicia, who yearns to have a son with his wife, Lucrezia. Nicia is persuaded to administer a potion, and to avoid the risk of falling victim to it, "gets somebody to sleep with her right after it; if he's with her one night, he'll draw to himself all the poison of the mandrake" (2.6).

Nor does Frate Timoteo—willing as he is, thanks to his cynical mind and his venality, to act as a go-between—appear "too bad" if it is he who persuades Lucrezia to couple with another prior to the coupling with her husband; his way of arguing, replete with hair-splitting sophisms (3.11), is inspired by a well-known comment on texts of canon law.[8] Even Messer Nicia, who in his simplemindedness is ready to march to the battle cry of "Saint Cuckoo," after Ligurio has explained to him that he is "the saint most honored in France" (4.9), does not have any qualms in causing the death of "the first young fellow" whom he will run into in the street, and he himself will see to it that he lies with his wife, to the point of ensuring, through his "touch with my hands," that the pair are coupling. He is therefore deceived because he himself is prepared to deceive, despite the dire consequences.

The plot thickly spun by the deception that pervades the whole play resolves itself in the night of passion between the two protagonists, and in the end Lucrezia, faced with the "cleverness" of Callimaco, the "stupidity" of her husband, the "folly" of her mother, and the "rascality" of her confessor, accepts with a good heart that which appears to be the fruit of "Heaven's wish that has ordered it so" (5.4). However, she solemnly makes a declaration that ties her for life to her lover. In this way the denouement manages to overcome the bitter irony of the joke, which is the raison d'être of *The Mandrake*. In effect, such tensions and the dark side of some of the characters have led to the question whether, beyond the joke, the play does contain something of a tragedy. Machiavelli's laughter, anything but lighthearted, is geared toward revealing human pettiness. Only love has the strength to make "sweet . . . every bitter thing that has been tasted," and the conclusion serves as a catharsis: the love between Callimaco and Lucrezia will also be a guilty one, but its strength makes it superior. Its power, celebrated in other impassioned verses, turns out to be triumphant, and in the song at the end of the third act praises are sung to the victory of love: "You conquer, with your sacred counsels alone / rocks, enchantments, and poisons."

In the prologue the author admits that perhaps "this material . . . does not befit a man who likes to seem wise and dignified," but he excuses himself, explaining "that he is striving with these trifling thoughts to make his wretched life more pleasant." Then again, "He has been cut off from showing other powers with other deeds." Almost by way of reproach, although *The Prince* had not led to any positive result, the performance of *The Mandrake* kindled the interest of Pope Leo X, who wanted it staged in Rome as well.[9] Only then did the long period of ostracism the Medici had imposed on Machiavelli finally end, concluding the long quarantine he had suffered. Perhaps this dawning of horizons also gave him the inspiration to write the only novella of his to have come down to us.[10] It is clear to anyone who knows Machiavelli's letters that the talent of a narrator lay within him; in these letters the erotic Veronese misadventure that he related to Luigi Guicciardini on 8 December 1509 and the ugly joke Giuliano Brancacci played on a friend, mentioned on 25 February 1514 in a letter to Vettori, follow the course of licentious accounts. Not for nothing did Matteo Bandello, a famous short story writer who was his friend, eulogize Machiavelli for his gifts as a narrator and the spirit with which he was able to entertain his friends.[11]

The tale, called *Favola*, which was sometimes referred to as the *Novella del demonio che pigliò moglie* and at other times as *Belfagor arcidiavolo*, sets forth a misogynistic theme, probably quite old and of Oriental origin, but reprised in Latin during the Middle Ages and published in French toward the end of the fifteenth century by Jehan Le Febvre in the *Lamentations de Mathéolus*. It is possible that Machiavelli became aware of it during one of his journeys to France. In this work, usually considered playful, Machiavelli depicts humanity in its most unhappy and petty aspects and ultimately in its tragic ones. The eighth chapter of *The Ass* comes to mind, where in the final verses written before leaving off the composition, Machiavelli had shown, through the words of the "fat porker," who refused to abandon his bestial condition, the unhappiness and the cruelty of men:

> One hog to another hog causes no pain,
> One stag to another; man by another man
> Is slain, crucified and plundered.[12]

Favola narrates the misadventures of an archdevil sent by Pluto into the world to learn how "all or most [of the souls who went to hell] complained that they were led to this great misfortune by nothing but marriage."[13]

One can conclude that in these reflections there could not have been any autobiographical reference: the wife of Machiavelli, Marietta Corsini, as far as we know, was a patient and affectionate woman who had raised six children and put up with the frequent escapades of her husband. At most she asked him for "a piece of light-brown camlet" as a gift.[14]

A Return to Business

Machiavelli's position was improving. After the death of the young Lorenzo de' Medici in May 1519, Cardinal Giulio de' Medici, having rushed to Florence to take the reins of government, appeared to intend to partly restore the republican institutions. To this end he consulted various people, including Machiavelli. He had been given free rein by the pope to do so, which we know from a letter dated 26 April 1520 that one of the frequenters of the Rucellai Palace, Battista della Palla, sent from Rome to Machiavelli:

> I have spoken of your affairs in detail with the pope and in truth, as far as can be seen, I have found him very well disposed toward you. . . . I have been asked to tell Cardinal de' Medici on behalf of His Holiness, when I am there, that he will be very pleased if the good will that His Reverend Lordship has toward your desires should henceforth be put into effect."[1]

In reality, the cardinal had already wanted to meet Machiavelli since March 10; Machiavelli was introduced to him by Lorenzo Strozzi, to whom, by way of thanks, *The Art of*

War would be dedicated. "The good will [of] His Reverend Lordship" would result in two important commissions: the request of an opinion in writing on the possibility of reforming the Florentine state and the task of writing the history of Florence.

The cardinal requested the piece on the reform of Florence against a background of consultations that the cardinal was having in Florentine circles following the death of every direct descendant of Cosimo de' Medici who had been capable of ruling. There were, it was true, two illegitimate sons: one, the future cardinal Ippolito, recognized as the son of Giuliano; the other, the future duke Alessandro, recognized as the son of Lorenzo; in reality, it appears that both were sons of Cardinal Giulio, the future pope Clement VII; the pair, however, were both still children. At that moment, members of the second-born branch of the family were not considered, which would have a valid representative in the mercenary who became famous as Giovanni dalle Bande Nere and who in 1537, through his son Cosimo, would take up the family succession. Thus, between the end of 1520 and the beginning of 1521, Machiavelli, to carry out the cardinal's request, would write *A Discourse on Remodeling the Government of Florence*, or in Latin *Discursus florentinarum rerum post mortem iunioris Laurentii Medices*, a short text addressed to Leo X, which exemplifies an ideal elaboration of *Discourses on the First Decade of Titus Livius*.

Even though he only recently had begun a relationship with the dominant family, Machiavelli did not shrink from expressing, right from the outset, a most unflattering opinion on the "system" of the Medici. The continual changes of government in Florence were occurring because "she has never been either a republic or a princedom having the qualities each requires."[2] So it happened, after the repression of the Revolt of the Ciompi in 1382, with "the republic of the Àlbizzi," which led Florence under the hegemony of that family, to be governed by the optimates for forty or so years, "and it would have been less permanent had the Visconti wars not ensued, which kept it united." But also "Cosimo's government," which followed—though enjoying, in contrast to its predecessor, the advantage of having been "established with the people's aid" and of being "controlled by the prudence of two such men as Cosimo and Lorenzo his grandson"—gave itself institutions so lacking in stability that it was continually necessary to resort to special measures, and "at the critical time of King Charles's expedition, the Medici government fell."

In a text to be laid before the Medici, we cannot expect to find a favorable opinion on the Soderini republic, but in any case the criticism of that regime is centered in turn on the fact that this too was "remote from a true republic" because of the ambiguous characteristics the office of gonfalonier for life assumed. The latter, if he were "intelligent and wicked," could make himself prince; if "good and weak, he could easily be driven out." For the first time Machiavelli pronounces a strong judgment, not of Pier Soderini, but of the gonfalonier for life, even if in some passages of *Discourses* we can catch a glimpse of some reservations toward this magistracy, which, since it was for life, could not adapt to changing times (3.9, in *Works* 1:453). In any event, the optimates wanted this situation, desirous as they were of installing a republic similar to that of Venice, and right from the beginning of *Discourse on Remodeling the Government of Florence* their arrogance was given as one of the causes of Florentine instability.

The various reforms introduced in the government of Florence had always been influenced by specific interests, and no scheme capable of elevating itself above the factions and provide a benefit to all the citizens had ever been conceived.

Machiavelli wrote: "The reason why all these governments have been defective is that the alterations in them have not been made for the fulfillment of the common good, but for the strengthening and security of the party."[3]

Perhaps the extraordinariness of the moment would finally offer the opportunity to install a true republic. The "opinions of many," who wished to restore the government established by Cosimo, a form of veiled lordship, was resolutely opposed. "A government of that sort is risky" because it is weak, Machiavelli declared without any ambiguity.[4] It was feasible in the time of Cosimo, although difficult, because the internal state of affairs was different: at that time, the government "had the approval of the people generally"; but now "the people" were "hostile" to it. With some courage, Machiavelli stated that after the experience of the Soderini republic, the Florentines would not tolerate a less free government: "The citizens of Cosimo's time had never experienced in Florence a government that gave greater power to the people; the present citizens have experienced one that they think more just and that pleases them better."[5] Moreover, the situation in Italy had changed profoundly: in the time of Cosimo, the Florentines were able to defend themselves from their enemies because the latter were only the other states of the peninsula; now, "since Spain and France are here," it was necessary to contend with those two powers, and complete freedom of action was unthinkable. The "former secretary" was well aware of the possible connections between external and internal politics, and that it was necessary to take these into account when giving shape to a new state. He added that the practice of high taxes that a state such as Cosimo's would have imposed was lost: Soderini's administration had restored Florentine finances to health, whereas the Medici restoration had immediately caused problems for the treasury. Moreover, during his time

Cosimo behaved with much "friendliness"; but now the Medici "have grown so great that, since they have gone beyond all the habits of citizens, there cannot be such intimacy" (*Works*, 1:105). In conclusion, Machiavelli sought to destroy nostalgic delusions: "Nor should anyone believe that men easily return to a way of life that is old and habitual, because in truth they do so when the old way of living is more pleasing than the new one, but when it pleases less, they do not return to the old way unless forced to, and they live in it only as long as that force lasts" (*Works*, 1:105).

He then tackled another difficult issue: the person of the "director," doubtless indispensable. If one had to think of an "unofficial director," undoubtedly one of the House of Medici would be preferable, but in dealing with an "official director," the latter would always be preferable to an "unofficial" one. And so the argument came back to the decisive point of a clear choice between a republic and a principality. "It is therefore not possible Your Holiness, if you wish to give Florence a firm government for your own glory and the security of your friends, to set up there other than a true princedom or a republic having its distinctive parts. Any other form would be useless and short-lived" (*Works*, 1:106).

In effect, the republic is the choice indicated as binding, and thus in the *Discourse* Machiavelli dwelled on the constitutional norms considered necessary so that it has a balanced foundation, at the same time giving instructions on the guarantees to be provided to the House of Medici. For the princedom, however, "there are no facilities for doing it" following the death of Lorenzo the Younger, since there is no one capable of assuming the succession. In Florence, moreover, there was a further obstacle to the creation of a principality: as Machiavelli had observed in *Discourses* (1.55), he repeated here that "where the citizens are accustomed to equality, a princedom cannot be set up except with the utmost difficulty," because "the establishment of inequality would be necessary; noble lords of walled towns and boroughs would have to be set up, who in support of the prince would with their arms and their followers stifle the city and the whole province."

If, as is easy to understand, the *Discourse* did not generally receive a warm welcome within Medici circles, these latter instructions did, however, find an audience. Measures against "equality," in fact, had been suggested to the Medici right after their return to Florence in 1512 by those connected to the Florentine secretary. In a piece of advice to Lorenzo the Younger, written in 1516 "to halt the State of Florence in its devotion to the Medici," a friend of Machiavelli, Lodovico Alamanni, recognized that the Florentines "were used to a certain stupidity sooner than freedom," and as a result had been persuaded to oppose courtly dress. He had therefore suggested a remedy; there was no doubt that "this fantasy of old would never stand up." Fortunately, however, "they are wise, and of the wise there is nothing to fear because they never do anything new"; on the contrary, "the young would easily be diverted from this citizenship," and it would suffice if Lorenzo would take them into his service, giving some of them military tasks, and others, "lettered" ones, roles such as "secretaries, agents, commissars and ambassadors." All of them "would grab the cloak and leave their hood," that is, they would abandon the simple dress of the citizen and assume courtly robes and, in changing clothes, "would act as if they had become friars, since they would renounce the republic and make profession to his order [Lorenzo's]."[6] In contrast to his brother Luigi, an assiduous frequenter of the Orti Oricellari who some years later would take part in the conspiracy against Cardinal Giulio, Lodovico Alamanni had sided with the Medici and had their political fortune at heart. However, he was friends with Machiavelli, as we know from a letter of 17 December 1517,[7] and we can conjecture that it was from Machiavelli himself that he had derived the ideas he was now espousing.

Filippo Strozzi, also a Florentine noble and a friend of Machiavelli who was destined to be remembered for the political struggle he waged in his final years against the Medici and, after having been made a prisoner in 1537 by Duke Cosimo I, for the tragic end that gave him the halo of republican martyr even during the Risorgimento, expressed similar ideas. After the second return of the Medici in 1530, when he was on the side of the restored regime, he suggested to Clement VII that he destroy that "civic equality" which had given strength to the Florentine Republic and had been revived in 1527 following the sack of Rome. To give stability to Medici power, which at that point had acceded to the princedom with Duke Alessandro, it was necessary to erase every trace of the former liberty. Strozzi therefore wrote that because it seemed that the strength of the state lay in its being ruled by a party that did not represent the people:

> it is recorded by some that it would be good perchance to elect all those who are friends, and that we think we have need of it, and also to be able to profit from running from house to house and declaring them noble through a public provision, admitting only these to the government and excluding everyone else as commoners.[8]

The distinction had to be a radical one: only those who had been declared noble would be able to accede to honors and public positions and to bear arms, "so that the difference between the common people and them might appear in all directions," and between the new nobles and the people an irremediable contrast might be born, to the lord's advantage.

These mechanisms of social tightening and stratification were destined to be confirmed in Italian life during the sixteenth century, while the artifices of constitutional engineering that Machiavelli suggested in order to give life to a stable republic would remain a dead letter. Nevertheless, the ending of the *Discourse* can be compared to the final chapter of *The Prince* for the nobility of its sentiments and human warmth. The spirit of the Florentine secretary continued to be open to hope for the future.

"The annals or the history of Florence"

Before sitting down to write the *Discourse*, Machiavelli was given another task, which allowed him to prepare his historiographic work.[1] In the summer of 1520 Cardinal Giulio decided to use his services in, once again, a financial mission. Again it concerned a disastrous piece of business: a merchant from Lucca, Michele Guinigi, belonging to one of the leading families of the small Tuscan republic. Due to his dissolute life, his father had disinherited him, but the illustrious family name had opened to him imprudently advanced loans in Florence. The Salviati, too, related to Leo X through the marriage of his sister Lucrezia with one of them, had been exposed to large losses. Even the signory of Florence became involved in the affair to the extent that it got negotiations under way with the government of Lucca starting in autumn 1519. On July 7 of the following year, Machiavelli was sent "to undertake and resolve this matter." The issue would drag on for so long that he could not resolve it (he would conclude it the following year), but when he returned to Florence the negotiations had been satisfactorily gotten under way.

In the course of the negotiations, Machiavelli had a lot of time to dedicate to other matters. He studied the government of the republic of Lucca, with the reform to be introduced in Florence in mind; but more important, he wrote *The Life of Castruccio Castracani of Lucca*, about a mercenary captain who in the fourteenth century had become lord of Lucca. This served as proof of Machiavelli's abilities as a writer of history, especially in view of the commission that he would receive in the autumn from the Studio Fiorentino to write *The History of Florence*. Leo X had in fact told Battista della Palla that he intended to ask him to commission Machiavelli "to do some writing" with reference to that work,[2] and on 6 September 1520, Zanobi Buondelmonti, who had read the life of the Lucchese mercenary, invited him to prepare for that more demanding enterprise, since "this model of a history of yours" had given him much pleasure and he had had the opportunity of discussing it with numerous other friends who had been frequenters of the Orti Oricellari.

In the autumn of 1520 the Studio Fiorentino, which was under the direct control of Cardinal de' Medici, commissioned from Machiavelli "the annals or else the history of the things done by the state and city of Florence."[3] This task was traditionally entrusted to the chancellors of the republic, and in some way this duty returned him to his former function, even if the compensation was little more than half of the salary he received as secretary. For this, Pier Soderini, who had previously offered him the position of chancellor of the Republic of Ragusa (a proposal that Machiavelli did not even consider, as he was too closely tied to Florence), now aware of the commission and of its related recompense, proposed to him on 13 April 1521 that he place himself in the service of the mercenary Prospero Colonna. He extolled the "stipend" that the latter was ready to give him: "Two hundred gold ducats and expenses . . . : much better than to stay there and write histories for *fiorini di suggello* [sealed florin]."[4] Evidently the ex-gonfalonier had not understood the mentality of his former colleague: for Machiavelli, obtaining a public position in Florence was more important than the salary, which is why he rejected the offer. One might think that this lack of understanding, besides the flight of 1512, may have dictated the derisory epigram that he composed upon the death in 1522 of his former employer: "That night when Piero Soderini died, his spirit went to the mouth of Hell. Pluto roared, "Why to Hell? Silly spirit, go up to Limbo with the rest of the babies."[5]

In fact, the position of historiographer did not just signify having his worth recognized and the regaining of authority; "writing histories" put him on an equal footing with two famous humanist chancellors of the republic, Leonardo Bruni and Poggio Bracciolini, whose works he would evoke in the preface to *The History of Florence*. It has also been observed that this work permitted him to "give a taste of the worth of his language and that of Florence," during a period when Italian men of letters had set in motion a debate on the language, which interested him so much that he took part in it.[6] With the drafting of *The History of Florence*, he would be able to try to restore to his city the literary prestige it had lost during the isolation into which Florentine literature had fallen at the beginning of the sixteenth century. Certainly, in the contract that was drawn up, he was left free to write "in whatever language—either Latin or Tuscan—may seem best to him";[7] but attributing his choice of Italian to a lack of familiarity with Latin would be to remove Machiavelli from the intellectual world of his time. If anything, we can observe that his preoccupation with writing the history of Italy in a "modern language" led him to pursue a style that departed from classical styles to a greater extent than he had done in *The Prince* and *Discourses* or even *The Art of War*, where he had been more faithful to the literary conventions of his age.

The writing of *The History of Florence* took four years, although it was interspersed with various other activities. It was not an easy task to write about the events in Florence after Cosimo took the reins at the command of a Medici pope (in November 1523 Cardinal Giulio had been elected pope with the name Clement VII). It is entirely understandable that on 30 August 1524 Machiavelli should confide in Francesco Guicciardini, with whom, as we shall see, he had sealed a strong bond of friendship:

> I have been staying and now stay on my farm to write the *History*, and I would pay ten soldi—I do not intend to say more—to have you by my side so that I could show you where I am, because, having come to certain particularities, I need to learn from you if I give too much offence either by raising or by lowering those things.[8]

Although he did not hide his thoughts on the situation in Italy and Florence, it was no doubt necessary that he exercise some caution. Donato Giannotti, who had frequented the Orti Oricellari, wrote later of having heard him say the following:

> I am not able to write this history from when Cosimo took the state up until the death of Lorenzo as I would write it if I were free in all respects; the events will be true, and I will not permit otherwise, save that I will leave in the background the discussion of the universal causes of things: words willing, I will tell of the events and the incidents that happened when Cosimo took over the state; I will leave in the background the discussion of how and by which means and astuteness someone can reach such heights, and anyone who wishes to

understand this further should note very well what I am going to make his enemies say, since that which I do not wish to say as though coming from me, I will make his enemies say.[9]

In truth, even if Machiavelli did harbor such scruples, the restrictions he placed upon himself were rather limited. Certainly, the worst faults and the gravest misdeeds of Cosimo, Piero, and Lorenzo were attributed mostly to their supporters, but the criticism that the powerful representatives of the Medici party acted in a partisan manner strikes out, by way of reflex, at those who dominate the government, and in *The History of Florence* we do not find pages that serve as an apology for the regime the Medici imposed. Suffice it to recall the severe reproach that Piero directed at his supporters, calling them to his house "to unburden his conscience and to see if he could make them ashamed," declaring at the beginning of his speech: "I would never have believed that there could come a time when the ways and habits of my friends would bring me to such a pass that I should love and mourn for my enemies." He continued: "You plunder your neighbor of his goods, you sell justice, you escape civil lawsuits, you oppress peaceful men, and the arrogant you make powerful. I do not believe that in all Italy there are so many examples of violence and avarice as in this city" (book 7, chapter 23).

By the end of 1524 the narration in the book had reached the death of Lorenzo the Magnificent, and in the first few weeks of 1525 the manuscript, elegantly copied, was ready to be offered to the man who had commissioned it, the pope. Unfortunately, the moment did not seem propitious; those were, in fact, tempestuous days. Francis I and Charles V had begun fighting each other in Italy, and Clement VII, after the French had taken Milan on October 1524, had formed an alliance with them. But on 24 February 1525 a decisive battle took place at Pavia, during which the king of France suffered a disastrous defeat and was taken prisoner. In this situation, Vettori hesitated to advise Machiavelli on whether he should "come with the book or not, because the times are opposed to reading and to gifts."[10] However, as he wrote to his friend on March 8, "the pope, on the first evening I arrived, . . . asked me about you on his own and inquired of me whether you had finished the *Historia* and whether I had seen it." Surprised by this curiosity, Vettori replied that Machiavelli had reached "the death of Lorenzo, and that it was something that would give satisfaction," so much so that he would have liked to have brought the manuscript to him, but, he added, "on account of the times," he himself had dissuaded him. At that point Clement VII had replied that he had been wrong to give him this advice: "He ought to come, and I feel for certain that his books are going to give me pleasure and be read willingly."[11] Thus, in May Machiavelli was in Rome and presented *History* to the pontiff, who, for the occasion, granted him 120 golden ducats. For the time being, the work was published only in manuscript form; the printed version would appear posthumously, in 1532, at the hand of the Roman typographer Blado and contemporaneously of the Florentine Benedetto di Giunta.

"The things done at home and abroad
by the Florentine people"

Whoever reads *The History of Florence* may pose a question: Do we have in front of us a complete work or not?[1] The opinions are contradictory. Felix Gilbert, an influential scholar, referring to some passages where Machiavelli writes that he intends not to stop with the death of Lorenzo the Magnificent, stated that "the *History of Florence* is not a complete work." Another scholar, no less than the authoritative Carlo Dionisotti, however, discounted the opinion that "Machiavelli would ever have seriously proposed, with Clement VII being pope, to continue his *History of Florence*," observing: "It was already a miracle that he had emerged unharmed from the published manuscript of a work that was provocative in so many of its aspects."[2]

Which elements and which information could make one think that something was missing? The evidence for the first is scarce. In the dedication to Clement VII, the author explains that "since, in writing, I have come to those times which, through the death of the Magnificent Lorenzo de' Medici, changed Italy's condition," he had wanted to assemble the work "in one volume" and to offer it to the pope. The promise to provide a sequel is rather vague: "Since the events occurring afterward have been loftier and greater, and must be set forth with a loftier and greater spirit," he had judged it opportune to present to the pope "all I have written up to those times." We can read this passage as an adjournment to a continuation, to be written in a subsequent period "with a loftier and greater spirit," but also as the sign of a period that has concluded, after which the changes that have taken place justify this interruption. In book 8, chapter 9, the birth of the future Clement VII is announced, and of his fortune and "virtù" we read, "When we come to present affairs, if God gives us life, we shall set them forth at length." Rather than a firm commitment to carry on, these words can be only an act of reverence and good wishes. Finally, the author concludes the dedication by writing that he would continue the work "if life does not desert me and Your Holiness does not forsake me." Even this can be seen as a customary greeting.

However, in a letter to Guicciardini written after 21 October 1525—that is, after tragic events in Milan had put an end to the hope that Spanish control over that duchy could be overthrown— he announced: "I received that addition, making a total of a hundred ducats, for *History*. I am now beginning to write again, and I relieve myself by blaming the princes, who have all done everything to bring us here" (*Works*, 2:987). We know, however, that the man who commissioned the work wished it to continue, so much so that he continued paying Machiavelli and even increased his compensation; thus the author was set to provide a sequel with the desire of "relieving himself." This makes it likely that Machiavelli intended to write to express the passion that had burst out of his letters in the last few years. However, nothing has reached us of this continuation, or at least so far nothing has been found.[3]

Machiavelli had not set aside the plan to continue the narration of the events that took place following the death of Lorenzo the Magnificent, even if he had described this time, with good reason, as the end of an era. He was certainly aware of the difficulty of discussing events in which he had been involved, and for our part we can lament not having his version of these episodes. In any event, in what concerns the historical work that we have, we see that it is endowed with a masterly construction and internal cohesion, allowing us to consider it complete.

On the choice of where to begin *History*, things are clearer. When Machiavelli wrote to Del Nero on the "substance of the contract," he did not define a starting date, leaving the question open; he would begin "from whatever time may seem to him most appropriate" (*Works*, 2:971). In the preface he stated that he had thought, "when I first decided to write of the things done at home and abroad by the Florentine people, to begin my narrative with the year of the Christian era 1434," in other words the ascent to power of Cosimo de' Medici. Subsequently, however, he changed his mind and decided to "begin my history with the origin of our city." He explained that he had become aware of the existence of a serious gap in the histories of Leonardo Bruni and Poggio Bracciolini, which prevented him from writing his own work, in line with the initial plan, as a continuation of those: the two authors had not talked sufficiently about "civil strife and internal hostilities, and the effects these have produced," and he criticized them for having "one part of them wholly silent . . . and the other part they describe so briefly that their readers can get no profit or pleasure."[4]

To tell the truth, the criticism aimed at his two predecessors has been called into question: it seemed, in fact, to be stretching the point to claim that in Bruni's and Bracciolini's works Florence's internal politics had not been discussed. We cannot exclude the fact that this criticism (with the consequent beginning that predated the ascent of Cosimo to power) was a mere expedience; since the work had been commissioned by a Medici cardinal (who later became pope), beginning the *History* in 1434 could have given the impression of an apologetic work, and, moreover, it would have been difficult to avoid a celebration of Cosimo's ascent to power.

There is, however, a real interpretative divergence that needs to be taken into account. When Machiavelli reflects on the outcome of events, the situation of Florence at the time of Cosimo and in his own time appears tightly linked to the old civil wars, and from that point of view, the way in which these were laid out in the histories of Bruni and Bracciolini was not acceptable to him. He was in fact led to give a negative opinion on the optimate-led government installed by the Àlbizzi during the years spanning the fourteenth and fifteenth centuries; therefore he could not endorse the panegyric by Bruni, who had hailed the republican regime of that period as *vera libertas,* to the extent that the intimate connection of ideals had been indicated between his *Historiæ* and his *Laudatio florentinæ Urbis.*[5] Equally, Machiavelli could not participate in Poggio Bracciolini's subsequent glorification of that government. The intention to celebrate the reconstruction of Florence's past had made the two humanists' works a pillar of the oligarchic republic's self-representation by affirming the combination of "libertas" and "equabilitas" in the lives of the citizens, an ideological statement that contradicted Machiavelli's ideas. It is clear that the authors, writing at the behest of Cosimo's descendant, would have been indecorous to indicate as a model the government of those who had wanted to eliminate the Medici from Florentine life. But this was certainly not Machiavelli's opinion, since precisely that government had been at the origin of the hybrid institutional situation he deplored at the start of *Discourse*, the work he wrote between November 1520 and February 1521 with the intent to propose a reform of the Florentine government. "The reason why Florence throughout her history has frequently varied her methods of government," Machiavelli observed in this piece of writing, "is that she has never been either a republic or a princedom having the qualities each requires."[6]

Moreover, previously in the *Discourses*, he had observed that "since at her origin she [Florence] was subject to Roman authority and had always lived under the control of others, she remained for a time humble, without planning for herself. Then, when came a chance for taking a breath, she endeavored to make her own laws."[7]

Not even the freedom granted allowed Florence to give itself satisfactory institutions, since those rules, "being mingled with old ones that were bad," would turn out to be flawed, leading Machiavelli to conclude: "And so she has gone on governing herself for the two hundred years for which there are trustworthy records, without ever having had a government because of which she could truly be called a republic."

Even this ambiguous situation, which caused the weakness of Florence, contributed to the complication of the Italian "crisis." In the moment in which Florence invited Cardinal Giulio de' Medici to establish a republic that supported him,[8] the chance of showing which events may have corrupted Florentine political life could be realized only by showing the course of the entire history of the city. The prevalence of private interests over public matters was one of its age-old characteristics. In the *Discourses* (1.4) Machiavelli had stated: "Those who condemn the dissensions between the nobility and the people seem to me to be finding fault with what as a first cause kept Rome free." In the *History* he could also now underline the difference between the Roman political struggles and the divisions in Florence. Thus, at the start of the third book he illustrated the radical difference between the two types of clashes and the contradictory effects that they would gave birth to: whereas in Rome the division was overcome with the promulgation of new laws or the institution of new magistracies that gave the republic greater fairness and stability, in Florence the victory of one party was marked by the killing of opponents or their banishment into exile; the clashes in Rome "always increased military power, those in Florence wholly destroyed it"; in Rome a more complex social articulation was reached, whereas Florence was brought to "a striking equality.⁹" Yet this led not to greater democracy but to a leveling, thus extinguishing every "ability in arms and boldness of spirit," such that the Florentine people "grew always weaker and more despicable."

The division between citizens was a problem he tackled with particular zeal in the episodes leading to the ascendance of the Guelph party. Through the historiographic expedience of oration, attributed to one of the "many citizens, [who were] moved by love for their country," Machiavelli highlighted the failures caused by "those who come together for the ruin of the republic" and unite in a faction, and who, to advance their own specific interests, "assemble . . . not for any public profit but for their own ambition."¹⁰ The speech ranges across the situation of all the Italian cities, which, "not having a strong rein to guide them, have organized their states and governments not as free but as divided factions." Italian political life thus suffocated from party interests and was shattered everywhere. These events occurred both in the state constitution, which was created by a dominant city and by the various centers subservient to it, and in the political action of the principal city, which developed as an alliance of ambitious individuals ready to place themselves at the head of factions, endowed with broad autonomy, and ready to fight to assert their own superiority.

Thus it becomes clear that *The History of Florence* has prefaces and orations as the cornerstones of its narration. In the first chapter of each book, original ideas are discussed, which outline the subsequent events, and the author uses this premise to strengthen the narrative. A simple chronological history of events could not have been satisfactory to someone who was able to lay out in such an original way his own historical reflections in the *Discourses on the First Decade of Titus Livius*. In the observations that open each book, Machiavelli thus traces the essential outline and the original characters of the events in Florence. Linking them together gave *The History* a unitary rhythm and impetus, which helped clarify his intentions. Thus, the preface immediately introduces the divisions of Florence; to all appearances, it reaches a eulogy of the city, powerful enough to know how to assert itself notwithstanding the internal disputes. But then a very persuasive reservation arises: "If Florence had had the good fortune . . . to take a form of government that would have kept her united, I do not know what form of republic, modern or ancient, would have been superior to her—with such ability in arms and in peaceful arts she would have abounded."[11] This had not happened, and the consequences had to be made evident to the reader.

The first chapter of the second book deplores the fact that the ancient Roman custom of founding new centers of habitation "where men can gather for convenient defense and farming" had fallen out of use.[12] The ancients were accustomed to "sending into conquered or empty countries new inhabitants," giving these population zones the name "colonies." It is a custom that is useful not only for keeping conquered lands, but also for preventing depopulated areas from being formed. Not all places "are . . . productive or healthful"; in some the inhabitants flourish, in others they are scarce, "and if there is no way for taking them from where they are plentiful and putting them where they are scarce, a province in a short time is ruined, for one part of it, through its small number of inhabitants, becomes desert, and another, through their excess, becomes poor." That is why "many parts . . . of Italy, have become, in comparison with ancient times, uninhabited."[13] It would be wrong to judge these words as only the fruit of admiration for the ancient Roman custom of controlling conquered territories through colonies. Machiavelli could not have forgotten the terrible consequences of the Black Death in 1348, which weighed heavily on the demography of Italy until the mid-fifteenth century, as the Florentine land registry of the time attests. Besides, someone who knew Livy, who was so attentive to the dislocation of the Etruscans and the Samnites, would certainly take into account the demographic upheaval of an Italy that, after the fall of the Western Empire, had witnessed the depopulation of its coastal areas both because of the degradation of the land, which had become swamp-ridden and malarial, and because of the Arab raids and incursions. Previously, in Giovanni Villani's *Chronicles* (page 34), the Florentine writer who in the fourteenth century had wanted to "recount and make memorial of the root and origins" of his city, Machiavelli woud have been able to read the following: "And note that of old the coasts were much inhabited, and albeit inland there were few cities, and few inhabitants, yet in Maremma and Maretima, towards Rome . . . there were many cities and many inhabitants, which to-day are consumed and brought to nought by reason of the corruption of the air" (1.50).[14]

The repopulation of the coasts, when it took place, had happened as a consequence of later events. Thus in *The History of Florence* we find the birth of Venice mentioned; it was "placed in a swampy and unhealthful site, yet the many inhabitants that at one time gathered there made it healthful." Equally Pisa, "because of the noxious air, was never full of inhabitants until Genoa and her shores were laid waste by the Saracens. This caused those people, driven from their native places, at one time to gather there in large numbers, which made her populous and powerful."

The discussion at the beginning of the third book on the consequences of factions has been mentioned; in some way the first chapter of the fourth book develops this line of thought, drawing attention to the evil rules that lead states to vary their governments "not between liberty and slavery, as many believe, but between liberty and license." "the promoters of license, who are the people, and promoters of slavery, who are the nobles, praise the mere name of liberty" (*Works*, 3:1187), and we should not overlook the fact that these comments open the book, which shows Florence during the years when the hegemony of the Àlbizzi was established. The hard polemic is nevertheless directed at all of the Florentine factions, whom Machiavelli accuses of being unwilling "to be subject either to the laws or to men." This leads to instability and the prevalence of "arrogant" or "stupid" men, who cause the ruin of the republic.[15]

The fifth book opens with the thorniest part of the work: the government of Cosimo de' Medici. If Machiavelli had intended to praise it, he would have found it easy to show that Cosimo had then initiated a new period for Florence, a new history, and that popular consent had favored the rise of the first of the Medici, overturning oligarchic power. However, Machiavelli succeeded in avoiding any laudatory or, worse, flattering, expression and, in keeping with some annotations to the *Discourses* (1.7 and preface to book 2), took as his starting point the continual "variations" of "worldly things," which, when they have "no further possibility for rising, . . . must go down. Likewise, when they have gone down and through their defects have reached the lowest depths, they necessarily rise, since they cannot go lower." There is, in short, an inevitable concatenation: from ability, which produces calm, one passes to idleness, and from there to disorder and ruin; then the cycle begins anew. If a period of quiet follows ability, "letters come after arms and . . . generals are born earlier than philosophers."[16] This observation would lead Machiavelli, in the eighth book, to play down of merits of the rebirth of letters and arts, attributed to Lorenzo the Magnificent; meanwhile in these pages, Machiavelli draws a negative picture of Italy during the period of the Medici government.

As he states, from the ruins of the Roman Empire no principality was born in Italy that was able to "proceed gloriously," even if the cities and the new political formations were given credit for freeing "Italy and defend[ing] her from the barbarians. Subsequently, "if . . . quiet through long peace did not result," nevertheless there were no tragic events of warfare "because those wars became so feeble that they were begun without fear, carried on without danger, and ended without damage."[17] At this point we can understand why, in the first book, the struggle between Gian Galeazzo Visconti and Florence was only hinted at,[18] and only to afford the opportunity to introduce the topic of mercenary armies. That struggle, which in the pages of Leonardo Bruni and Poggio Bracciolini had assumed epic tones, to the point of symbolizing the fight between liberty and tyranny,[19] is mentioned here quickly in the same way as the wars between Italian states. Machiavelli, far from expressing admiration for the government of Florence, which was fighting the expansionism of the Duke of

Milan, did not see it—as we can observe later on—as being particularly animated by republican energies.

The beginning of the sixth book presents a harsh argument against military customs and fighting methods, echoing the criticisms of Machiavelli in *The Art of War*. In the seventh book we find the ruinous results of factions and of the partisans of some citizens, who abuse their power to the detriment of public life. Finally, the first chapter of the eighth book develops the preceding thoughts: factions have brought the Medici to power, and their authority over other citizens causes their adversaries to fight them and seek recourse in conspiracies. "Since the beginning of this eighth book lies between two conspiracies, one already narrated, which was carried on in Milan [against Galeazzo Maria Sforza in 1476], and the other to be related, which occurred in Florence [that of the Pazzi against Lorenzo and Giuliano de' Medici in 1478],"[20] it would be proper to deal specifically with this kind of political event "if in another place I had not spoken of them." In fact, in the *Discourses* (3.6), Machiavelli had amply illustrated the difficulties that conspiracies met with and had in some way shown their ineffectiveness. But he had also observed that conspirators are generally "men of rank or . . . those very close to the prince";[21] conspiracies are in fact born from an internal fracture among the ruling class, which in the Italy of the time was extremely restricted. This is why a failed conspiracy leads to a tougher government by the man it seeks to bring down, but because of repression the prince's power ends up being weakened. If the prince does not become a victim of the conspirators"—which seldom happens—[he] rises to greater power. Many times, indeed, having been good, he becomes wicked" as a result of the fear he has experienced. This leads to a vicious circle, because fear leads the prince to seek ways of "making himself safe," and "making himself safe" from "conspiracies . . . gives him reasons for doing harm," leading to the ruin of the prince himself.[22] It almost seems to be an advance warning of an unwritten page of *History*: the casting out of Piero di Lorenzo de' Medici in 1494.[23]

The question arises whether Machiavelli's freedom of expression, notwithstanding the regard he owed to the addressee of the work, may be explained by the particular situation in which the Medici government in Florence found itself in those years, since it was lacking a family member who might rule the city directly. The letter of Donato Giannotti, who refers to Machiavelli's declaration that he did not feel "free in all respects" in writing on the Medici regime, has been noted; but, as mentioned, if Machiavelli's conscientiousness reflects well on him, the conditions imposed upon him appear rather minor. Even the eulogy to Lorenzo the Magnificent at the end of the work appears very limited, despite the fact that in those years his reputation was already being formed. His figure seems to correspond rather to the picture he drew of him in the *Discourse* for the reform of the Florentine Republic, in which Machiavelli suggested to Cardinal de' Medici that he assume the behavior of "a wise lawgiver" and give a new order to Florence.[24] If anything, a sympathetic light is shone on the negative parts in the conclusion (8.36), and it seems to find some point of contact with the character of Machiavelli himself, when he writes that there cannot be "any vices . . . brought up against him that soiled his great virtues." In fact, it does not suit the author to criticize Lorenzo for being "in affairs of love . . . wonderfully involved," nor to reproach him if he welcomed the company of "witty and keen men"; the reference to "observing both . . . his pleasure-seeking conduct and his serious conduct" reminds one of Machiavelli's taste for "important matters" together with "empty things."

The confidence he made to Giannotti on the opportunity of using the speeches of the Medici's adversaries to explain what he had been unable to express in the first person is confirmed by the words, obviously softer and more cautious, in the dedication to the pope. Machiavelli was eager to point out "how far I am from flattery" and, as confirmation, gave as an example what he said "in the public speeches and private conversations." The function of the speeches attributed to particularly high-profile people is therefore clear. However, his resort to this expedience, according to a traditional model of classical historiography taken up by the humanists, has been the target of various criticisms. To mention just one name, Eduard Fueter, the author of the famous manual on the history of historiography, deplored "the fatal influence" of "ancient artistic theory" on Italian humanistic historiography, which led to the "rhetorical manipulation of the reality" through direct orations. Following this usage, Machiavelli introduced speeches that "often grossly violate the exterior verisimilitude."[25] For his part, Felix Gilbert believed in excusing the author of *The History of Florence* for having kept this type of exposition, putting forward alleged "clues" of his concern for humanist precepts, which he considered "more a literary convention than a valid guide to writing history."[26] This is a curious criticism of the historiography of the fifteenth and sixteenth centuries, founded on the misguided adoption of current methods of studying the past; within the different practices it does not grasp a historical issue that is not only about culture but also about mentality.

Machiavelli's leading biographer, Pasquale Villari, developed his thoughts in this regard much more appropriately, observing that the speeches in *The History of Florence*, "although also imaginary, expose the feelings, the very thoughts of the author regarding historical events," and they express in a profound way "that which the facts themselves aid and in-spire."[27] In fact, we should consider the way in which Machia-velli took advantage of the expedience of orations in *The History of Florence*. The orations are no longer the statement of an *alto sentire* that can be pointed out as an example for the admiration of readers, as generally happened in ancient as well as humanistic historiography, but rather serve to lay bare Flo-rentine politics, and not just those of the Medici. We can therefore propose a model in a negative sense also.

One shrewd analysis of the function of speeches in human-ist historiography, which examines especially the novelty that Machiavelli introduced by resorting to this rhetorical form, has pointed out the role of direct speech in highlighting "the turning points" in the episodes related, as well as "the intrinsi-cally dialogic essence of politics and the multiplicity of its ac-tors.[28] In fact Machiavelli used speeches to represent not only important individuals in specific historical situations but also groups of men. Thus the first important speech is the one that "part of the Signors" gave before the Duke of Athens in Sep-tember 1342 (2.34) to dissuade him from imposing his lord-ship and "make a slave of a city that has always lived free." If that page of republican eloquence was meant to extol exem-plary principles with sage advice for the common good and the liberty of the citizens, and perhaps—it has been suggested—also for the purpose of influencing the mind of the man to whom *The History of Florence* was dedicated and to encour-age him to deliver the reform set forth in the *Discourse*, it is important for us to observe how various points of the speech echo some passages in *The Prince* and *The Discourses*. We note, once again, a profound coherence of ideas in Machiavelli's works.

The use of the principles as a model can also be expressed in a negative form, in speeches that are in sharp contrast to commonly accepted ideas. An eloquent case is the speech of Rinaldo degli Àlbizzi—following the exile that Cosimo de' Medici imposed on him—to incite Filippo Maria Visconti to wage war against Florence (5.8). "Love for a man's native land is caused by nature," Machiavelli had stated in *The Art of War*,[29] and at the start of the *Discorso o dialogo intorno alla nostra lingua (Discourse or Dialogue Concerning Our Language)*, in a passage inspired by Plato's *Crito*,[30] he had sharply criticized Dante because "he persecuted beyond all humanity" his native land to exact revenge "for the offence of his exile."[31] Equally, the Florentine nobleman is moved by a similar desire for vendetta, and yet his speech has tones and movements that make him pronounce words that are, notwithstanding everything, appreciative: "That city deserves to be loved which loves all her people equally, not that city which, neglecting all the others, bows down before a very few of them."[32] A warning follows, which, even in our own times, sounds familiar: a people deprived of liberty is certainly not driven to defend the interests of those who tyrannize them and can welcome the enemy when he raises the hope of overturning the regime that oppresses it. The consequences are those that Machiavelli expressed at other times for princes who do not base their power on the people: the continual danger of conspiracies and the impossibility of having recourse to their "own arms," and therefore the need to use mercenary arms.

The speech upon which commentators' analysis is most often concentrated is attributed to an anonymous commoner in the early days of the Revolt of the Ciompi, led by wool carders in 1378 (3.13). From the orator's words emerges the deep fracture that the social struggle had caused between the leading groups and the rebel party. While Leonardo Bruni had in his turn made some of the heads of the factions talk, attributing to them the language of collectivity and the common interest, Machiavelli makes a common wool worker intervene to illustrate the reasons for the protest and to denounce the pretense hidden behind the call to a collective good. Those words had moved Marx to annotate his copy of *The History of Florence* comparing the Florentine rebel to Sallust's Catiline, and Pasquale Villari would later make a similar observation.[33] However, a recent comparison with the speeches attributed by Sallust to Mithradates, and by Tacitus to the chief of the Britons Calgacus with the intent to incite war against the Romans, is more suitable. These display a reality that had been reversed to serve the rulers' interests; the identification of power with violence and robbery also destroyed the "official" truth in the speeches made by these two enemies of Rome.[34] Thus the words of the wool carder denounce economic factors as the driving force of the events that led to the insurrection: few people have taken possession, through fraud or force, of wealth and power, contravening the law of nature that created all men equal. "Strip us all naked; you will see us all alike."[35]

Machiavelli did not agree with the arguments of the rebellious man of the people; rather, he concluded: "These arguments so greatly inflamed their spirits, which were of themselves already hot for evil." He did not, however, want the rebels' reasons to be ignored, because he realized the violent tension that the political struggle had led to. And within this lies the innovation of his account. It is possible that in his sources there may have been some word in consonance with the wool worker's speech, because, for example, the *Chronicle* of Alamanno Acciaioli, which we know was used in *History*, reports trials of imprisoned rebels. But the strength of the rebel's intervention, carried out with coherence and rhetorical ability, certainly cannot be compared with admissions in piecemeal confessions, usually extracted through force.

Also, only this example can illustrate the functionality of the expedience adopted to show to the reader how dramatic the situation was. I should also point out the turning point that these events represent in the history of Florence: until then internal struggles had led to the elimination of upper classes and that leveling out of the social scale which, according to Machiavelli, had ended up wearing out the republic; after the defeat of the minor guilds that had been the soul of the revolt, power was concentrated in the hands of the supporters of a single, particularly powerful family, and in this regard it does not make a great difference whether the Àlbizzi prevailed before 1434 or the Medici afterward.

It is necessary to take into account the outcome, albeit for a brief moment, of the revolt. Its conclusion was relatively peaceful and in some way similar to that of the revolts of ancient Rome: reforms were introduced, new elements entered the government, the guilds were enlarged, and a new, more representative signory was created. The humble wool carder Michele di Lando was elected gonfalonier, "a sagacious and prudent man, more indebted to Nature than to Fortune" (*Works*, 3:1166), that is, endowed with political intelligence; once in government, he turned out to be not a party man, but worthy "to be numbered among the few who have benefited their native city.... His goodness never let come into his mind a thought opposed to the general good" (*Works*, 3:1168).

The reaction of the optimates led to his fall and to the take-over by the Àlbizzi, ending with the assumption of power by a faction that would govern Florence in a violent and tyrannical way; Machiavelli's assessment is extremely severe. If we read *The History of Florence* with the *Discourse*—the text on the reform of the Republic of Florence which he presented in 1521 to Cardinal Giulio de' Medici—in mind, we can dwell on some reflections regarding the basis of a wise government, which were certainly not taken into consideration: "Those who organize a republic ought to provide for the three different sorts of men who exist in all cities, namely, the most important, those in the middle, and the lowest." To give an eminent place to the first and an adequate one to the second, "to satisfy the third and final class of men, which is the whole general body of citizens," it is necessary to "[reopen] the Hall of the Council of One Thousand, or at least of the Six Hundred Citizens,"[36] that is, to restore the institutions that gave the people representation and the possibility of making themselves heard. If Bruni's and Bracciolini's histories had comprised two fundamental texts on the Florentine life of their time, and in some way an illustration of the bases on which the city was ruled, Machiavelli hoped that his work could fulfill a similar duty for the republic and might be born after the death of Lorenzo the Younger. To that end he described the negative actions of the past, offering documentation of the evils to be avoided when reorganizing the city. The old political struggles had led to the creation of an unstable order—neither republic, nor principality. Now it was necessary to find a way of founding a republic that was firm in its principles, since the House of Medici no longer seemed to have a member capable of ruling the government. Machiavelli's hope was destined to remain unfulfilled, but the anxiety for the future that fueled his thoughts, which could envision new political horizons and unite common sense with a passionate patriotism, cannot fail to make an impression.

It may seem futile at this point to reprise the old dispute over whether Machiavelli was a "true" historian. Certainly, he does not display behavior that, for historians of the nineteenth century, starting with Leopold Ranke, had to be a chief characteristic of those who investigate the past, which is summarized in the motto "Tell it the way it really was." "Historical detachment" is not a virtue practiced in *The History of Florence*, and it suffices to show the contempt that led the author to write, at the end of the first book, "of these slothful rulers and of these dastardly armies my history will be full."[37] Nevertheless, it is difficult not to agree with someone who has observed that the issues Machiavelli proposed were "yeast and ferment, in a direct or indirect manner, in our historiographic literature of the sixteenth century and beyond."[38] Precisely because the issue of Italian liberty was the inspiring impulse behind the entire work, his representation of the past places before us the first example of a national history.

The Friendship with Guicciardini

At the start of the 1520s, Machiavelli had forged a bond of friendship with Francesco Guicciardini. Their relationship may be surprising if we think back to the hostile behavior of the Florentine aristocrat toward the government of Pier Soderini and if we bear in mind the aversion that is evident in the pages that Guicciardini dedicated to his former right-hand man in his early work, *The History of Florence*. There was also a significant age difference of fourteen years between them, even if for Machiavelli this could be an incentive, rather than an obstacle, to sharing his thoughts, trusting as he was toward someone who had a broader experience of life. Even their personalities were very different; whereas Machiavelli was extroverted and cordial, Guicciardini was closed and reserved. This can also be seen in their behavior as writers: Machiavelli loved to have his works known; Guicciardini always wrote for himself and did not so much as publish a single line in his lifetime; only when he ended his political life did he dedicate himself to a work that he probably would have liked to see published, the *History of Italy*, but he lacked the time to do so. In any event, the friendship of two personalities of their caliber should also be considered in the light of the significance that it assumes in the general picture of the history—political and intellectual—of that period.

The two had met much earlier: in 1509 at the latest. In that year, on November 29, Machiavelli wrote to Luigi Guicciardini, affectionately addressing him "as his dearest brother," and in closing he asked to be remembered to "your Messer Francesco," Guicciardini's younger brother. It appears that the latter did not reciprocate this affection at the time, and while Francesco Guicciardini certainly had dealings with the secretary of the Council of Ten when in January 1512 he was sent as ambassador to Spain, it does not seem that he had other opportunities to meet after that. When Machiavelli was thrown out of the chancery, their paths had diverged; Guicciardini, returning from the embassy in Spain in 1514, held government posts in Florence and then, from 1516 to 1527, obtained important positions in the administration of the Papal States;[1] Machiavelli, after his confinement in the countryside, remained isolated for a long period in Florence, deprived of any involvement with the city's public life. Nevertheless, there must have been some connection between them; otherwise the visit that Machiavelli paid to Guicciardini at Modena in May 1521 would make no sense.

At that time, the Florentine signory sent Machiavelli as its own representative to the chapter general of the Franciscan order, which was meeting at Carpi, an important mission for the republic, contrary to what one might be led to believe by the letters exchanged between Machiavelli and Guicciardini. In fact, the activities of the Franciscan monasteries in the city and elsewhere on Florentine territory were quite important, and Florence wanted the order's chapter general to divide its own province of Tuscany into two parts, so as to take the governing of it from the Sienese, who controlled it at that time. The chapter general, on that occasion, would resolve the matter with a compromise, maintaining the unity of the province but electing as its commissioner someone welcome to Florence, instead of, as it seemed before the meeting, the Sienese Bernardino Ochino.

Having to pass through Modena, Machiavelli decided to stop there between May 15 and 16, visiting Guicciardini, who was governor of Modena in the name of the pope. "Nature had made these two men very different," wrote their greatest biographer, Roberto Ridolfi, "and fortune had still further divided and set them apart."[2] Nevertheless, those few hours they passed together were enough to seal their friendship: "Besides the fascination of his intellect, Machiavelli shone with a human warmth which broke the ice with Guicciardini." Thus, right from the first letters that followed, their rapport was intimate and couched in terms of a lively cordiality.

As in the correspondence with Vettori, in this exchange of letters the playful tone alternated with serious and often anxious reflections. The very next day after their meeting in Modena, Guicciardini, who knew about an additional task commissioned by the wool carders' guild from Machiavelli that since he was at the Franciscan chapter of Carpi he might select a renowned preacher for them, and well aware of Machiavelli's opinions on the subject, mocked the "reverend consuls" of that corporation and wrote that it is as if "the task had been given to Pachierotto, while he was alive, or to Ser Sano [two well-known Florentine homosexuals] to find a beautiful and graceful wife for a friend." On the same day a prank was played on Machiavelli's hosts, probably arranged during the meeting at Modena; while he was in Carpi, the governor swiftly sent to him a crossbowman who, "making a bow down to the earth," delivered a missive, causing considerable sensation among those present, who were led to believe that the Florentine envoy and the governor of Modena might be ex-

changing particularly urgent news. The scene repeated itself
the following day with another messenger, who carried a "great
bundle of letters," such that "the smoke of it has gone up to the
sky," and everyone started asking the man who was now considered a person of great importance news of the wider world
of politics. Machiavelli did not need to be asked twice; he
showed the chancellor of the lord of Carpi, whose guest he
was, "those sections about the Swiss and the king [of France].
He thought it a great thing. I spoke to him of the sickness of
Caesar and of the states that he wished to buy in France; in
such a way it made him drool."[3]

The style of the correspondence is intentionally comic and
may suggest that of Machiavelli's recent work, *The Mandrake*.
The beginnings of the letters have a burlesque flavor: "Magnificent Sir, Ruler to be Most Respected. I was on the privy
seat when your messenger arrived." Or "Magnifice Domine,
cazzus! One needs to manage cleverly in dealing with that fellow." Equally worthy of the play is the description of some
scenes, and Ser Nicia comes to mind when we hear of those
who surrounded Machiavelli upon the courier's arrival: "They
all stood with open mouths and with their caps in their hands;
and while I write I have a circle of them around me, and seeing
me write at length they are astonished, and look on me as inspired; and I, to make them wonder more, sometimes hold my
pen still and swell up, and then they slaver at the mouth."

In the scenes from *The Mandrake*, the replies of Callimaco,
who in the play was dressed in the solemn clothes of a doctor,
may remind us of Machiavelli turning to his host, who was
burning with curiosity: "I reply to him in a few words and
badly put together, and rely on the flood that is to come, or the
Turk who is going to cross over [into Italy], and if it would be
a good thing to carry on a Crusade in these days, and similar
stories for tavern benches."[4]

But between the joke and the scorn, serious thoughts alternate. Guicciardini thinks with melancholy about his friend's fate:

> When I read your titles as ambassador of the republic and of friars, and I consider how many kings, dukes, and princes you have negotiated with in the past, I am reminded of Lysander, to whom, after so many victories and trophies, was given the task of distributing meat to those very same soldiers whom he had so gloriously commanded.

The Spartan general, celebrated by Plutarch, was certainly a familiar personality, since the Greek historian writes that Lysander knew how to sew around himself the fur of a wolf and that of a lion, as Machiavelli had wished his prince might do. But Guicciardini's thoughts contrast with that same vision of human destiny: "You see that, with only the faces of the men and the extrinsic colours changed, all the very same things return; and we do not see any incident that has not been seen in other times. But changing the names and forms of things means that only the prudent recognize them; therefore history is good and useful."[5]

They are thoughts upon which Guicciardini often reflects. Thus in the *Ricordi* (76) he writes the following: "Whatsoever has been in the past or is now will repeat itself in the future; but the names and surfaces of things will be so altered, that he who has not a quick eye will not recognise them, or know to guide himself accordingly, or to form a judgment on what he sees."[6]

His friend thinks no differently and in the *Discourses* (3.43), echoing Ecclesiastes,[7] had written:

Prudent men are in the habit of saying . . . that he who wishes to see what is to come should observe what has already happened, because all the affairs of the world, in every age, have their individual counterparts in ancient times. The reason for this is that since they are carried on by men, who have and always have had the same passions, of necessity the same results appear.

It is the very principle of the repeatability of human affairs, illustrated in the introduction to the first book, where he affirms the necessity of imitating the ancients, taking issue in a polemic against those who do not believe it possible: "As if the sky, the sun, the elements, men, were changed in motion, arrangement, and power from what they were in antiquity."

From Guicciardini's letter of May 18 we can infer, not surprisingly, that he had been able to read at least some pages of the *Discourses*, since he observed the following: "I believe this legation will not be completely useless for that, because in these three days' idleness you will have imbibed the whole Republic of Clogs and you will make use of that model for some purpose, comparing it or measuring it against some of those forms of yours."

The allusion can be only to the second chapter of the *Discourses*, where Machiavelli showed "how many kinds of republics there are." If therefore there were also diverging points of view between the two friends on important political choices, as well as on some of their thoughts—including a few statements in the *Discourses*, as Guicciardini's *Observations* would later attest—we note, in connection with some general lines of their view of matters, a consonance of feeling that certainly contributed toward their relationship and overcame their differences of opinion.

In the following years their correspondence became less frequent, or perhaps some letters were lost. For example, only a fragment remains of the letter in which Machiavelli expressed the desire to consult his friend on the subject of *The History of Florence*. In any event, their relationship continued to alternate between serious moments and playful episodes. In June 1525, after having presented the pope with *The History of Florence*, Machiavelli, who evidently always enjoyed a reputation as a military technician, had suggested to the pontiff that he institute in Romagna a militia that might serve to defend the region in the difficult situation created by the French defeat at Pavia. The memory of the "armies" assembled in those lands by the Valentino had endured, and Clement VII sent him to Guicciardini, governor of that region, with a letter in which he warmly recommended the measure that, with some grandiloquence, he defined as "salvation of the ecclesiastical State, in the whole of Italy and almost the entire Christendom."

Guicciardini was not as convinced. Romagna, he wrote to Cesare Colombo, his agent in Rome, on June 22, was in no condition to permit putting "arms in the hands of the people," both because of the hatred and factions that divided it and because "the Church has no friends in Romagna," and the pope could not "avail himself of the love of the people." This, in particular, may have been a persuasive argument even for Machiavelli, who abandoned the enterprise without having done anything.

Notwithstanding this incident, the relationship between the two friends remained cordial. Thus, on July 29 Guicciardini wrote to him in bantering tones that "after your departure Mariscotta [a famous courtesan] spoke of you very flatteringly." For his part, Machiavelli had promised to visit two estates that Guicciardini had bought in the Mugello without having seen them, and on 3 August he informed him accurately of the inspection he had carried out. He confirmed the good condition and fertility of one of the two, called La Colombaia, but preceded this news with information on the other, called Finocchieto. "Stony Arabia," he observed, "is not different," adding a depressing description of that land and the advice to "get rid of it." Guicciardini jokingly replied four days later, pretending that the response had been written by "Milady Property of Finocchieto": she "wished health and clarified judgment to Machiavelli" and wrote a long defense of her own virtues and merits, stating that if she appears so displeasing to people, she does so because she only wants to please the owner whom she loves and whom she knows loves her in return.[8]

Clizia and the Musical Madrigals

Guicciardini, meanwhile, had read *The Mandrake* and had appreciated it so much that he wanted to have it staged at Faenza in the following year's carnival. Machiavelli brightened up, and it is probable that in September, on his return from a trip to Venice, where he had gone to recover some goods for Florentine merchants, he stopped at his friend's, who must have confided in him issues that had perplexed him while reading the play. Thus in mid-October, the author sought to clarify some of the play's witty remarks and terms with a letter that has a whimsical flavor, a jokingly erudite tone, where he even ended up citing the second decade of Livy, which had disappeared without a trace.[1] But Guicciardini wanted more; the prologue did not seem appropriate to him for an audience from Faenza, and he also asked for some interlude to be recited between the acts. Machiavelli would please him generously; not only did he compose a new prologue, but on 3 January 1526 he wrote to him: "We have made five new canzone suited to the comedy—and they are to be set to music to be sung between acts." He had in fact introduced an innovation, the sung madrigal, which he had thought of in the previous year for a new play he had written, *Clizia*. According to an illustrious musicologist, there were no prior examples of musical madrigals for the theater; Machiavelli used the services of a French musician then living in Florence, Philippe Verdelot, who was renowned at the time.[2]

It is possible that the idea of introducing music to his plays may have suggested itself to Machiavelli by his desire to please "la Barbera," a singer and actress to whom he had taken a fancy in that period. From 1523 he had become a regular visitor to a rich man of the people, Iacopo Falconetti, called il Fornaciaio because, at the huge farm outside Porta San Frediano, where he lived, he owned a great kiln, which supplied a good part of his wealth. After having been a member of a signory council, he had been removed for unknown reasons and confined to his estate for five years. Under this house arrest, however, he lived cheerfully; important people from Florence visited him and were welcomed with lunches and parties.

It is probably here that Machiavelli met Barbara Salutati Raffacani, and when in 1525 the Fornaciaio wanted to organize a theatrical performance, suggesting a repeat performance of *The Mandrake*, the author preferred to write another play, *Clizia*. He wanted to satisfy his new lover, who would show off her gifts as a singer, thanks to the songs set to music that Machiavelli introduced between the acts.

He had derived the play's plot from Plautus's *Casina* and, with his sense of humor, succeeded in adding originality to the work. He wanted to link it to *The Mandrake*, timing its events two years after those of Callimaco and Lucrezia and inserting references to the characters of the other work. The principal character in *Clizia*, an aged father who has fallen in love with the young woman he himself had found and brought up, introduces an element of self-irony to the plot, since Machiavelli gives him a name that repeats the first letters of his own first name and surname, Nicomaco. The old man's attempt to marry Clizia to one of his servants so that he himself can become her lover is foiled by the old man's wife, and the final recognition of the young woman, revealed to be of noble birth, makes possible her marriage with the young Learco, who loves her.

The play's humor is inferior to that of *The Mandrake*. In the latter the deception has a lightness capable of breathing life into the events, which take place with polished precision. Only the simplemindedness of Messer Nicia introduces farcical tones, which almost never overstep the bounds of the great burlesque tradition. But in the amorous restlessness of old Nicomaco, the ridicule culminates in his final mortification, and rarely do we rediscover the happy unpredictability of the earlier play. The figures of the two silent nudes evoked at the end of each play can appear emblematic of the differences in humor. The body of Callimaco, denuded and admired by Nicia, is described in terms of his youthful attractiveness: "You never saw finer skin, white, soft, smooth; and don't ask me about the other things." However, the servant Siro, "raised up on the bed, all nude," and turned in a priapic pose toward Nicomaco, who believed he was lying in bed with Clizia, makes a face at him with an obscene gesture. In the end the old Nicomaco is reduced to a state that elicits even his wife's compassion: "The poor man has entirely lost heart; it seems to him he's disgraced."[3]

The Fornaciaio spared no expense, and since the stage set of *The Mandrake* had been painted by Andrea del Sarto and Bastiano da Sangallo, he gave the latter the task of painting the set for *Clizia*. At the party for the performance of *Clizia*, together with other illustrious guests, there were the two young men descended from the House of Medici, Ippolito and Alessandro. One can understand why Filippo de' Nerli, a friend from

Modena who would later make a name for himself as a historiographer, enthusiastically sang the praises of the performance:

> Fornaciaio and you, you and Fornaciaio have managed things so that the fame of your revelries has spread and continues to spread not only through all Tuscany but also throughout Lombardy. . . . The fame of your comedy has flown all over. You should not believe that I have heard these things from friends' letters, but rather I have heard it from wayfarers who go all about the roads preaching "the glorious celebrations and great spectacles" of Porta San Frediano.[4]

Even years later, the party at the Fornaciaio's house in all its magnificence and the performance of the play would be remembered in *Repubblica fiorentina,* written by another friend from the Orti Oricellari, Donato Giannotti.[5]

Final Act

The Italian political scene was turning ever darker. The Battle of Pavia has been mentioned; on that day the victory of the army of Charles V sealed the peninsula's fate. The Duchy of Milan, by now firmly in the grip of the imperial forces, was governed by a Sforza who had the autonomy of a puppet. His minister, Girolamo Morone, wanted to turn the situation on its head and unite with an anti-imperial coalition, seeking to attract to it also the Marquis of Pescara, Charles V's lieutenant. The attempt, too fraught with danger, failed. "Morone was seized," wrote Machiavelli to Guicciardini at the end of October 1525, "and the dukedom of Milan is overthrown." Machiavelli believed that now Clement VII himself was in danger and—citing, from memory as always, Dante: "I see into Alanga the fleur-de-lis entering, and in his Vicar etc."[1]— seemed to foretell the sack of Rome in 1527. The letter, which closed by accusing the Italian princes "who have all done everything to bring us here," was signed "Niccolò Machiavelli, Historian, comic writer, and tragic writer."[2]

On 18 March 1526, Francis I, a prisoner in Spain following his defeat at Pavia the previous year, was set free by Charles V. The event seemed incredible to Machiavelli, who in his letters to Guicciardini, especially one dated March 15, when the news was already circulating, fully debated the various issues. After having set forth the potential arguments that the king of France might have deployed to obtain his freedom, he concluded: "Nevertheless all the reasons that can be brought forward do not guard the Emperor from being stupid,"[3] and in those days he composed an epigram against "That brainless / Charles King of the Romans."[4] It quickly became common knowledge that the decision regarding the fate of Francis I was much disputed even among the emperor's closest collaborators, and the discussion would later be narrated by Guicciardini.[5] The subsequent course of events would show that in reality the emperor, if he had not managed to obtain much of an advantage—since Francis I, almost as soon as he had reentered his kingdom, had declared null all the concessions extorted from him while he was deprived of liberty—had at least freed himself from an embarrassing situation, being unable to keep the king of France prisoner for much longer. Now the latter, before the European political world, had played the part of breaker of his word and betrayer of his own sons, delivered as hostages in exchange for his own freedom. At the same time, the state of his kingdom was not such as to permit him to immediately deal with a conflict with Charles V.

In fact, the League of Cognac, signed on 22 May 1526 among France, the pope, Venice, Florence, and the Duke of Milan, was more of a threat on paper than on the battlefield. Francis I could not or did not wish to intervene right away in Italy, and the Italian potentates were the same incompetent ones that Machiavelli had denounced in his writings. A hope had again flashed before him for a brief moment: in Giovanni de' Medici, the mercenary known as Giovanni dalle Bande Nere, he believed he had found someone equal to the situation. Aware of his risky proposal, on March 15 he wrote to

Guicciardini about it with much caution: "I say one thing that will seem to you crazy; I shall bring forward a plan that will seem to you either foolhardy or ridiculous." But the situation was moving swiftly, and "these times demand decisions that are bold, unusual and strange." He therefore reported a rumor that "a few days ago . . . was said throughout Florence." He was well aware that "the people are uncertain and foolish"; nevertheless, "often they say that something is being done that should be done." The rumor was that Giovanni de' Medici "was raising the flag of a soldier of fortune to make war where he had the best opportunity." Could he perhaps be the "redeemer" invoked in *The Prince*, the character that Fabrizio Colonna had hoped for, capable of imitating Philip of Macedonia, who with the force of arms had unified Greece? Probably not even Machiavelli dared hope as much, but it was at least possible that this man of arms, who was "bold, prompt, has great ideas, is a maker of great plans," might succeed in showing the Spanish that it was not possible to ruin "Tuscany and the Church without any hindrance." There would be no need for the pope to expose himself to too much risk, he pointed out; he could surreptitiously finance his enterprise against the Spanish in the territory of Milan. And the king of France, who "would see that he has to do with people who are alive and, in addition to arguments, show him deeds," would definitely be forced to fight.[6]

But the "bold decisions" were certainly not in line with Clement VII's nature, let alone the distrust of the firstborn Medici toward the cadet branch of the family. The slap in the face arrived quickly. On March 31 Filippo Strozzi wrote to Machiavelli that he had read his letter to Guicciardini and did not agree with the proposal regarding an action in Lombardy by Giovanni de' Medici. He added that this was also the position of the pope, with whom he had talked about this plan;

the objection was that the pope would remain equally exposed, since "if our Lordship offers him [Giovanni de' Medici] money, the venture becomes his." For the moment, Clement VII did not want to place himself at risk in any way. Nevertheless, Machiavelli did not give up, and after hearing of the popular revolt unleashed in Milan at the end of April against the Spanish, he again wrote to Guicciardini on 17 May 1526:

> I have heard the rumours from Lombardy, and it is recognized on every side how easy it would be to get some rascals from that region. This opportunity, for the love of God, should not be lost, and remember that Fortune, our bad advice and our worse officials would have brought not merely the King [of France] but also the Pope to prison. . . . Provide now, for the love of God, in such a way that His Holiness will not go back into the same dangers, from which you will never be secure until the Spanish are so completely taken out of Lombardy that they cannot return.

It is one of Machiavelli's most moving and agitated letters in all of his correspondence, where twice we find the phrase "the love of God." The close of the letter has an equally passionate tone: "You know how many opportunities have been lost; do not lose this one or trust any more in standing still, turning yourself over to Fortune and to Time, because with Time there do not come always the same things, and Fortune is not always the same."

And at the end, with a phrase from Livy, he launched a desperate plea: "Free Italy from long anxiety."[7] It upset him to know that popular ferment continued in Milan and that the duke, besieged in the castle, was resisting the Spanish, while those who should have intervened in his aid delayed as they fell prey to uncertainty, more because of their distrust of the other Italian potentates than the danger the Spanish power represented. Finally, toward the end of June, the allies made their move. They were not united, however; the pope had one captain general, the Florentines another, and the Venetians had hired the Duke of Urbino; paid by the king of France, Giovanni dalle Bande Nere also took part. The attack on Lombardy, however, was so listless that, after occupying Lodi, the league's army made camp before Milan without advancing to take the city, hoping that the Milanese, with their allies at the gates, would rise up. But the Spanish oppression had achieved its aim, and no revolt was unleashed. Shortly afterward, the Duke of Urbino abandoned the siege and retired to Marignano. The attack had failed.

In mid-July, Machiavelli arrived at the camp, but the military operations had almost ceased. Shortly before, he had been nominated chancellor of the new magistracy of the directors of the walls, charged with the defense of Florence, and it is not clear how he came to be in Lombardy; perhaps he had been called there by Guicciardini, who was sent by the pope as his lieutenant general. The situation must have immediately appeared dire to him, for on July 18 Guicciardini wrote to Roberto Acciaiuoli: "Machiavelli is here. He had come to reorder this militia, but seeing how corrupt it is, he doesn't trust that it has any honor; He was so busy laughing at the mistakes of the men that he couldn't manage to correct them."[8]

His laugh, however, could not have been very cheerful. As he had already written in verse:

> Io spero e lo sperar cresce 'l tormento,
> io piango e il pianger ciba il lasso core,
> io rido e el rider mio non passa drento . . .
> Così sperando, piango, rido e ardo,
> e paura ho di ciò che io odo e guardo.

I hope and hope increases my torment,
I weep and weeping feeds the weary heart,
I laugh and my laughter does not touch my
   soul . . .
Thus hoping, I weep and laugh and burn,
And I fear what I hear and see.[9]

A few days later even the castle was forced to surrender to the Spanish, and the forces of the league withdrew from Milan. On July 30 they attacked Cremona, thinking it easy prey, but again they turned out not to be up to the task. The city would not capitulate until September 23, after the allies had missed the opportunity to move on to Genoa to prevent the disembarkation of reinforcements from Spain. A letter from Machiavelli to a young friend, Bartolomeo Cavalcanti, outlined the dramatic lack of the allies' effectiveness:

The reason why the Pope started this war before the King of France sent his soldiers into Italy and took action in Spain according to his agreement, and before all the Swiss arrived, was his hope in the people of Milan and his belief that six thousand Swiss, whom the Venetians and the Pope had sent on learning of the first rebellions in Milan, would be so prompt that they would arrive at the same time as the Venetians arrived with their army. Besides, he believed that the King's soldiers, if they were not so prompt, would at least be early enough to aid in carrying through the undertaking.[10]

Since Francesco Sforza was besieged inside the castle and it was necessary to go to his rescue, the allies moved there, hoping that the war could be concluded rapidly. But of their "presuppositions," "two of the most important" were missing: the

Swiss did not arrive, and the Milanese did not rise up. The league's army fell back on Marignano; then, after the Swiss came, it returned to Milan but did not attack. It was decided to assault Cremona while leaving part of the forces in Milan: "This was contrary to a rule of mine that says it is not a wise plan to risk all one's Fortune and not all one's forces."[11] In conclusion, "We have . . . lost this war twice: once when we went to Milan and did not stay there; the second time when we sent [part of the forces] and did not go to Cremona."

Matters subsequently got worse: the Colonna family, in league with Spain, attacked the Kingdom of Naples and entered the Papal States, reaching Rome and sacking it. Clement VII, also troubled by the news of the victory of the Turks at Mohács the previous August, which opened the way for them to advance on Hungary, now wanted to make peace with the emperor and signed a truce with the viceroy of Naples. The League of Cognac ended up dissolving, and the situation in Italy began to spin out of control.

From Germany, bands of *Landsknechts* descended on Italy, gathered by a Lutheran fanatic, Georg von Frundsberg, who wanted to punish the "Antichrist" who ruled in Rome. The Venetians held well back from confronting them, content to limit their plunder to the lands through which they passed. Giovanni de' Medici planned to bar the crossing of the Po, but on November 25 he was mortally wounded in combat.

In the letters that Machiavelli wrote between February and April 1527—he had once again been sent to Guicciardini by the Florentine signory—we are able to follow the Landsknechts' march on Rome, which unfolded with an inexorable inevitability. Although on paper the forces that should have stood against the Landsknechts were superior to them, despite the latter having met up near Piacenza with the rabble soldiers of the Bourbon constable en route with Francis I, the German bands continued their advance, attracted by the mirage of the booty promised by the sacking of the pope's capital. Not even the anarchy in which they found themselves when in March they were left without a leader after an apoplectic fit struck Frundsberg during a violent rage, leading to his death, put a brake on them.

The pope, who in the days of negotiations for the formation of the League of Cognac had been opposed to it until the Duke of Ferrara had joined the alliance, now invoked the latter's help, willing to give in marriage to the duke's son Ercole his own niece, the future queen of France, Catherine de' Medici. The duke replied that he had already reached an agreement with Charles V and, angry with Clement VII because he had not made the Florentines restore the rock of San Leo to him, a stronghold that threatened his capital, remained in his own duchy, indifferent to the situation.

We know from a letter Machiavelli sent to Francesco Vettori on 5 April 1527 that Guicciardini had outlined to the pope the choice he had to make: either to vigorously take up hostilities against the Spanish again or to firmly make peace with them. Truce was only a middle way, and one that did not avert the dangers.[12] But once again Clement VII balked when faced with a difficult decision. The advance of the Landsknechts put Florence at risk: if the viceroy of Naples prevented them from attacking Rome, they would probably turn their attention to Florentine territory. Therefore Machiavelli urged Vettori to take steps to ensure that Pisa, Pistoia, Prato, and, naturally, Florence were prepared for their defense. However, the march of the Landsknechts continued undisturbed, and the subsequent incitements of Machiavelli remained unsuccessful, with the allies coming on relentlessly, without any regard for the agreement of truce, the Spanish being the first not to respect it. There was still the possibility of putting forces together and compelling the invaders to retreat. Machiavelli wrote, "Now we cannot hobble any more, but must go like mad," and he recalled that "often desperation finds remedies that choice has been unable to find." But to achieve this, resolute decisions were needed, because—he concluded in the letter to Vettori— "through the experience that sixty years have given me, . . . I do not believe that ever more difficult articles than these were struggled with, where peace is necessary and war cannot be abandoned."[13]

On April 22 he returned to Florence; the following day Guicciardini also arrived to check on the measures taken for the defense of the city. Despite the inept trio of cardinals who governed the city——Silvio Passerini, Niccolò Ridolfi, and Innocenzo Cybo—Florence appeared to the Landsknechts to be sufficiently well defended that they left it alone. However, before this became public knowledge, a group of young men asked for arms to fight these ferocious bands. The arms were promised but were not delivered, and on April 26 a revolt was unleashed that frightened the cardinals so much that they abandoned the city. The palazzo was occupied, and the signory was forced to declare the Medici in rebellion and to restore regulations in force prior to their return in 1512. The league's troops, however, who had not been deployed against the Landsknechts, were now used by the cardinals to reenter the city and compel the rebels to reach an agreement; their impunity was guaranteed and the power of the Medici was restored.

But on May 6 the bands of lance troops and of the Constable of Bourbon (killed in the assault on the walls by a shot from a harquebus that Benvenuto Cellini bragged about having fired) entered Rome, ferociously sacking it. Five days later the news reached Florence, and this time the republic was definitively established.

Of Machiavelli in these days we have little news. Probably on April 26, the day of the youth revolt, he was already heading to Rome to meet the forces deployed to assist the pope. Guicciardini too had left Florence for the same reason. The news of the sack of Rome reached them when they were near Orvieto, and having received news of the Medici's being thrown out of their own city, they both decided to return there. Machiavelli went first, by sea from Civitavecchia to Livorno. The ex-secretary hoped to resume his former position in the restored republic, although it appeared that he was aware that his recent collaboration in the service of Clement VII would count against him. In fact, on June 10 the Florentine government appointed to the secretaryship another functionary who had been in that position under the Medici government.[14]

At this point, Machiavelli had only a few days of life left; in fact, he would die on 21 June 1527. He had been ill for some time, although we do not really know whether it was his stomach or his colon that ailed him. Writing to Guicciardini on 17 August 1525, he had exaggerated the beneficial effects of pills that the latter had had prepared and sent to him.[15] It is probable that they hastened his end. Paolo Giovio, in the brief biography he wrote, attributed his death to that "drug."[16] It has been said that he transferred onto Machiavelli—whom he described as "ridiculous and aetheist"—that which Saint Jerome had written about Lucretius, the Latin poet equally famous for his impiety, who would fall victim to a love potion. But if we strip away Giovio's denigratory intentions from this accusation, it is probable that Machiavelli's end may really have been caused by the drug. The pills, which Machiavelli eulogized for their purgative effects, contained an ingredient he called "carman deos"; this probably means "germander," a substance that, with constant use, can seriously damage the liver, so much so that nowadays it is banned from pharmaceutical use.

It is related that Machiavelli told the friends who came to visit him shortly before he died—Zanobi Buondelmonti and Luigi Alamanni, who had just returned from the exile imposed on him after the conspiracy of 1522; Filippo Strozzi; Francesco del Nero; and Jacopo Nardi—of a dream he had had in those days: he had seen a crowd of poor people dressed in rags—famished, crippled, and down-at-heel people—and heard talk that they were the blessed spirits of heaven of whom it was written *Beati pauperes, quoniam ipsorum est regnum cælorum* (Blessed are the poor in spirit, for theirs is the kingdom of heaven [Matthew 5:3)]. Then appeared a group of personages full of solemnity and majesty; it seemed to be a senate intent on discussing affairs of state. Among them he recognized Plato, Seneca, Plutarch, Tacitus, and other famous ancient literary figures. These, he was told, were condemned to hell, because it was written *Sapientia huius sæculi inimica est Dei* (The wisdom of this world is the enemy of God). When he was asked with whom he wanted to go, he replied that he preferred by a long shot to be in hell with those great minds, to talk with them about affairs of state, rather than with the rabble that had been shown to him.[17]

It is possible that the account is a myth, and we know that in the seventeenth century it was exploited by anti-Machiavellian writers, yet those who knew him had previously referred to it.[18] Sensibly, Sasso observed that the question to pose was not whether it was true or false, but how much it seems "to conform to what Machiavelli actually imagined, put in story form, thought, and wrote."[19] These images of heaven and hell might be seen in the context of criticisms of Christianity in the *Discourses*, "interpreted . . . according to sloth and not according to vigor" (2.2, in *Works*, 1:331). In the months preceding the restoration of the Florentine Republic and again in the few days Machiavelli lived in Florence until his death, the revival of Savonarolian tendencies may have created this contentious behavior of scorn for the *pauperes*, the personification of Christian virtue, as well as respect for the *sapientia huius sæculi* (the wisdom of the world). For his part, Villari had previously noted consonances between the spirit of that dream and other writings of Machiavelli.[20] In *The Mandrake* (4.1) Callimaco, anxious to know whether Frate Timoteo had succeeded in persuading Lucrezia to take the potion, gives vent to his feelings: "How anxious I've been and still am!" And after having debated the various possibilities, he says to himself: "The worst you can get from it is you'll die and go to Hell: But how many others have died! And in Hell how many worthy men there are! Are you ashamed to go there?" As is well known, Pope Leo X reconciled himself with Machiavelli immediately after having seen the play. Besides, in *The Life of Castruccio Castracani* a no less scandalous saying is attributed to the Lucchese mercenary: "Being asked if in order to save his soul he ever considered making himself a friar, he answered that he had not, because it seemed to him strange that Brother Lazarus should be going to Heaven and Uguccione della Faggiuola to Hell."[21] We have noted that the *The Life of Castruccio* was a kind of writing test for Machiavelli, who wanted to obtain from the future pope Clement VII the commission of writing *The History of Florence*. If in the era of the Counter-Reformation the anti-Machiavellians used the account of the dream to demonstrate the impiety of the author of *The Prince*, then when Machiavelli was alive, a witticism had already been welcomed with affection.

Notes On the Use of the Word *Stato* in Machiavelli

Nowadays the concept of *stato* is often bundled into meanings that unite, in a contradictory manner, an exacerbated wish for control and discipline together with a lack of sufferance for the restrictions that the institution imposes. So, complaints arise regarding *troppo stato* (too much government), which burdens society, but also concerning abandonment, with citizens left to face difficulties on their own; or we hear calls to tighten laws that regulate public order and, at the same time, to mitigate norms about infractions that are no less disastrous for general security. These criticisms show the separation between civil society and the state, which resulted from profound transformations in economic life and international relations that took place in previous decades. Nevertheless, even half a century earlier, Bobbio had indicated the controversial relationship between state and liberty, outlining two lines of thought:

> That which runs from Locke to Kant, according to which the principal task of the state is to guarantee natural liberty, and therefore to effectively permit that existence according to liberty that in the state of nature remains

necessary, but unfulfilled, for which the task of the state is not to superimpose its own laws on the natural ones but to make sure, through the exercise of coercive power, that the natural laws are truly working. The other direction, which runs from Rousseau to Hegel, assigns to the state the task of totally eliminating natural liberty, which is the liberty of the isolated individual, and to transform it into civil liberty, that is into liberty meant as the perfect adaptation of the individual will to the collective one, and is the more properly democratic tradition.[1]

Useful clues can perhaps be found by going back to previous years, when the notion of state began to take shape, before it developed fully and reached, in the liberal era, a vision of an ideal political body, collective and sovereign, whose interests—according to a democrat of that period who was open to liberal tendencies—"affect all citizens and often do not affect anyone in particular: they are not linked in a tangible way to the interests of each citizen."[2] They were rules respected by those who, it was said, "have the sense of the state." Marx would go on to clarify how the interests of the dominant classes succeeded in etching themselves on the life of organized society and had yearned for the final extinction of the state, which could be achieved thanks to the incessant revolutionary progress of norms capable of jointly ensuring equality and liberty. The dramatic failure of that route and, in reaction, the aggressive individualism that developed at the end of the "short century" have influenced the very institutions and regulations created to guarantee public and general interest.

Machiavelli, to breathe life back into the "mixed bodies" that states are, suggested "to carry them back" to their origins; an examination of his writings can provide food for thought and enable us to understand through which avenues the notion of state was being formed. A terminological examination has already been made in some works,[3] which in general have highlighted how *stato*, in the language of the Florentine secretary, differed from the conception we have of it nowadays. Nevertheless, it is worth going over that ground again, albeit by limiting the review to a brief sample of the hundreds of passages in which this word appears and bearing in mind attributions and duties that are related to it.

❧

In chapter 3 of *The Prince* we read that in medicine it is necessary to "foresee far ahead" to prevent an illness from becoming untreatable: "So it is in things of state [stato]; on early recognition . . . the maladies that spring up in a state can be healed speedily."[4] A little further on, we find a strong criticism of the policy of Louis XII, who "did the opposite of what should be done in order to hold a new possession [stato] in a province differing from his old dominion." The term *stato* recurs, therefore, not many lines after, but with a different meaning: in the first instance it has institutional connotations, approaching those of political individuality, which assumes organic characteristics through a relationship, charged with vitality, with the human body; in the second instance, however, it designates the territorial domain. We find yet a third meaning, for example in chapter 9, where, on the subject of civil principalities, Machiavelli observes: "These civil princedoms [stati] are in danger when they are in the process of shifting from republic to tyranny." Here *stato* indicates that which we would nowadays term "regime," and its dynamism brings to mind the following observation in the *Discourses on the First Decade of Titus Livius* (1.6, in *Works* 1:210), repeated more than once in his works: "Since all human affairs are in motion and cannot remain fixed, they must needs rise up or sink down."[5] In this case, the idea of movement and transformation superimposes itself over the original meaning of the term—"condition," "manner of being"—and casts it in a historical light.

We have before us three comparable examples in passages written within a very short period. Although convinced that Chabod was correct in supposing that *The Prince* was written in one go over a few months starting in the summer of 1513, I have preferred to confine myself to pages contained in what is generally considered the nucleus of the work: the first eleven chapters.[6] In any case, the observations suggested by examining them do not contrast with those that can be deduced from other writings by Machiavelli: the term *stato* is never defined; at the same time, these various meanings always seem to be alternating, even if with different shades of meaning, and in none of his works is *stato* used in a more circumscribed or unambiguous manner. Even a decade or so after *The Prince* was written, in *The History of Florence*, its semantic meaning has the same variations. We find, for example, *stato* in the sense of territorial domain, in the mention of the Battle of Agnadello, when "in one day the Venetians were deprived of the territory [stato] which in the course of many years they had gained with boundless expense" (1.29, in *Works*, 3:1069); in the sense of "government," or "regime," in the speech attributed to one of the citizens who protested before the signory in 1371 about the arrogance of the Guelph party, lamenting that liberty had been crushed by "a state [stato] of aristocrats or a popular government" (3.5, in *Works*, 3:1146); and in the institutional sense, where Machiavelli writes of the mismanagement of the Duke of Athens, which had provoked among the "citizens . . . indignation when they saw the majesty of their state [stato] ruined" (2.36, in *Works*, 3:1127–28).

We can therefore discount the hypothesis that, starting with the first work written *post res perditas* (after all was lost) and taking up the *quondam segretario* (former secretary) when he began to develop his political thoughts, it is possible to follow in Machiavelli's writings the continual progression of the notion of *stato*. Nor should we consider the opposite possibility, however: that such a notion is clear from the beginning. Norberto Bobbio, starting with the opening sentence of *The Prince*, "All the states, all the dominions that have had or now have authority over men have been and now either are republics or princedoms," observed that "Machiavelli would have been unable to write that sentence at the start of the work if the word in question [stato] were not already in current use."[7] We can read, almost as confirmation of this observation, the famous letter of 10 December 1513, where Machiavelli told Vettori of having "composed a little work *On Princedoms*," adding that once it was read, people "would see that for the fifteen years while I have been studying the art of the state, I have not slept or been playing" (*Works*, 2:929–30). The expression "art of the state"—which became famous after Burckhardt, writing of the lords and princes of the Italian Renaissance, defined their states as a "work of art"—under Machiavelli's pen refers not to the original creation of a single personality but rather to his activity in the Florentine chancery, comparable to the apprenticeship of a master craftsman and equal to those in the trade guilds of the time. And the term *stato* here refers to a structurally complex political entity, which comprises not only the administrative apparatus of the republic but also its normative regulations; in summary, the modern meaning of this notion begins to emerge.

All of this appears indisputable. However, before *The Prince*, Machiavelli did not use *stato* in the institutional sense. Fredi Chiappelli, subjecting Machiavelli's writings from the early period of the Florentine chancery to analysis, concluded that these belong to "a phase in the history of the term that displays greater uncertainty and fluctuation than in *The Prince*.[8] In Machiavelli's private correspondence, as well as in written reports from his diplomatic missions, *stato* is generally used to indicate the Florentine Republic: "Lo stato nostro" (our state, 5 June 1499), "questo stato" (this state, 5 October 1499), and so on, or various states that are specifically mentioned: "The Duke of Ferrara and Marquis of Mantova were closely united under the shadow of defending their states [li stati loro]" (21 November 1500). We can conclude that it is easy to move on from this sense of the word to its general institutional-political meaning.

This, however, does not happen in the *First Decennale*, where the term is repeated five times: in verses 72 ("You set up a citizens' republic [stato]"), 286 ("And your government [stato] too did not understand how to make decisions"), 308 ("that set its foot in your domain [stato]"), 420 ("to recover lost realm [stato] and honor"), and 464 ("the state [stato] of his duke of Valence");[9] in verse 286 the semantic value is analogous to the one we saw in governmental writings; it designates not an abstract individuality but the Florentine Republic; in the other verses it indicates the territory, other than in verse 72, where it signifies "government" or "regime." While the term *stato* does not appear in the *Capitoli*, in the writing *Ai Palleschi* of 1512, *stato* is used more than once to designate "government" or "regime."

Let us reconsider, then, the sentence at the beginning of *The Prince*: "states," we note, is united with "dominions," almost as though the *hendiadys* is useful to better clarify the concept, and therefore not far from the "multiple notion" noted by Chiappelli "in the attempt to resolve the issue even in analytical periphrasis," as in the example that he cites: "Ciptà e libertà nostra" (The city and our freedom). We may then remember that, to indicate the state generically, we often also encounter *repubblica*. Thus, at the beginning of the *Discourses* (1:2, in *Works* 1:203), we read: "Some who have written of states [repubbliche] say that they have one of three kinds of government [stati], called princedom, aristocracy and popular government"; a little further on, having described the events that led such societies to vary their manner of rule, he concludes: "And this is the circle in which all states revolve as they are governed and govern themselves." Here *repubblica* has the ancient Latin meaning that Bodin also would use, and *stato* defines the "reggimento" (rules), a term often adopted in the time of Machiavelli but rarely by Machiavelli himself. So the sense attributed to *stato* varies not only in his writings; what for us is a concept that can be defined with that word alone is also indicated by another term.

❧

Stato takes time to appear with a precise semantic value. In the chapter that Alberto Tenenti dedicated to the notion of the stato between the fourteenth century and the early 1500s, giving examples both in Latin and in the vernacular,[10] we see early evidence of the territorial sense of the term, while only in the early 1400s is its significance "often wedded to that of arrangement." However, as "the supreme reference of political action," it recurs in various deliberations of bodies in Venice but takes time to become established in Florence, and I would be inclined to observe that not all the examples adopted in that sense are persuasive. I do not agree at all with the final observation, in which Tenenti maintains that Machiavelli, "although he wrote of the 'majesty' [of the state], . . . never truly caught what may have been the true nature of its internal blood clot." Certainly, we never find a definition that completely explains the essence of the word; nevertheless, Chabod, in his analysis, cited some examples where he believed he saw a "modern meaning."[11] The study, then, of various passages relating to state functions allows us to mark out a concept that is close to the more developed one: for example, the famous passage in chapter 3 of *The Prince*, which refers to Machiavelli's reply to the "Cardinal of Rouen," who had claimed "that the Italians know nothing of war." The Florentine secretary hit back with the words "and the French know nothing of politics [stato]," by which he meant not just an abstract notion of the institution but the political action required to safeguard it.

To grasp the full complexity of the use of *stato*, it is also worth examining other references. In the *Dizionario del linguaggio italiano storico ed amministrativo* by Giulio Rezasco, we find various definitions in a list that takes into account the plurality of meanings that *stato* acquired over time.

The oldest examples are those that come across as "condition" or "way of being," and the word had already appeared in this sense in Dante's *Divine Comedy*.[12] With this meaning, the term can be extended to the position that not only an individual but also a family name occupies in the city, according to usage that has an important precedent in the *Libri della famiglia* by Leon Battista Alberti and that returns in Guicciardini.[13] If in Rezasco's *Dizionario* we see that it takes time for a meaning close to the modern one to appear, in its sense of "dominion" there are, however, citations that do not distinguish between examples from Villani and those from Machiavelli, while the headword "essenza del reggimento" (essence of government) is illustrated in a passage from Bernardo Segni's *Trattato de' governi*: "The state, in the cities, is a type of arrangement through which political appointments [of magistrates] must be made as well as deciding which [political] party should rule and control the city." The meaning is analogous to that of *reggimento*, which Guicciardini had defined twenty-five years earlier: "To meditate on government and public administration, on which our health and our life depend—as do all the notable deeds that are performed in this earthly life below!"[14] And in Machiavelli the use of *stato* for "government" and "regime" is earlier still.

If we were to proceed to an analysis of the term *stato* in the writings of Guicciardini,[15] we would also see the idea that the state is based on forceful action. In *Ricordi* (48), we read: "States cannot be established or maintained by conforming to the moral law. For if you look to their beginnings, all will be seen to have had their origins in violence."[16] He clarifies, however: "Save only the authority of commonwealths within the limits of their own territory." Therefore, in the narrow environment of the city of Guicciardini's birth, republics— evidently not principalities—are established thanks to a pact between the citizens, whereas they impose themselves with arms, that is, conquest, and often with acts of repression on the surrounding territory. The observation evidently implies a negative judgment, also as a result of the subsequent reference to the "twofold violence" that the "priests" use, "constraining us at once with weapons spiritual and temporal."[17] Machiavelli's assessment appears to differ: for him "expansion," or the conquest of territories, is a function of the internal arrangements of the republic that carries it out, and he cites the examples of Sparta and Venice on the one hand and Rome on the other (*Discourses* 1.6, in *Works*, 1:209). Earlier he observed that only "with power" could men "make themselves safe," and thus the founding of a new city should take place "in very fertile places, where, since the richness of the site permits the city to expand, she can both defend herself from those who assail her, and crush whoever imposes himself to her greatness." Further examples can be given, but this seems sufficiently explicit.

Although Machiavelli accepts that a state should use violence to acquire territory, or better still views its expansion favorably, as when he speaks of the ability of the "Roman state" to arrive "at the greatness it reached" (1.6, in *Works*, 1:209), he disapproves of any form of oppression in the internal government of a state. He does not explicitly write that seeking consensus is indispensable to the foundation on which one must build and maintain a political framework, yet he points to consensus as the most suitable instrument to give it a secure base. Even in the case of the Valentino, who may be the most eloquent example of the "ruler" whose scepter was "dripping with tears and blood," he highlights how the Valentino instead won over the people of Romagna "through their getting a taste of well being" and dwells on the ways in which he had governed that duchy, "because this matter is worthy of notice and of being copied by others" (chapter 7, in *Works*, 1:31).

He states this principle more clearly in the *Discourses* (3.7, in *Works*, 1:448), when, having posed the question "Why, of the many changes made from free government to tyranny, and the opposite, some are made with bloodshed, some without it," he explains: "That depends on the following: any government that is changed came into existence with violence or not. Since when it originates with violence, it must originate with injury to many, of necessity on its fall the injured try to revenge themselves; from this desire for revenge come bloodshed and deaths. But if that government was established by the common consent of a large group that made it great, there is no reason, if then the said large group falls, for injuring anyone else than its leader."

In fact, in the previous chapter, dedicated to conspiracies (3.6, in *Works*, 1:428), "by far the most important" reason that leads conspirators to plot against a prince is outlined as being "hated by the people generally." Consistent with this, in 1520, having to give his opinion on the government to be installed in Florence, he wrote: "Without satisfying the generality of the citizens, to set up a stable government is always impossible."[18] In *The Prince* he had observed that "well-ordered states and wise princes with the utmost attention take care not to make the rich desperate, and to satisfy the people and keep them contented," in other words, to obtain the support of the "group." Nevertheless, he states, it is easier to secure for oneself the support of the people and, writing of the civil principality (chapter 9, in *Works*, 1:39–40), he notes: he who "comes to the princedom with the aid of the rich maintains himself with more difficulty" than he who reaches it "with the aid of the people." In fact, he encounters greater obstacles by imposing himself on the rich, whereas it is easier to "satisfy the people, because the people's object is more creditable than that of the rich: the latter wish to oppress and the former not to be oppressed." By following this course, the prince also protects himself from conspiracies and can take "little heed [of them] when his people are well-disposed" (chapter 19, in *Works*, 1:68).

When, in *The History of Florence*, he addresses the first attempt, by the Duke of Athens, to impose on Florence a signorial power *in perpetuo*, he places the condemnation of the violent methods of ruling a state in the mouth of a member of the signory, having him state in his speech—the first in the work—the very principles of civil living (2.34, in *Works*, 3:1124):

> You seek to make a slave of a city that has always lived free. . . . Consider, My Lord, what great forces are needed to hold as a slave so great a city. Those whom—foreigners—you can always get are not enough. Those inside you cannot trust, because they who are now your supporters and who encourage you to make this

decision, first through your authority will overcome their enemies, and then will try to find a way for destroying you and making themselves rulers.

It is the risk previously outlined to the prince who thinks of leaning on the rich; it was imprudent, in Machiavelli's opinion, "because as prince he finds himself surrounded by many who think themselves his equals."[19] But Walter of Brienne, the Duke of Athens, cannot even count upon the people: "The common people, in whom you trust, are whirled about by any accident, however slight. Hence in a short time you must fear that all this city will be hostile. This will give cause for her ruin and yours."[20] And the subject of the dangers the prince faces returns, previously discussed in the *Discourses*: "Against this evil you can find no defense; because those rulers only can make their rule secure who have few enemies . . . but in the middle of universal hatred no security is ever to be found."

The "desire for liberty," warns the orator, does not lessen with time, because "one often sees it taken up again by men who have never experienced it," but the memories handed down from their fathers, and the "public buildings, the offices of the magistrates, the insignia of the free organizations recall it" (*Works*, 3:1124). And no enterprise would be sufficient to counterbalance the mourning for liberty: "Not if you should join to this state all of Tuscany," since the glory would not be felt as the Florentines' own, who "would gain not subjects but fellow slaves" (*Works*, 3:1125). Nor could the citizens be comforted, "though your conduct be holy . . . because to one wonted to living unbound, every chain has weight and every bond pinches." Moreover, it is not given "to find a violent government joined with a good prince." In conclusion: "You must then believe either that you can hold this city with the utmost violence . . . or must be content with what authority we have given you. To this we encourage you by reminding you that only authority freely given is durable."

The secure state, therefore, is one that has a broadly accepted government. It may astonish us to find no mention in *The History of Florence* of the *florentina libertas* when discussing the struggle between Florence and the Visconti; naturally, the dangers run by the city are cited, but there is no hint of the idealistic reasons traditionally invoked by the Florentine humanists in support of their fight against the Milanese "tyrant" and in celebration of the republican state.

Must we interpret this silence as a prudential form adopted in a work commissioned by a Medici? I would be inclined to exclude that possibility, given that the values of liberty are not silenced in the speech directed at the Duke of Athens, to the extent that historians have supposed that Machiavelli may have introduced it to make Pope Clement VII aware of the necessity to restore to Florence—following the death of Lorenzo di Piero de' Medici, duke of Urbino, ruler of Florence from 1513 to 1519—its republican liberty, reprising and expanding upon the arguments presented in the *Discourse on Remodeling the Government of Florence*.[21]

In fact, the stato that arose from the defeat of the Ciompi and held power in the years of the war with Milan is treated very harshly in *The History of Florence*: the faction that ruled it governed in a way that was "harmful to the Florentine citizens" (3.22, in *Works*, 3:1175). If this was the judgment that Machiavelli came to pass on it, he would have found it difficult to share the hymn to liberty in, for example, Bruni's *Laudatio florentinæ urbis*. It must have seemed more convincing to show the dangers of tyranny at a moment when liberty had been placed in jeopardy by a lord than singing its praises at a time when the reaction of the "rich" had become arrogant and oppressive. The government that came to power after 1381 dictated to Machiavelli the comments with which he opened the fourth book of *History* (*Works*, 3:473):

> Those cities, especially such as are not well organized, that are administered under the semblance of republican government, often vary their rulers and their constitutions not between liberty and slavery, as many believe, but between slavery and license. The promoters of license, who are the people, and the promoters of slavery, who are the nobles, praise the mere name of liberty, for neither of these classes is willing to be subject either to the laws or to men.

The man who wrote those words would have found it difficult to share in Bruni's celebrations of that *stato*: "Hæc est vera libertas, hæc æquitas civitatis" (This, then, is true liberty, this equality in a commonwealth).²² From that different judgment of the Florentine state we can better understand the polemic hint with which, in opening his historiographic work, Machiavelli expressed his own critical reservations toward the works of Leonardo Bruni and Poggio Bracciolini.²³ Garin was undoubtedly correct when he observed that "Bruni . . . sets in motion a theoretical explanation, beginning from classical history and historiography, but in order to construct an original vision of political life in a continuous dialogue with the ancient historians." Nevertheless, it is necessary to bear in mind his warning: "Bruni may constitute a fertile prologue to Machiavelli, a point of reference, *even though often by means of a contrast.*"²⁴

∼§

In Machiavelli's eyes, the social basis of a state characterizes it through its institutions and its strength. Thus, in the fourth chapter of *The Prince* (1.20–22), he poses the question of how Alexander the Great became "lord of Asia in a few years." The answer leads him to an original digression on "two different ways" in which a monarchy may be ruled: "In one there is a prince, and all the others are as servants who, through his favor and appointment, assist as agents in governing the kingdom. In the other, there is a prince, with barons who hold their rank not through the ruler's favor but through their ancient blood."

The greater or lesser complexity of the structure is reflected in the particular features of the kingdom: "States governed by a prince and his servants think their prince more powerful, because in all their territory they receive no superior except him." This determines the very nature of the state, and to illustrate the differences, two contemporary examples are considered:

> Examples of these two different methods of governing in our times are the Turk and the King of France. The whole monarchy of the Turk is governed by one ruler; the others are his servants; dividing his kingdom into sanjaks, he sends them various administrators, and changes and varies these as he likes. But the King of France is placed amidst a long-established multitude of lords acknowledged by their own subjects and loved by them; such lords have their vested rights; these the king cannot take from them without danger to himself. On considering, then, both of these countries, you see that there will be difficulty in gaining the Turk's country but, when it is conquered, great ease in holding it. So, on the contrary, you see that in some respects the country of France can be more easily occupied but that it can be held only with great difficulty.

The compactness of the Turk's *stato* is due to the crushing of all the subjects into servitude and to the lack of a social articulation, and therefore to the direct administration of the sovereign and to the absence of princes who can support an invasion or place themselves at the head of a revolt. In the kingdom of France, however, such possibilities exist,[25] but precisely because of this, the former, whenever its land is occupied and its sovereign killed, would be wholly deprived of focal points of resistance; in the latter case, however, "victory . . . brings in its train countless difficulties, both with those who have aided you and with those you have overcome." One would therefore see a network of resistance, which would make it difficult to "hold [that state]."

For Chabod, this step is one of the first formulations of the idea of Europe, which has several specific characteristics.[26] "Europe," he observes, "this time is really Europe; the Christian religion, Machiavelli has completely forgotten." It is a feature "rich with consequences, as it favors the development of virtue, that is, the ability to do, the creative energy." The geopolitical juxtaposition assumes specific significance because this is examined "in our times": the Aristotelian distinction between the kingdoms of ancient Greece and the monarchy that is "typical of many barbarian peoples" living in Asia, who being "more servile than the Greeks," tolerate "a despotic power" more easily, is adapted to the states of the Turk and the king of France.[27] Medieval theorists, from Saint Thomas Aquinas to Marsilius of Padua and onward, had reprised the difference between the two forms of monarchy, repeating the allusion to the Asiatic characteristics of despotism, but in *The Prince*—apparently for the first time—the example of the ancient oriental empires is not given, except as a starting point, and the emphasis is placed on the differences between the great powers of the time. The difference between the Turkish empire and the kingdom of France, noted Procacci, would return in the writings of Le Roy and in the work of Bodin, as they also would in the arguments ignited during the Wars of Religion.[28] The focus, however, would move to the servile characteristic of despotism, and scant attention would be paid to the social complexities of the two types of state, at least until Montesquieu, who in *Esprit des lois* would dwell at length upon the peculiarities of despotism.

Nevertheless, later still, the issues Machiavelli highlighted would be neglected: the difficulty of conquering the *stato* of the Turk and the ease of keeping it, in contrast to the kingdom of France. Only Hume, in *Political Essays* and, in his footsteps, Tocqueville, in *Democracy in America*, would return to this issue, citing especially chapter 4 of *The Prince*.[29]

Such characterization invites us to follow further analogies with Machiavelli's views, right up to the thoughts on leadership by Gramsci, dictated by the observation that the empire ruled by czarist despotism differed profoundly from western states, the latter being much more complex. As is well known, Gramsci reflected on the Russian Revolution: "In the East the state was everything, civil society was primordial and gelatinous"; therefore the revolution was a "war of maneuver." On the other hand, the proletariat's ascent to power in the West was influenced by its capacity to sustain a "war of position," since "there was a proper relation between state and civil society, and when the state tottered, a sturdy structure of civil society was immediately revealed. The state was just a forward trench; behind it, stood a succession of sturdy fortresses and emplacements."[30] It is not necessary to push beyond the analogy in the comparison of the two types of state and society; nevertheless, we should not neglect the permanence of the interpretative categories used to understand the profound organization of political life.

◆

With which principles does one rule a state? As Chiappelli observed, it is opportune to determine not only what the state is but also what it does.[31] And so we read the following in *The Prince* (chapter 13, in *Works*, 1:47): "The principal foundations of all states, the new as well as the old and the mixed, are good laws and good armies." The passage records the observation with which Machiavelli had opened *La cagione dell'Ordinanza* (*The Reason for the Militia*) in 1506: "Everyone knows that whoever speaks of empire, kingdom, principality, or republic and whoever speaks of men who command, starting from the highest rank and descending to the captain of a brigantine, speaks of justice and arms" (*Opere*, 1:26).

He also repeated this principle in other writings, using the same or similar words. Thus, in the *Discourses*, he writes: "There cannot be good laws or anything else good" where there is no "good military organization" (3.31, in *Works*, 1:500). And to show that "the discord between the people and the Roman Senate made that republic free and powerful" (1.4, in *Works*, 1:202), he observed the following in a polemic against those who did not understand that force of arms had to be accompanied by good government: "I cannot deny that Fortune and the military system were sources of the Roman power; but it surely seems that these objectors do not realize that wherever there are good soldiers there must be good government, and it seldom happens that such a city does not also have good Fortune."

Quaglioni, maintaining that "a Machiavelli ignorant of the jurispolitical culture of his time" was unthinkable, brought attention back to "the blunt Justinian theme" that runs through his work: the nexus between justice and arms placed at the start of the constitution *imperatoriam maiestatem* [the imperial majesty], who "should be armed with laws as well as glorified with laws."[32] He therefore asked: "Is it permissible to hypothesize that Machiavelli wanted to remind us, constantly, that 'justice and arms,' 'good arms,' and 'good laws' are the foremost principles of the entire *Corpus* of Justinian, and therefore the authoritative foundation of the science of public law?"

Quaglioni's analysis of Machiavelli's language sheds light on the latter's legal training and explains his "insistence on the issue of *ordini* ['rules'],[33] that is of statutory laws and forms of government."[34] I may add that in *The Art of War* "ancient ways" dictate the most solemn affirmation of the union that these two foundations of the state must hold tightly: "All the arts that are provided for in a state for the sake of the common good of men, all the statutes made in it so that men will live in fear of the laws, and of God, would be vain if for them there were not provided defenses," that is, "military support." And a little later in the book, Fabrizio Colonna would declare: "Weapons borne by citizens or subjects, given by the laws and well regulated, never do damage; on the contrary they are always an advantage, and cities keep themselves uncorrupted longer by means of those weapons than without them" (*Works,* 2:566 and 584). If "the majesty of the state"—an expression that recurs (with some variations, "principality," "empire") in *The Prince,* in the *Discourses,* and in *The History of Florence*—is ensured by the Justinian binomial, the importance of "rules" constitutes almost a leitmotif in Machiavelli's work, inasmuch as it is a foundation of civil living. The "rules" given by Cyrus, Romulus, and Theseus, he observes in *The Prince* (chapter 6, in *Works,* 1:25), do not appear "different from those of Moses, who had so great a teacher" (God himself), and such "rules" "the methods of those whom I have set up as your aim"—offer an "opportunity" that is "very great" for the salvation of Italy

(chapter 26, in *Works*, 1:94). Even the rules the Valentino
founded his state on appear exemplary and, if they "did not
bring him success," this was due only to "an unusual and utterly malicious stroke of Fortune" (chapter 7, in *Works*, 1:29).
In the *Discourses*, the comments begin with "those cities
that . . . governed themselves by their own judgment . . .
[which] have had diverse beginnings, diverse laws and institutions." "Laws and institutions" is another binomial that is essential in Machiavelli's political vision; the norms that regulate
the life of the state and the fundamental statutes that constitute it are the very reason for the solidity of a republic or a
principality. The grandeur of Rome was born from the "revolts," which gave rise to "laws and institutions conducive to
public liberty" (1.4, in *Works*, 1:203). Without giving too
many examples, I can turn to an "extravagance," the verses of
The Ass, where the hero, left alone by his "guide," turned his
thoughts "to lessen[ing] . . . the great fire that was consuming
my heart," to the "variations in earthly things," and realized "it
is true that a power is wont to exist long or but briefly according as its laws and methods are more or less good" (chapter 5,
vv. 19–21, 36, and 76–78, in *Works*, 2:762–63).

Good methods must guarantee the primacy of the public
good. The distinction in Machiavelli between public benefit
and private benefit is a very strong one. When this distinction
is abused, corruption reaches its highest level, whereas "living
freely" sees harmony reign between the two principles:

> All cities and provinces that live in freedom anywhere in
> the world . . . make very great gains. They do so because
> their populations are larger, since marriages are freer and
> more attractive to men, and each man gladly begets those
> children he thinks he can bring up, without fear that his
> patrimony will be taken from him; he knows not merely

that they are born free and not slaves but that by means of their abilities they can become prominent men.

In such conditions the state flourishes:

> Riches multiply in a free country to a greater extent, both those that come from agriculture and those that come from industry, for each man gladly increases such things and seeks to gain such goods as he believes, when gains, he can enjoy. Thence it comes that men in emulation give thought to private and public advantages; and both kinds keep marvelously increasing." (*Discourses* 2.2, in *Works*, 1:332–33)

Certainly, the variation of human affairs ensures that wealth leads to corruption, since citizens who become rich tend also to wish to acquire rank and honors, and their ambition puts the public good at risk. From this stems the warning that "well-ordered republics ought to keep their treasuries rich and their citizens poor" (1.37, in *Works*, 1:272).[35]

Ambition is mentioned as a constant danger; Machiavelli already said so in the *Tercets on Ambition*, writing that ambition had been sent among men "to deprive us of peace and to set us at war, to take away from us all quiet and all good" (vv. 28–29, in *Works*, 2:736). From private ambition are born factions and partisans, which bring a republic to ruin. Machiavelli was not opposed to internal battles in a political entity, as demonstrated by his famous comment about the "revolts" in Rome, thanks to which that republic became "free and powerful."[36] That situation, however, concerned two bodies of citizens, "the plebeians and the senate," with both fighting to assert their rights but able in the end to reach an agreement in the name of the "public good," thus giving life to new institutions. Factions, however, which are caused by private disagreements and by the ambition of powerful citizens who wish to create their own groups of supporters, fight to overthrow each other. One of the most significant passages is in the chapter of the *Discourses* that deals with "the bringing of charges" and "slanders" (1.8, in *Works*, 1:214–17). The slanders that had spread in Florence caused "hate [which] went on to divisions, from divisions to parties, from parties to ruin." The example—not mentioned in the text, but clear enough for Guicciardini to guess[37]—is Cosimo de' Medici, who "among other things" also availed himself of slanders aimed "against powerful citizens who oppose themselves to his thirst for power," and "by taking the side of the popular party and confirming its low opinion of its opponents, he makes it friendly to himself." In this way he managed to take power. In *The History of Florence* the episode would be recounted in the seventh book, and in the first chapter Machiavelli explains which "divisions" damage or are useful to a republic: "Those do harm that are accompanied with factions and partisans; those bring benefit that are kept up without factions and without partisans" (*Works*, 3:1336). Then follow the mechanisms with which factions and party supporters strengthen themselves and end up prevailing to the ruin of the "common good." On the other hand, in the opening of the third book (*Works*, 3:1140–41), Machiavelli had clarified—via a comparison with the "enmities" that kept Rome and Florence "disunited"—which divisions had produced beneficial effects and which ones had been disastrous. Where the citizens had argued with each other by "debating" and had overcome the dispute "by law," their battle had been beneficial to liberty and the state; where, however, the conflict had made enemies of them and the winning party had triumphed "by the exile and death of many citizens," the success of the winning faction, "harmful and unjust," had ended by extinguishing every virtue.

In summary, the primacy of private interests over the public good could not happen without the dominion of injustice, and this is the most garish symptom of corruption, which overwhelms a society and all of its political life. The citizens who had risen up against the violence of the Guelph party in 1371 addressed a speech to the signory, where they lament that the party's followers were seeking "the satisfaction of having conquered the others" and had "usurped" the sovereignty of the republic (3.5, in *Works*, 3:1146):

> Hence they make laws and statutes not for the public benefit but for their own; hence wars, truces, alliances are decided not for the common glory but for the pleasure of a few . . . the laws, the statutes, the methods of government here . . . are managed not as required by free government but as required by the ambition of the party on top.

In the *Discourses*, to demonstrate that "the multitude is wiser . . . than a prince," Machiavelli resorts to an almost paradoxical argument: "The cruelties of the multitude are against a man who they fear will seize the property of them all; the cruelties of a prince [are] against any man who the prince fears will seize his individual property" (1.58, in *Works*, 1:317). But precisely in this extreme defense of the "common good" is the affirmation of the necessity of the law and of that equality among citizens which is the soil from which the republic can grow.

The relationship between equality and republic is almost one of cause and effect; in any case, the first is the indispensable condition for the second (*Discourses* 1.55, in *Works*, 1:306).

Thus, as proof that in the German cities "government has been kept orderly and uncorrupted," Machiavelli reveals that they "do not allow any citizen of theirs to be a gentleman or to live in the fashion of one." As the highest examples of corruption are those who, besides great fortunes, "command castles and have subjects who obey them." The presence of these "gentlemen," who "crowd the Kingdom of Naples, the City of Rome, the Romagna, and Lombardy," is incompatible with "well-ordered government, because men of these types are altogether hostile to all free government." This term ["*civiltà*" in the original, translated by Gilbert as "free government"] is another word that throws light on a vision of organized political life; it appears, therefore, not to be contained solely within the term *stato* or *repubblica*: civil life, ruled by "good statutes and laws," cannot remain free of corruption if it contains divisive elements, which, in the case of a republic, are factions, and in a principality, the "gentlemen who command castles." "Equality," as in the three Tuscan republics of Florence, Siena, and Lucca, is a political foundation of such strength "that a prudent man, understanding the ancient forms of society, could easily have introduced there well-regulated government." On the contrary, where "the matter is so corrupt that the laws are not restraint enough," such as in the "lands" full of gentlemen, only "a kingly hand . . . with absolute and surpassing power" can put a "check on the over-great ambition and corruption of the powerful." The figure of the prince reappears, imbued with a "surpassing" power, which evokes the ghost of the Valentino (*Discourses* 1.55, in *Works*, 1:308–9).

One clarification is striking, which was confirmed a few years after Machiavelli's death. In that same chapter of the *Discourses,* we read: "He who wishes to set up a kingdom or a principality cannot do so unless he draws away from that equality many men of ambitious and restless spirit and makes them gentlemen in fact." As I have mentioned, Filippo Strozzi, who was present at Machiavelli's deathbed and who appears to have listened to him recount his "celebrated dream,"[38] showed that he had drawn a valuable lesson from that teaching after the fall of the Florentine Republic in 1530, when, to "give a different form of government to the present one," in other words to found a principality in Florence, he advised Pope Clement VII to proceed with an "an election of all of those who are friends . . . and declare them noble through public provision, admitting only these to the government, and excluding everyone else as commoners";[39] that is, to introduce that "inequality" which Machiavelli judged a basic element of a principality.

Considered in its semantic aspect, the word *stato* therefore turns out to be still fluctuating in Machiavelli's writings; the warning from the *Discorsi* can be applied to this too: "For forces easily acquire names, but names do not acquire forces," and the "forces" of the state were at the time undergoing development (1.34, in *Works*, 1:267). Nevertheless, an open examination of the various implications of this collective political organism in Machiavelli's writings reveals a qualitative richness and a search for an internal unity that, while drawing on the Roman tradition, propel themselves toward the idea that was formed in later developments, in particular if we bear in mind the one Bobbio called the "direction from Rousseau to Hegel." Perhaps because this view outlines a "democratic" vision of the state, it has been misunderstood by those, such as Gentile, who sought in the Florentine secretary a consonance with their own philosophy. But to describe Machiavelli's thoughts as being closed "inside a subjectivity in which there can be no room for a state that has a true moral value, and that can be considered an absolute common or universal good," signifies only that Machiavelli did not develop the idea of an "ethical state," not that he had no notion of the state.[40] Now, the approximation focusing on an author of the past, if it fails, reveals the error not of the man being critiqued but of the critic himself, who has used inappropriate interpretative criteria.

One other point deserves to be reconsidered, however: not only Gentile, but also Croce, pointed out that in Machiavelli the idea of politics is not identified with the idea of the state; leaving aside the value judgment contained in their observations, it may be useful to take a cue from them, as some have sought to do, to grasp in its complexity a vision of "civil life" that incorporates the idea of state and that therefore leads to an examination of the various phenomena relating to the diverse "generations of men" organized in society.

NOTES

Preface

1. N. Machiavelli, "Discourses on the First Decade of Titus Livius," preface to bk. 1 of the *Discourses*, in *The Chief Works and Others*, 1:190. Unless otherwise stated, Machiavelli's writings are quoted from the three-volume edition translated by Allan Gilbert and published by Duke University Press, 1989.

2. J. Burckhardt, *The Civilization of the Renaissance in Italy* (London: Penguin Books, 1990), pp. 185ff.

3. L. Pulci, *Morgante*, 25:228–36: the wise devil Astaroth informs the knight Rinaldo that "the other hemisphere, yes, can be reached," where equally there are "castles, towns and reigns" and populous lands. English translation by Joseph Tusiani, introduction and notes by Edoardo Lèbano (Bloomington: Indiana University Press, 1998).

4. Joannes de Sacrobosco (John Holywood), in his work *De sphæra mundi*, written around the mid-thirteenth century, explained that the Earth is split into five zones, of which only two, the temperate ones of the Northern and Southern Hemispheres, were habitable. The others were not only uninhabitable but also inaccessible due to the extremes of cold and heat, which even set fire to ships that ventured into those waters. *De sphæra mundi* was the reference used to study the characteristics of the Earth, and it had a vast and prolonged fame, so much so that it was continuously published

until the sixteenth century and beyond; thus, the University of Padua, as late as 1592, signed a contract with Galileo that stipulated he would read and explain this work. On the other hand, we know from the *Libro di ricordi* by Niccolò Machiavelli's father, Bernardo (ed. C. Olschki [Rome: Edizioni di storia e letteratura, 2007], with a postscript by L. Perini), that the latter owned the commentary on Cicero's *Somnium Scipionis* by Macrobius, the Latin writer of the fifth century, which contains an illustration showing the division of the world into five zones, only two of which are habitable.

5. *Orlando Furioso*, 15:21–22; English translation by Guido Waldman (Oxford: Oxford University Press, 1983).

6. "These voyages have not only confuted many things which had been affirmed by writers about terrestrial matters, but besides this, they have given some cause for alarm to interpreters of the Holy Scriptures who are accustomed to interpret those verses of the Psalms [18.5] in which it is declared that the sound of their songs had gone all over the earth and their words spread to the edges of the world, as meaning that faith in Christ had spread over the entire earth through the mouths of the apostles: an interpretation contrary to the truth" (F. Guicciardini, *The History of Italy*, trans. and ed. Sidney Alexander [Princeton: Princeton University Press, 1984], p. 182).

7. Thus wrote Copernicus in the letter of dedication to Pope Paul III in the *De revolutionibus orbium cælestium* (see the edition translated by Charles Glenn Wallis, *On the Revolution of the Heavenly Spheres* [Amherst, MA: Prometheus Books, 1975], p. 5). Based on this information, the earliest idea of the "astronomical revolution," which would negate the geocentric vision of the universe, would have been conceived by Copernicus while he was still studying at the University of Padua (1501–1506) or immediately after.

8. For a picture of the intellectual developments of this period, see C. Vasoli, "La tradizione scolastica e le novità umanistiche filosofiche del tardo Trecento e del Quattrocento," in *Le filosofie del Rinascimento*, ed. P. C. Pissavino (Milan: B. Mondadori, 2002), esp. pp. 126ff.

9. *Discourses* 1.40, in *Works*, 1:284. All works by Machiavelli are listed here without his name.

10. Vettori to Machiavelli, 20 August 1513, and Machiavelli to Vettori, 26 August 1513, in *Machiavelli and His Friends: Their Personal Correspondence*, trans. and ed. James B. Atkinson and David Sices (DeKalb: Northern Illinois University Press, 1996), pp. 251 and 257. This adhesion to reality, however, impels him to seek confirmation in juridical texts corresponding to real-life situations; to cite just one particularly effective writing, see D. Quaglioni, "Machiavelli e la lingua della giurisprudenza," in *Langues et écritures de la république et de la guerre: Études sur Machiavel*, ed. A. Fontana, J.-L. Fournel, X. Tabet, and J.-C. Zancarini (Genoa: Name, 2004), pp. 177–92.

11. The phrase is repeated in *Discourses* 1.6 and 2 , preface to bk. 2, in *Works*, 1:210 and 322, and in *History of Florence*, bk. 5.1, in *Works*, 3:1232.

12. This behavior too would give rise to misunderstanding. Thus, Bodin, who recognized in Machiavelli the experience "of the republic," adduced the testimony of Giovio for Machiavelli's poor knowledge of the classics: "Jovius reports that he lacked this qualification, and the work speaks for itself"; Bodin stated that Machiavelli would have been a more truthful writer "if he had combined a knowledge of the writings of ancient philosophers and historians with experience." See. J. Bodin, *Method for the Easy Comprehension of History*, trans. Beatrice Reynolds (New York: Columbia University Press, 1945).

13. F. De Sanctis, "Conferenze su Machiavelli," in *L'arte, la scienza e la vita*, ed. M. T. Lanza (Turin: Einaudi, 1972), p. 76.

14. It is superfluous to refer the reader to the imposing work of J. M. De Bujanda, but see at least *Index de Rome, 1557, 1559, 1564* (Sherbrooke, Québec: Centre d'Études de la Renaissance, 1990).

15. *Lettere di Giovambattista Busini a Benedetto Varchi*, ed. G. Milanesi (Florence: Le Monnier, 1860), p. 241.

16. On these issues, an important work is G. Procacci's *Machiavelli nella cultura europea dell'età moderna* (Rome: Laterza, 1995).

17. Ibid., pp. 347ff. As is well known, this is the interpretation of Ugo Foscolo in *The Sepulchres*, vv. 155–58.

18. J.G.A. Pocock, *The Machiavellian Moment: Florentine Political Thought and the Atlantic Republican Tradition* (Princeton: Princeton University Press, 1975). For some aporias on Pocock's interpretations, see M. Viroli, *Machiavelli's God*, trans. Antony Sugaar (Princeton: Princeton University Press, 2010), pp. 24–25.

19. See M. Gaille-Nikodimov, "L'annexion républicaine de Machiavel dans la pensée anglo-saxonne," in *Machiavel aux XIXe et XXe siècles*, ed. P. Carta and X. Tabet (Padua: Cedam, 2007), pp. 287–307.

20. See H. Baron's preface to to Leonardo Bruni Aretino's *Humanistisch-philosophische Schriften* (Leipzig: Teubner, 1928), where for the first time the term *Bürgerhumanismus* (civic humanism) appears. The development of this concept is naturally contained in his book *The Crisis of the Early Italian Renaissance* (Princeton: Princeton University Press, 1962), on which see A. Molho, "Hans Baron's Crisis," in *Florence and Beyond: Culture, Society and Politics in Renaissance Italy; Essays in Honour of John M. Najemy*, ed. D. S. Peterson with D. L. Bornstein (Toronto: Centre for Reformation and Renaissance Studies, 2008), pp. 61–90.

21. Atkinson and Sices, *Machiavelli and His Friends*, pp. 134–36.

22. The word *virtù*, here in its adjectival form, is used in a specific sense in Machiavelli that does not translate readily into English, its meaning denoting "strength," "ability," and "spirit."—Trans.

Chapter 1. A Shadowy Period

1. Machiavelli to Francesco Vettori, 16 April 1527 (*Works*, 2:1010).

2. See B. Machiavelli, *Libro di ricordi*.

3. R. Ridolfi, *The Life of Niccolò Machiavelli*, trans. Cecil Grayson (London: Routledge and Kegan Paul, 1963), p. 2.

4. Machiavelli to Francesco Vettori, 18 March 1513, in *Works*, 2:899. The dating of the letter here to "1512 [1513]" reflects the fact that in Florence during Machiavelli's time, "it was the custom to begin each new year not on 1 January but on 25 March; Florentines used the designation 'in the year of the Incarnation' " (Atkinson and Sices, *Machiavelli and His Friends*, pp. 433–34). In *Works*, Gilbert gives the date of the letter as rendered by Machiavelli, with the corresponding year based on the calendar starting on January 1 each year afterward in square brackets; here the dates of the letters in question have been rendered in modern style, with the new year beginning on January 1.—Trans.

5. See the appendix to the second volume of the work by A. Verde, *Lo studio fiorentino, 1473–1503* (Florence: Leo S. Olschki, 1973–1994), dedicated to Machiavelli when he was a student (p. 537). According to Verde, Machiavelli did not attend the University of Pisa, contrary to the custom of young Florentines of his status, because, as mentioned in Bernardi's *Ricordi*, the latter was able to provide for his education without recourse to public teaching. Bernardo had—Verde explains—a good knowledge of books on law, history, and literature and could therefore give the young Niccolò a thorough cultural education. At the same time, one should note that a university degree was not required to accede to public positions, and the diploma conferred by the Arti (the guilds) sufficed.

6. P. Giovio, *Elogia clarorum virorum . . . apud Michaelem Tramezinum, Venetiis 1546* (quoted from the English translation by Florence Alden Gragg published as *An Italian Portrait Gallery* [Boston: Chapman & Grimes, 1935], p. 124).

7. From Bernardo's *Libro di ricordi* (p. 138) we know that Machiavelli began to "far de' latini" (do Latin) with Paolo da Ronciglione, who also taught the humanist Pietro Crinito; this detail casts doubt on Giovio's statement.

8. Previously J. H. Whitfield, in *Discourses on Machiavelli* (Cambridge: W. Heffer & Sons, 1969), p. 197, had put forward the hypothesis that Machiavelli knew book six of Polybius thanks to

philhellene circles in Florence, and C. Dionisotti, in *Machiavellerie: Storia e fortuna di Machiavelli* (Turin: Einaudi, 1980), pp. 139–40, quotes a passage from the *Liber de urbe Roma* by Bernardo Rucellai that hints at the reading of this text in Latin.

9. C. Ginzburg, in "Machiavelli: L'eccezione e la regola," *Quaderni storici* (2003): 112, and L. Perini, in the postscript to the *Libro di ricordi*, have identified many of the books Bernardo Machiavelli mentioned. For Machiavelli's readings, see also C. Ginzburg, "Diventare Machiavelli: Per una nuova lettura dei 'Ghiribizzi al Soderini,' " *Quaderni storici* 121 (2006): 151–64.

10. *Libro di ricordi*, pp. 14 and 35. It is unknown in what way Niccolò Alamanno (or della Magna) may have utilized the work of Bernardo Machiavelli because none of the editions of Livy that this printer produced has come down to us.

11. In 1971 Mario Martelli published the article "Preistoria (medicea) di Machiavelli" in *Studi di filologia italiana*, 29:377–405, in which, taking as a foundation the manuscript Laurenziano 41.33 from the hand of Biagio Buonaccorsi, he attributed the composition of Machiavelli's *Poscia che a l'ombra sotto questo alloro* and *Se avessi l'arco e le ale* to a date prior to 1494, and therefore hypothesized a youthful frequentation of Medici circles. Subsequently, however, in "Machiavelli politico, amante, poeta," *Interpres* 17 (1998): 252, Buanoccorsi stated that "the earlier conclusions, provisional at the time and formulated as provisional, have to be radically revised" and that the "pastoral should be restored to its time (1515 or 1518)." Thus there would disappear that glimpse into the period prior to Machiavelli's entry to the chancery, which, however, could have explained his relationship with Giuliano de' Medici after the fall of the Republic of Florence.

12. S. Bertelli, "Noterelle machiavelliane: Un codice di Lucrezio e di Terenzio," *Rivista storica italiana* 73 (1961): 544–53; id., "Noterelle machiavelliane: Ancora su Lucrezio e Machiavelli," ibid., 74 (1964): 774–90. As is well known, the poem by Lucretius was discovered by Poggio Bracciolini when he went to the Council of Constance in 1415.

13. *Works*, 2:927–31.

14. Thus Ginzburg, in *Machiavelli: L'eccezione e la regola,* pp. 197ff., has noted in a dialogue in *The Mandrake* the indirect quotation of a canon lawyer, whose work was in the possession of Bernardo Machiavelli.

CHAPTER 2. The Relationship with Savonarola

1. Machiavelli to Ricciardo Becchi, 9 March 1498, in *Works,* 2:889.

2. *Discourses on the First Decade of Titus Livius* 1.45 (*Works,* 1:288).

3. Ibid. On the entire episode, see I. Cervelli, "Savonarola, Machiavelli e il libro dell'Esodo," in *Savonarola, democrazia, tirannide, profezia,* ed. G. C. Garfagnini (Florence: Edizioni del Galluzzo, 1998), pp. 243–98.

4. Machiavelli to Ricciardo Becchi, 9 March 1498, in *Works,* 2:889-90.

CHAPTER 3. The Activity in the Chancery

1. The episode is related by Philippe de Commynes, the French historian who accompanied Charles VIII on his expedition (*The Memoirs of Philip de Commines,* vol. 2, ed. Andrew Scoble [London: Henry G. Bohn, 1856], p. 138): In Pisa

> a great number of men and women cried out to him, "Liberty, Liberty," begging of him, with tears in their eyes, that he would vouchsafe to restore it to them.... The king not understanding what they meant by that word liberty ... replied he was willing it should be so; though (to speak truth) he had no authority to grant it, for the town was not his own and he was

received into it only for friendship, and to relieve him in his great necessities.

2. *Discorso sopra Pisa*, in *Opere*, Biblioteca della Pléiade, vol. 1 (Turin: Einaudi-Gallimard, 1997), pp. 3–4, and Machiavelli to a councilor of Lucca, 5 October 1499, in *Opere*, vol. 2 (1999), p. 19.

3. For these arrangements, see D. Marzi, *La Cancelleria della Repubblica fiorentina*, rist. anast. [facsimile] (Florence: Le Lettere, 1987); G. Guidi, *Lotte, pensiero e istituzioni politiche nella Repubblica fiorentina dal 1494 al 1512* (Florence: L. S. Olschki, 1992), and for that which relates to Machiavelli: N. Rubinstein, "The Beginnings of Niccolò Machiavelli's Career in the Florentine Chancery," *Italian Studies* 11 (1956): 72–91.

4. See E. Garin, "I cancellieri umanisti della repubblica fiorentina," in *La cultura filosofica del Rinascimento italiano* (Florence: Sansoni, 1961), pp. 3–37.

5. See S. Bertelli, "Machiavelli e la politica estera fiorentina," in *Studies on Machiavelli*, ed. M. P. Gilmore (Florence: Sansoni, 1972), p. 51.

6. Atkinson and Sices, *Machiavelli and His Friends*, p. 355.

7. Political judgments in annotations to chronicles and diaries have been highlighted by E. Cutinelli-Réndina, J.-J. Marchand, and M. Melera-Morettini, "Ipotesi per una ricerca: L'emergenza del discorso politico dalla storiografia toscana minore tra Quattro e Cinquecento," in *Langues et écritures*, ed. Fontana, Fournel, Tabet, and Zancarini, pp. 29–50. For the relationship between historical narration and political reflection, according to a cultural trend previously witnessed in the 1400s in Tuscany, see E. Cutinelli-Réndina, J.-J. Marchand, and M. Melera-Morettini, *Dalla storia alla politica nella Toscana del Rinascimento* (Rome: Salerno, 2005).

8. *The Art of War* 7, in *Works*, 2:721.

9. Ridolfi, *Vita*, p. 468. See also the introduction by G. Inglese in his edition of the *Capitoli di Machiavelli* (Rome: Bulzoni, 1981), pp. 28ff.

10. Atkinson and Sices, *Machiavelli and His Friends*, p. 27.

11. Ibid., p. 33.
12. Ibid., p. 31.
13. Ibid., p. 50.
14. *Works*, 2:947.
15. Atkinson and Sices, *Machiavelli and His Friends*, p. 59.
16. Ibid., p. 208.
17. On the Florentine world in this period, see in particular *I ceti dirigenti in Firenze dal gonfalonierato di giustizia a vita all'avvento del ducato*, ed. E. Insabato, intro. R. Fubini (Lecce: Conte, 1999). Some information, then, in F. Gilbert, "Bernardo Rucellai and the Orti Oricellari: A Study on the Origin of Modern Political Thought," *Journal of the Warburg and Courtauld Institutes* 12 (1949): 105, and id., "Le idee politiche a Firenze al tempo di Savonarola e Soderini," in *Machiavelli e il suo tempo* (Bologna: il Mulino, 1977). See also L. Martines, *The Social World of the Florentine Humanists* (Princeton: Princeton University Press, 1963), and id., *Lawyers and Statecrafts in Renaissance Florence* (Princeton: Princeton University Press, 1968), and R. Burr Litchfield, *Emergence of a Bureaucracy: The Florentine Patricians, 1530–1790* (Princeton: Princeton University Press, 1986), which, moreover, tackles issues with more general interests.
18. *Works*, 2:961.
19. Atkinson and Sices, *Machiavelli and His Friends*, pp. 190-1.

CHAPTER 4. The Correspondence with Functionaries of the Domain

1. In 1971 the publisher Laterza had set in motion the publication of Machiavelli's writings from the chancery, comprising both the letters from his diplomatic missions, given in full, and a selection of the governmental writings, edited by F. Chiappelli and J.-J. Marchand, but this edition, published under the title *Legazioni, commissarie, scritti di governo* was halted after publication of the fourth volume, ending with 31 December 1505. Now the Edizione

Nazionale delle Opere di Machiavelli has resumed the publication of a selection of the governmental writings, entrusted to J.-J. Marchand and his colleagues.

2. N. Machiavelli, *Legazioni. Commissarie. Scritti di governo*, vol. 1 (1498–1500), ed. J.-J. Marchand (Rome: Edizione Nazionale delle Opere di Machiavelli, 2002), pp. 17–18.

3. Ibid., p. 20.

4. *Ghiribizzi al Soderino*, Machiavelli to Giovan Battista Soderini, 13–21 September 1502, in Atkinson and Sices, *Machiavelli and His Friends*, p. 135.

5. *Legazioni. Commissarie. Scritti di governo*, 1:23.

6. Ibid., vol. 2 (1501–1503), ed. F. Chiappelli, with the collaboration of J.-J. Marchand (Rome: Laterza, 1973), p. 11.

7. *Legazioni. Commissarie. Scritti di governo*, vol. 2 (1501–1503), ed. E. Cutinelli-Réndina (Rome: Edizione Nazionale delle Opere di Machiavelli, 2003), pp. 82–83.

8. Machiavelli to Vettori, 10 December 1513, in *Works*, 2:930.

9. Ibid., 9 April 1513, in *Works*, 2:900.

10. *Works*, 1:57.

11. *Opere*, 1:26–31.

12. *Works*, 1:333.

13. See E. Fasano Guarini, "Gli statuti delle città soggette a Firenze tra '400 e '500: Riforme locali e interventi centrali," in *Statuti, città, territori in Italia e Germania tra Medioevo ed Età moderna*, ed. G. Chittolini and D. Willoweit (Bologna: il Mulino, 1991), pp. 69–124.

14. Ibid., p. 24. On these issues, see the doctoral thesis of A. Guidi, "L'esperienza cancelleresca di Niccolò Machiavelli. L'Arte dello Stato' e la milizia nei dispacci della Cancelleria fiorentina," Istituto di Studi Umanistici di Firenze, 2008.

CHAPTER 5. Diplomatic Activity

1. *Opere*, 2:622–28.

2. Always of value are the comments of F. Chabod, "Alle origini dello Stato moderno," in *Scritti sul Rinascimento* (Turin: Einaudi,

1967), pp. 625–50. See also A. Tenenti, "La nozione di 'stato' nell'Italia del Rinascimento," in *Stato: Un'idea, una logica; Dal comune italiano all'assolutismo francese* (Bologna: il Mulino, 1987), pp. 53–97. I also refer the reader to my appendix here, "Notes Concerning the Use of the Word *Stato* in Machiavelli."

3. See G. Mattingly, *Renaissance Diplomacy* (Harmondsworth, UK: Penguin Books, 1955).

4. See A. Fontana, "Les ambassadeurs après 1494: La diplomatie et la politique nouvelles," in *Cahiers de la Renaissance Italienne* (Paris: Presses de la Sorbonne Nouvelle, 1995), esp. pp. 164–65.

5. *Discourses* 3.39, in *Works*, 1:516.

6. *Opere*, 1:729–32.

7. See Mattingly, *Renaissance Diplomacy*, pp. 201ff.

CHAPTER 6. The Experience of the Early Missions

1. *The Prince*, chap. 3, in *Works*, 1:20. This statement, which in the text evidently refers to foreign policy reports, was used in general terms by the French anti-Machiavellian movement in the second half of the sixteenth century to accuse the Italians at the court of Catherine de' Medici of wishing to alter, with their immoral maxims, the laws on which the kingdom was founded; see P. Carta, "I fuorusciti italiani e l'antimachiavellismo," in *Francesco Guicciardini fra diritto e politica* (Padua: Cedam, 2008), pp. 159ff.

2. See. E. Cutinelli-Réndina, *Chiesa e religione in Machiavelli* (Pisa: Istituti editoriali e tipografici, 1998).

3. *Opere*, 1:126.

4. Ibid., pp. 4–7.

5. Ibid., pp. 56–68 and 77–84.

6. "Rapporto di cose della Magna," translated as "Second Report on the Affairs of Germany," in *The Historical, Political and Diplomatic Writings of Niccolo Macchiavelli*, trans. C. E. Detmold, vol. 4 (Boston: James R. Osgood and Company, 1882).

7. *Works*, 1:163–69; for the report to the signory of Florence, see *Opere*, 2:801–5.

8. *Works*, 2:962.

9. *Opere*, 2:1703.
10. Detmold, trans., *Writings of Niccolo Macchiavelli*, 3:144.
11. Ibid., p. 259.
12. *Opere*, 2:804.
13. *The Prince*, chap. 7, in *Works*, 1:31.

CHAPTER 7. Changes of Fortune and the *Ghiribizzi al Soderino*

1. Detmold, trans., *Writings of Niccolo Macchiavelli*, 4:10.
2. *Discourses* 27, in *Works*, 1:255.
3. The text, which has come down to us via the transcription of Giuliano de' Ricci, was titled, until the rediscovery of the signature, "Ghiribizzi scripti in Raugia al Soderino," and the lines were therefore thought to have been addressed to the ex-gonfalonier Pier Soderini, who upon the return of the Medici to Florence in 1512 had taken refuge at Ragusa, the mercantile republic on the Adriatic (see Ridolfi, *Vita*, pp. 477–78). The reading of the signature allows us to understand that *Ghiribizzi* had been "written in Perugia"— addressed not to Ragusa but to Soderino, who was not Piero but his nephew Giovan Battista—in reply to Giovan Battista's letter of 12 September 1506 (see Atkinson and Sices, *Machiavelli and His Friends*, p. 133).
4. G. Sasso, "Qualche osservazione sui 'Ghiribizzi al Soderini,'" in *Machiavelli e gli antichi ed altri saggi*, vol. 2 (Milan: Ricciardi, 1988), p. 12.
5. On the assertion of Ptolemy and its implications, see E. Garin, "Aspetti del pensiero di Machiavelli," in *Dal Rinascimento all'Illuminismo: Studi e ricerche* (Pisa: Nistri-Lischi, 1970), pp. 57ff.
6. *Discourses* 1.56, in *Works*, 1:311. Also Francesco Guicciardini, in his *Ricordi: Counsels and Reflections of Francesco Guicciardini*, ed. G. R. Berridge (Leicester, UK: Allandale Online Publishing, 2000), wrote: "That spirits do exist may, I believe, be affirmed. I mean what we call spirits, that is to say, certain airy beings conversing famil-

iarly with men. For I myself have had such proof of their existence as makes it seem to me past a doubt" (p. 211).

7. L. Febvre, *Il problema dell'incredulità nel secolo XVI: La religione di Rabelais* (Turin: Einaudi, 1978).

8. Atkinson and Sices, *Machiavelli and His Friends*, p. 103. Valuable information on Bartolomeo Vespucci can be found in Sasso, *Qualche osservazione sui "Ghiribizzi,"* pp. 32ff.

9. E. Garin (*Astrology in the Renaissance: The Zodiac of Life*, trans. Carolyn Jackson and June Allen, translation revised in conjunction with the author by Clare Robertson [London: Routledge & Kegan Paul, 1984], p. 20) records that at San Marco, Savonarola's convent, a manuscript belonging to Cosimo de' Medici, the *Introductorium maius in astronomiam* by Albumasar, the great astrologer of Baghdad, was preserved; the manuscript states the impossibility of altering the determination of the planets and negates any choice by man or his initiative on their influence. We may doubt whether Machiavelli had direct knowledge of this text, but similar ideas probably circulated outside this cloister.

10. *Works*, 2:624.

CHAPTER 8. The Florentine Ordinance

1. See C. Dionisotti, "Machiavelli, Cesare Borgia e don Micheletto," in *Machiavellerie*, pp. 3–59.

2. Atkinson and Sices, *Machiavelli and His Friends*, p. 107.

3. Dionisotti, *Machiavellerie*, p. 17.

4. F. Guicciardini, *The History of Florence*, trans. and ed. Mario Domandi (New York: Harper & Row, 1970), p. 258.

5. Luca Landucci, *A Florentine Diary from 1450 to 1516*, trans. Alice de Rosen Jervis (New York: Arno Press, 1969), p. 218.

6. Cardinal Francesco Soderini to Machiavelli, 15 December 1606, in Atkinson and Sices, *Machiavelli and His Friends*, p. 150.

7. *Opere*, 1:26–31.

8. *Works*, 2:744.

9. Guicciardini, *History of Florence*, p. 258.

10. Detmold, trans., *Historical, Political and Diplomatic Writings of Niccolo Machiavelli*, 4:158.

11. Ibid., pp. 161–64.

12. *Works*, 2:740.

13. Guicciardini, *History of Florence*, p. 277.

14. Francesco Vettori to the Ten, 8 February 1509, in *Opere*, 2:1099.

15. See "Il Rapporto di cose della Magna," in Detmold, trans., *Writings of Niccolo Machiavelli*, 1:69–77.

CHAPTER 9. The Venetian Defeat and the Reconquest of Pisa

1. In Machiavelli's writings the battle is given the name of another location near the scene of the fighting, namely Vailate (in the texts, Vailà).

2. *Opere*, 2:1170.

3. Detmold, trans., *Writings of Niccolo Machiavelli*, 4:165–66.

4. Ibid., p. 178.

5. Agostino Vespucci to Machiavelli, 8 June 1509, in Atkinson and Sices, *Machiavelli and His Friends*, p. 181 (Nisi crederem te nimis superbire, oserei dire che voi con li vostri battaglioni tam bonam navastis operam ita ut non cunctando sed accelerando restitueritis rem florentinam).

6. *Opere*, 2:1231. Equally, in the *Tercets on Ambition* (v. 132), he wrote: "[Never] before now the sun has looked upon such savagery" (*Works*, 2:738).

7. Detmold, trans., *Writings of Niccolo Machiavelli*, 4:207.

8. *Works*, 2: 736.

9. Machiavelli to Alamanno Salviati, 28 September 1509; addressed to "The Noble Alamanno Salviati, Most Worthy Captain of Pisa, Honored Patron, etc."; the letter can be found in Atkinson and Sices, *Machiavelli and His Friends*, pp. 426ff. See Salviati's reply of October 4 to "My Dear Niccolò Machiavelli," ibid., pp. 186–87.

10. *Works*, 2:739.

CHAPTER 10. The End of the Republic and the Return of the Medici

1. Machiavelli to the Ten, 1 December 1509, in Detmold, trans., *Writings of Niccolo Machiavelli*, 4:211.

2. Guicciardini, *History of Italy*, p. 46.

3. Pier Soderini to Machiavelli, 20 June 1510, in Detmold, trans., *Writings of Niccolo Machiavelli*, 4:221.

4. See A. Renaudet, *Le concile gallican de Pise-Milan: Documents florentins (1510–1512)* (Paris: Champion, 1922).

5. The work of A. Renaudet is essential on these issues; see his *Préréforme et humanisme à Paris pendant les premières guerres d'Italie (1494–1517)*, 2nd ed. (Paris: Librairie d'Argences, 1953).

6. *Discourses* 2.15, in *Works*, 1:361.

7. Machiavelli to "a lady," Florence, after 16 September 1512, in *Works*, 2:890–95. The identification of the "gentildonna" [lady] as Isabella d'Este is by B. Richardson; see "La 'lettera a una gentildonna' del Machiavelli," *La bibliofilia* 84 (1982): 271–76.

8. *Opere*, 1:87–89.

CHAPTER 11. The Confinement at Sant'Andrea

1. On 13 March 1513 Machiavelli immediately told Francesco Vettori of his liberation; see *Works*, 2:898.

2. Vettori to Machiavelli, 30 December 1514, in Atkinson and Sices, *Machiavelli and His Friends*, p. 307.

3. Machiavelli to Vettori, 18 March 1513, in *Works*, 2:898.

4. Machiavelli to Vettori, 13 March 1513, ibid., p. 898.

5. "By the Blessed Spirits," in *Works*, 2:880.

6. For this exchange of letters, which lasted from 9 April to 26 August 1513, see Atkinson and Sices, *Machiavelli and His Friends*, pp. 228–60, and *Works*, 2:900–26. On this correspondence and the subsequent one of 1513 in connection with *The Prince*, see F. Chabod, "Sulla composizione de 'Il Principe,' " in *Scritti su Machiavelli* (Turin: Einaudi, 1964), pp. 177ff.

CHAPTER 12. "I have composed a little work *On Princedoms*"

1. "Io ho, Giuliano, in gamba un paio di geti" (I have, Giuliano, on my legs a set of fetters) and "In questa notte, pregando le Muse" (Last night, beseeching the Muses), in *Works*, 2:1013–15. Later he wrote a third sonnet to Giuliano, about sending thrushes (ibid., p. 1014), probably in the autumn of 1514. H. Jaeckel and R. Fubini, in "I 'Tordi' e il 'Principe Nuovo': Note sulle dediche del 'Principe' di Machiavelli a Giuliano e a Lorenzo de' Medici, e Postilla ai 'Tordi,' " *Archivio storico italiano* 156 (1998): 73–92 and 93–96, suggested that the sonnets masked the gift of the prince. We cannot discount the fact that the relationship with Giuliano dates from the last days of Lorenzo the Magnificent; see the article by Martelli, "Preistoria (medicea) di Machiavelli."

2. After his exit from prison he wrote, on 18 March 1513, of having to owe "all of life that is left me . . . to the Magnificent Giuliano de' Medici and your Pagolo," and on April 16: "His Magnificence Giuliano will come there, and you will naturally find a chance to do me good."

3. *The Prince*, chap. 26, in *Works*, 1:93.

4. See F. Gilbert, "The Humanist Concept of *The Prince* and *The Prince* of Machiavelli," *Journal of Modern History* 11, no. 4 (December 1939): 449–83.

5. See D. Quaglioni, "Il modello del principe cristiano: Gli 'specula principum' fra Medio Evo e prima Età Moderna," in *Modelli nella storia del pensiero politico, a cura di V. I. Comparato* (Florence: L. S. Olschki, 1988), 1:103–22.

6. Atkinson and Sices, *Machiavelli and His Friends*, p. 233.

7. A general summary of the inaccuracies and errors in the references in *Discourses on the First Decade of Titus Livius* can be found in M. Martelli, *Machiavelli e gli storici antichi* (Rome: Salerno, 1998).

8. See J.-L. Fournel, "Retorica della guerra, retorica dell'emergenza nella Firenze repubblicana," *Giornale critico della filosofia italiana* 2, no. 3 (September–December 2006): 389–411.

9. See his letter quoted in the introduction to my *Discorsi sopra la prima deca di Tito Livio* (Turin: Einaudi, 2000), p. xxiii.

10. See Ridolfi, *Vita di Niccolò Machiavelli*, p. 620, and Sasso, *Niccolò Machiavelli*, 1:330.

11. Atkinson and Sices, *Machiavelli and His Friends*, p. 261.

12. *Works*, 2:927–931.

13. See F. Chabod, "Del 'Principe' di Niccolò Machiavelli," in *Scritti su Machiavelli* (Turin: Einaudi, 1964), pp. 29ff. and esp. p. 35n3, and F. Meinecke, "Anhang zur Einführung," in *Der Fürst und kleinere Schriften*, ed. Meinecke (Berlin: R. Hobbing, 1923).

14. "Il 'Principe' ebbe due redazioni?" now in Sasso, *Machiavelli e gli antichi*, 2:197–276.

CHAPTER 13. The "Myth" of *The Prince*

1. Selections from the *Prison Notebooks of Antonio Gramsci*, ed. and trans. Quintin Hoare and Geoffrey Nowell Smith (London: Lawrence and Wishart, 1971), p. 125.

2. The comments by G. Chittolini are always valuable; see *La formazione dello stato regionale e le istituzioni del contado: Secoli XIV e XV* (Turin: Einaudi, 1979).

3. It is best to remember that, in the course of the Wars of Religion in France, anti-Machiavellian writers, without taking into consideration the appreciation of the "good constitutions" of that kingdom (*Opere*, 1:169, 316, 419ff.), read those observations "as an incitement to install in France too a regime in line with the Turkish one." See Procacci, *Machiavelli nella cultura europea*, pp. 174–75.

4. *The Prince*, chap. 6, in *Works*, 1:25.

5. *Works*, chap. 8, 1:38.

6. Ibid., 3:1345.

7. Detmold, trans., *Writings of Niccolò Machiavelli*, 4:409.

8. See, in particular, *A Discourse on Remodeling the Government of Florence*, in *Works*, 1:101–15.

9. Ibid., p. 421.

10. Ibid., p. 43.

11. Sasso, "Il 'Principe' ebbe due redazioni?"

12. *Works*, 1:47.

13. Commines, *Memoirs*, p. 153.

14. G. Inglese, "Il *Principe (De Principatibus)* di Niccolò Machiavelli," in *Letteratura italiana: Le opere*, ed. A. Asor Rosa, vol. 1 (Turin: Einaudi, 1992), p. 914.

15. B. Croce, "Machiavelli e Vico," in *Elementi di politica* (1925), then reprinted in *Etica e politica* (Bari: Laterza, Bari 1931), esp. pp. 251--53.

16. *The Prince*, chap. 17, in *Works*, 1:61.

17. Guicciardini, *History of Italy* (bk. 6, chap. 4).

18. *Works*, 1:58.

19. Ibid., p. 67.

20. *Aeneid* 1.563.

21. D. Cantimori, "Niccolò Machiavelli: Il politico e lo storico," in *Storia della letteratura italiana*, ed. E. Cecchi and N. Sapegno, vol. 4, *Il Cinquecento* (Milan: Garzanti, 1966), pp. 38–39.

22. This observation is by Procacci, *Machiavelli nella cultura europea*, esp. pp. 36ff, which refer to S. Seidel Menchi's *Erasmo in Italia* (Turin: Bollati Boringhieri, 1987).

23. In *History of Florence* (1.9), Machiavelli recalled how the popes, through the misuse of excommunication and arms, had rendered excommunication ineffectual (after Luther's revolt against indulgences) and were at the mercy of other powers when it came to arming themselves.

24. E. Garin, *Italian Humanism: Philosophy and Civic Life in the Renaissance*, trans. Peter Munz (Oxford: Basil Blackwell, 1965), p. 221. See also D. Cantimori, "Retorica e politica nell'Umanesimo italiano," now an appendix to *Eretici italiani del Cinquecento* (Turin: Einaudi, 1992), pp. 485–511.

25. *Works*, 3:1461, vv. 182–83. The *Second Decennale* was written at a time very close to that of *The Prince*: 1514 or 1515.

26. *Works*, 1:89 (chapter 24).

CHAPTER 14. Frequenting the Orti Oricellari

1. Ibid., 2:945.
2. See Ridolfi, *Vita di Niccolò Machiavelli*, p. 254 (the warning, issued by Cardinal Giulio de' Medici, is dated 15 February 1515).
3. On this work, see in particular G. Sasso, "L'Asino: Una satira antidantesca," in *Machiavelli e gli antichi*, 4:39–128, in which Sasso discusses and rejects the hypothesis, advanced in 1920 by L. F. Benedetto and taken up in 1990 by M. Martelli, of a beginning date of 1512, immediately after the fall of the republic.
4. *The [Golden] Ass*, chap. 1, lines 46ff., in *Works*, 3:751.
5. This is why Giuliano de' Ricci did not make copies of the play, which was then lost; see O. Tommasini, *La vita e gli scritti di Niccolò Machiavelli nella loro relazione col machiavellismo* (Rome: Loescher, 1911), 2:305n.
6. *Works*, 2:898.
7. Ibid., p. 752.
8. Ibid., p. 770.
9. Ibid., p. 777.
10. See Gilbert, Bernardo Rucellai and the Orti Oricellari.
11. *Discourses*, bk. 2, preface, in *Works*, 1:324. The preceding quotations are from the dedication to *Discourses*, in *Works*, 1:188–89.
12. *The Art of War*, vol. 7, in *Works*, 2:726.

CHAPTER 15. An Original Comment on Livy

1. Dionisotti, *Machiavellerie*, pp. 233ff. The observation of G. Inglese could approach this interpretation; while highlighting that the *Discourses* cannot "indicate any authentic model," Inglese notes: "Machiavelli experiments with a kind of brilliant crossroads between the treatment of political material, ordered by theme, and humanist comment, as a continuous series of glosses to the texts of the classics." See G. Inglese, *Per Machiavelli: L'arte dello stato, la cognizione delle storie* (Rome: Carocci, 2006), p. 97.

2. An interesting comparison of the case records of lawyers and doctors in an effort to show the methodical work that led Machiavelli to follow the diagnostic procedures of doctors is by L. Zanzi, *I "segni" della natura e i "paradigm" della storia: Il metodo del Machiavelli; Ricerche sulla logica scientifica degli "umanisti" tra medicina e storiografia* (Manduria: Lacaita, 1981) (I owe this citation to my friend L. Perini, whom I thank).

3. I. Calvino, *Six Memos for the Next Millennium*, trans. Patrick Creagh (London: Vintage, 1996), p. 116.

4. *Discourses* 1.4, in *Works*, 1:202.

5. Ibid., 1.2, *Works*, 1:197.

6. Ibid., 2.2, *Works*, 1:333.

7. This quotation and the following ones are ibid., 2.2, *Works*, 1:332.

8. Ibid., 1.11, *Works*, 1:225.

9. Ibid., 1.18, *Works*, 1:243.

10. Ibid., 1.55, *Works*, 1:307.

11. Ibid., 1.37, *Works*, 1:272.

12. Ibid., 3.25, *Works*, 1:486.

13. These statements were immediately refuted by Machiavelli's earliest critics. Thus, the first evidence of anti-Machiavellism is found in the work of Juan Ginés de Sepúlveda, the historian and chaplain of Charles V (then tutor to his son Philip), who in 1535, naturally without considering the link Machiavelli made between liberty and strength of mind, contested these observations, writing how the idea of the Crusade had been inspired by the Spanish reconquest. See Procacci, *Machiavelli nella cultura europea*, pp. 85–87.

14. As G. Procacci observed in the introduction to N. Machiavelli, *Il Principe e Discorsi sopra la prima deca di Tito Livio*, ed. S. Bertelli (Milan: Feltrinelli, 1960), p. lx, "Religion, in the sense of the Latin word 'religio,' does not only link men to one god or several gods, but essentially links men to one another."

15. Cf. I. Berlin, "The Originality of Machiavelli," in *Studies on Machiavelli*, ed. M. P. Gilmore (Florence: Sansoni, 1972), pp. 157–206.

16. *Discourses* 1.55, in *Works*, 1:308–9.

17. Ibid. 3:9, in *Works*, 1:453.

18. Guicciardini, *Ricordi*, p. 98.

19. The classsic work of F. Meinecke, *L'idea della ragion di stato nella storia moderna* (1924), trans. Dino Scolari (Florence: Sansoni, 1942), begins with this research. B. Croce, in *Storia dell'età barocca* (Bari: Laterza, 1953), pp. 75–76, places the comments of the Florentine secretary under the heading of reason of state.

20. Thus A. Prosperi, *Tribunali della coscienza: Inquisitori, confessori, missionari* (Turin: Einaudi, 1996), pp. xix–xx.

21. G. Botero, *Della ragion di stato*, ed. C. Morandi (Bologna: Cappelli, 1930), p. 9.

22. Viroli, *Machiavelli's God*, pp. 6–7.

23. Ridolfi, *Vita di Niccolò Machiavelli*, p. 258.

CHAPTER 16. *The Art of War*

1. *The Art of War*, in *Works*, 2:566.

2. Giovanni Salviati to Machiavelli, 6 September 1521, in Atkinson and Sices, *Machiavelli and His Friends*, p. 342.

3. *The Art of War*, in *Works*, 2:567.

4. Ibid., p. 576.

5. Ibid., pp. 723–25.

6. Ibid., p. 725.

7. *The Art of War*, in *Works*, 2:726.

CHAPTER 17. A New Season in Machiavelli's Life

1. Machiavelli to Giovanni Vernacci, 15 February 1516, in *Works*, 2:964. The quotation (as capitalized) in the title of part 3 (see above) is from Machiavelli to Guicciardini, after 21 October 1525, in *Works*, 2:987.

2. Ridolfi, *Vita di Niccolò Machavelli*, p. 264.

3. The date established by Ridolfi, ibid., pp. 532–35, is confirmed, as that scholar has noted, in the scene between Frate Timoteo and a widow (3.3), where the latter expresses the fear that the Turk may enter Italy, a fear that had spread toward the end of 1517.

4. Tommasini, *La vita e gli scritti di Niccolò Machiavelli,* 2:305n.

5. Machiavelli to Vettori, 31 January 1515, in *Works,* 2:961.

6. E. Raimondi, *Politica e commedia* (Bologna: il Mulino, 1972).

7. See G. Aquilecchia, "La favola Mandragola si chiama," in *Schede di italianistica* (Turin: Einaudi, 1976), pp. 102ff.

8. See C. Ginzburg, "Machiavelli, l'eccezione e la regola," 197ff.

9. The success of *The Mandrake* was spectacular in Venice, where for three evenings in February 1522 the performance had to be stopped, "such was the great number of people," wrote M. Sanudo in *I diarii* (Venice: Visentini, 1879–1903), vol. 32, cols. 458 and 466. In 1526 the performance of the *Menaechmi* by Plautus, staged by a company of Venetian gentlemen, was abandoned because it was being performed at the same time as the *Comedia de Callimaco* (*Opere,* 2:417).

10. Recently, however, P. Stoppelli, in *Machiavelli e la novella di Belfagor* (Rome: Salerno, 2007), has advanced the hypothesis, based on Machiavelli's handwriting, that the novella dates from 1525–26.

11. M. Bandello, *Novelle,* in *Tutte le opere di Matteo Bandello,* ed. Francesco Flora, 2 vols. (Milan: Mondadori, 1952), 1:40.

12. *Opere,* vol. 3 (2005), p. 78.

13. Ibid., pp. 159ff.

14. Machiavelli refers to this request for a length of camel-hair cloth in his letter to his nephew Giovanni Vernacci dated 8 June 1517 (*Works,* 2:966). On Machiavelli's love life, including the suggestion that he had homosexual relations, see M. Martelli, "Machiavelli politico, amante, poeta," *Interpres* 17 (1998): 211–56.

CHAPTER 18. A Return to Business

1. Battista della Palla to Machiavelli, 26 April 1520, in Atkinson and Sices, *Machiavelli and His Friends,* pp. 324–25.

2. *A Discourse on Remodeling the Government of Florence*, in *Works*, 1:101–3.

3. Ibid., p. 103.

4. Ibid., p. 104.

5. Ibid.

6. R. von Albertini, *Firenze dalla repubblica al principato* (Turin: Einaudi, 1970), pp. 376–84.

7. *Works*, 2:966–68. It is the letter in which Machiavelli wrote to him: "I have just been reading *Orlando Furioso* by Ariosto, and truly the poem is beautiful, and in many places is wonderful. If he is there, give him my regards, and tell him I am sorry only that, having spoken of so many poets [at the end of the poem], he has left me out like a dog."

8. See the letters and documents published as an appendix to the tragedy by G. B. Niccolini, *Filippo Strozzi*, ed. P. Bigazzi (Florence: Le Monnier, 1847). The letter cited is on pp. 183–84.

CHAPTER 19. "The annals or the history of Florence"

1. The chapter title is from Machiavelli to Francesco Del Nero, about 8 November 1520, in *Works*, 2:971.

2. Battista della Palla to Machiavelli, 26 April 1520, in Atkinson and Sices, *Machiavelli and His Friends*, p. 325.

3. This is "the substance of the contract" that Machiavelli mentioned to his brother-in-law Francesco Del Nero, chief administrator of the Florentine Studio, or university. See Atkinson and Sices, *Machiavelli and His Friends*, p. 329.

4. Ibid., p. 334. For *fiorini di suggello*, see Totto Machiavelli to Niccolò Machiavelli, 27 August 1500, in Atkinson and Sices, *Machiavelli and His Friends*, pp. 438–20n2. We should remember that Machiavelli, in his letter to Vettori dated 10 June 1514—where, once again disappointed at not being able to obtain some job from the Medici, had written: "I shall continue, then, among my lousy doings"—had hinted at the eventuality of being "forced" to "become secretary to a constable" (*Works*, 2:945).

5. *Works*, 3:1463.

6. Machiavelli probably wrote the *Dialogo intorno alla nostra lingua* in 1524. Dionisotti noted this in *Machiavellerie*, p. 379.

7. Thus Machiavelli himself mentioned "the substance of the contract" to Francesco Del Nero in the letter he sent to him in the autumn of 1520 (Atkinson and Sices, *Machiavelli and His Friends*, p. 329).

8. *Works*, 2:978.

9. See L. A. Ferrai, "Lettere inedite di Donato Giannotti," in *Atti dell'Istituto Veneto di Scienze, Lettere ed Arti* 6, no. 3 (1884–1885): 1570ff.

10. Atkinson and Sices, *Machiavelli and His Friends*, pp. 354–55.

11. Ibid.

CHAPTER 20. "The things done at home and abroad by the Florentine people"

1. The chapter title is from the preface to *The History of Florence*, in *Works*, 3:1030.

2. F. Gilbert, "Istorie fiorentine di Machiavelli," in *Machiavelli e il suo tempo*, pp. 291–318 (esp. pp. 309ff.), and Dionisotti, *Machiavellerie*, p. 392.

3. On Machiavelli's intention to continue *The History of Florence* and on the absence of any text that might have come down to us, see Ridolfi, *Vita di Machiavelli*, pp. 350 and 578–79n17.

4. *Works*, 3:1031.

5. See E. Garin's preface to *Storie fiorentine*, by L. Bruni and P. Bracciolini (1476; repr., Arezzo: Biblioteca della Città di Arezzo, 1984).

6. *A Discourse on Remodeling the Government of Florence*, in *Works*, 1:101.

7. *Discourses* 1.49, in *Works*, 1:296.

8. *Opere*, 1:737.

9. *History of Florence* 3.1, in *Works*, 3:1140.

10. Ibid. 3.5, in *Works*, 3:1145.

11. Ibid., in *Works*, 3:1032.

12. Ibid., in *Works*, 3:1080.

13. Ibid. 2.1, in *Works*, 3:1080–81.

14. Giovanni Villani, *Selections from the First Nine Books of the Croniche fiorentine of Giovanni Villani*, trans. Rose E. Selfe, ed. Philip H. Wicksteed (Westminster, UK: Archibald Constable, 1896).

15. *History of Florence* 3.5, in *Works*, 3:1187.

16. Ibid., in *Works*, 3:1232.

17. Ibid., in *Works*, 3:1233.

18. Ibid., in *Works*, 3:1073: "Giovan Galeazzo Visconti killed Bernabò his uncle and seized all of the territory of Milan; and since it was not enough for him to have become Duke of all Lombardy, he wished also to conquer Tuscany. But when he thought he was about to get control and then to be crowned King of Italy, he died." Gian Galeazzo is spoken about in similar terms in the third book (ibid., p. 1179).

19. See the classic work by Baron, *Crisis of the Early Italian Renaissance*.

20. Ibid., p. 1383.

21. *Works*, 1:431.

22. Ibid., 3:1383–84.

23. Francesco Guicciardini discussed similar ideas in his *History of Florence*, written between 1508 and 1512 (but unpublished), observing that, following the Pazzi plot, Lorenzo "acted as free and complete arbiter, indeed almost as lord of the city." He saw this as the way

> civil discord and strife end: the one side is exterminated, the head of the other becomes lord of the city. His supporters and adherents, once companions, become almost subjects; the people and the multitude become slaves; power is passed on by inheritance, and very often it passes from a wise man [Lorenzo] to a madman [Piero] who then plunges the city into the abyss. (P. 36)

24. See P. Larivaille, "Sul ritratto machiavelliano di Lorenzo il Magnifico nel capitolo finale delle 'Istorie fiorentine,'" in *Laurentia Laurus*. *Per Mario Martelli*, ed. F. Bausi and V. Fera (Messina: Centro interdipartimentale di studi umanistici, 2004), pp. 11–37.

25. E. Fueter, *Storia della storiografia moderna*, trans. Altiero Spinelli (Naples: Ricciardi, 1943), 1:21, 80.

26. F. Gilbert, *Machiavelli e Guicciardini: Pensiero politico e storiografia a Firenze nel Cinquecento* (Turin: Einaudi, 1970), p. 203.

27. P. Villari, *Niccolò Machiavelli e i suoi tempi* (Milan: Hoepli, 1914), 3:238.

28. G. Pedullà, "Il divieto di Platone: Machiavelli e il discorso dell'anonimo plebeo," in *Storiografia repubblicana fiorentina (1494–1570)*, ed. J.-J. Marchand and J.-C. Zancarini (Florence: Franco Cesati Editore, 2003), pp. 209–66.

29. *Works*, 2:662.

30. See Sasso, *Machiavelli e gli antichi*, 3:286–89.

31. "A New Translation of the Discorso o dialogo intorno alla nostra lingua," in *Politics, Patriotism and Language, Niccolò Machiavelli's "Secular Patria" and the Creation of an Italian National Identity*, ed. W. J. Landon (New York: Peter Land Publishing, 2005), p. 129.

32. *Works*, 3:1242.

33. See *Ex libris Karl Marx und Friedrich Engels. Schicksal und Verzeichnis einer Bibliothek*, ed. Institut für Marxismus-Leninismus (Berlin: Dietz, 1967), pp. 136–37, and Villari, *Niccolò Machiavelli*, 3:249.

34. See Pedullà, *Il divieto di Platone*, pp. 247–49, which showed the analogy of the speech of the wool carder with those by Mithradates and Calgacus thanks to A. Schiavone's analysis in *La storia spezzata: Roma antica e l'Occidente moderno* (Rome: Laterza, 1996), pp. 92–93.

35. *Works*, 3:1160–61.

36. Ibid., 1:107–10.

37. Ibid., 3:1079.

38. Cantimori, "Niccolò Machiavelli," p. 51.

CHAPTER 21. The Friendship with Guicciardini

1. Guicciardini's thoughts on such positions are well known; see his *Ricordi*:

> I know no man who feels deeper disgust than I do at the ambition, avarice, and profligacy of the priesthood, as well because every one of these vices is odious in itself, as because each of them separately and all of them together are utterly abhorrent in men making profession of a life dedicated to God. Besides which, these vices are by nature so contrary to one another, that they can coexist only in some monstrous subject. And yet the position I have filled under several Popes has obliged me for personal reasons to desire their greatness. But for this I should have loved Martin Luther as myself: not that I would be loosed from the laws prescribed by the Christian religion as commonly interpreted and understood, but because I long to see this pack of scoundrels brought within due bounds, that is to say, purged of their vices or stripped of their authority. (P. 26)

2. R. Ridolfi, *The Life of Francesco Guicciardini*, trans. C. Grayson (New York: Alfred A. Knopf, 1968), p. 91.

3. *Works*, 2:971–75.

4. Machiavelli to Francesco Guicciardini, 8 May 1521, in *Works*, 2:974.

5. This and the passage previously quoted are in Guicciardini's letter to Machiavelli of 18 May 1521 (Atkinson and Sices, *Machiavelli and His Friends*, pp. 338–39).

6. Ed. Berridge, p. 96.

7. The observation is by Garin, "Aspetti del pensiero di Machiavelli," p. 73, referring to verse 3.15: "Quid est quod est? Ipsum quod fuit."

8. Atkinson and Sices, *Machiavelli and His Friends*, pp. 357–60.

CHAPTER 22. *Clizia* and the Musical Madrigals

1. The letter was written between 16 and 20 October 1525; ibid., pp. 367–68.

2. See N. Pirrotta, *Li due Orfei: Da Poliziano a Monteverdi* (Turin: Einaudi, 1975), pp. 143–69 (the musical scores of Machiavelli's madrigals are reproduced in *Opere*, 3:832–41). Important books have been dedicated to these pieces of music: see A. Einstein, *The Italian Madrigal* (Princeton: Princeton University Press, 1949), 1:250–51, and W. Osthoff, *Theatergesang und darstellende Musik* (Tutzing: Schneider, 1968), 1:213–49 (the chapter titled "Verdelot Musik zu Machiavelli-Komödin und das Madrigal") and 2:68.

3. *The Mandrake*, 5.2, and *Clizia*, 5.2 and 4 (*Works*, 2:817, 859, and 862).

4. Filippo de' Nerli to Machiavelli, 22 February 1525, in Atkinson and Sices, *Machiavelli and His Friends*, p. 354 (the last sentence is a quotation from Poliziano, stanza 1, verse 1).

5. D. Giannotti, *Repubblica fiorentina*, ed. G. Silvano (Geneva: Droz, 1990), pp. 208–9.

CHAPTER 23. Final Act

1. *Purgatory* 20, vv. 86–87, in *Works*, 2:987.

2. *Works*, 2:987.

3. Machiavelli to Guicciardini, 15 March 1526, in *Works*, 2:992.

4. See the epigram "Argus" in *Works*, 3:1463.

5. In *History of Italy* l.16, chaps. 14 and 16, Guicciardini mentions the contradictory opinions of the great chancellor Mercurino di Gattinara and Charles de Lannoy, the viceroy of Naples, on the liberation of Francis I.

6. Machiavelli to Guicciardini, 15 March 1526, in *Works*, 2:993–94.

7. Ibid., pp. 997–98.

8. In Ridolfi, *Vita di Machiavelli*, p. 357.

9. *Opere*, 3:18.

10. Machiavelli to Bartolomeo Cavalcanti, about 6 October 1526, in *Works*, 2:1003–6.

11. See *Discorsi* 1:22–23.

12. *Works*, 2:1007.

13. Machiavelli to Vettori, 16 April 1516, ibid., 2:1010. It is the letter in which he declares: "I love my native city more than my soul."

14. See Villari, *Niccolò Machiavelli*, 3:364 and 477.

15. Ibid., pp. 402–3 (the ingredients of the pills).

16. Giovio, *Elogi dei letterati illustri*, p. 259.

17. The most complete account of the dream has come to us via P. Bayle, *Dictionnaire historique et critique*, in the entry "Machiavel," note L:

> He [Machiavelli] saw a small company of poor scoundrels, all in rags, quite starved, ill-favoured, and in short in a very bad plight. He was told that these were the inhabitants of Paradise, of whom it is written, *Beati pauperes, quoniam ipsorum est regnum cœlorum*. After these were retired, an infinite number of grave majestick personages appeared: they seemed sitting in senate, where they were canvassing of very important state affairs; there he saw Plato, Seneca, Plutarch, Tacitus, and others of the like characters. When he demanded who these venerable gentlemen were, he was informed that they were the damned, the souls of the reprobated, *Sapientia huius sæculi inimica est Dei*. After this he was asked to which of those companies he would choose to belong. He answered he would much rather go to hell with those great genius's [*sic*] to converse with them about affairs of state, than be condemned to the company of such lousy scoundrels as they had presented to him before. (The translation is from the *General Dictionary, Historical and Critical*, vol. 7, ed. Thomas Birch et al. [London, 1738])

18. See G. Milanesi, ed., *Lettere di G. B. Busini a B. Varchi* (Florence: Le Monnier, 1860), pp. 82–83 (letter of 23 January 1549), and B. Varchi, *Storie fiorentine* (Rome: Edizioni di storia e letteratura, 2003), p. 266n4. On the dream, see G. Sasso, "Il 'celebrato sogno' di Machiavelli," in *Machiavelli e gli antichi*, vol. 3 (Milan: Ricciardi, 1988), pp. 211–300.

19. Sasso, "Il 'celebrato sogno,' " p. 271.

20. Villari, *Niccolò Machiavelli*, 3:368–70.

21. *Works*, 2:558.

APPENDIX: Notes on the Use of the Word *Stato* in Machiavelli

1. N. Bobbio, "Della libertà dei moderni comparata a quella dei posteri," in *Politica e cultura* (Turin: Einaudi, 1955), p. 186.

2. É. Garnier-Pagès, *Dictionnaire politique* (Paris: Pagnerre, Paris), under the entry "État."

3. The text taken from the university course of F. Chabod is particularly effective; see *Alle origini dello stato moderno* (prior to 1956–57), reprinted in his *Scritti sul Rinascimento*, pp. 625–50. The analysis by F. Chiappelli is exemplary; see *Studi sul linguaggio del Machiavelli*, pp. 59–73. See also F. Ercole, *La politica di Machiavelli* (Rome: Anonima Romana Editoriale, 1926), esp. pp. 65–96, and O. Condorelli, "Per la storia del nome 'stato' (Il nome 'stato' in Machiavelli)," *Archivio giuridico Filippo Serafini*, s. 4, vol. 5 (1923), pp. 223–35, and 6 (1924), pp. 77–112. Hannah Arendt, in *Sulla rivoluzione* (1963; repr., Milan: Comunità, 1983), p. 37, notes that the term *stato* in Machiavelli's time was new but had been used before; she writes that it derives from *status rei publicæ*, meaning "form of government," adding that in this sense it also occurs in Bodin's *Method for the Easy Comprehension of History*..

4. *Works*, 1:16–17.

5. E. Garin observes that this deals with a Hippocratic theme (*Rinascite e rivoluzioni: Movimenti culturali dal XIV al XVIII sec-*

olo [Bari: Laterza, 1975], p. 136), a topic taken up by L. B. Alberti (*Theogenius*, in *Opere volgari*, ed. Grayson, 2:87ff.).

6. The hypothesis of F. Chabod, "Sulla composizione de 'Il Principe' di Niccolò Machiavelli" (1927), in his *Scritti su Machiavelli*, pp. 139–93, starts form the declaration in the letter of 10 December 1513 to Francesco Vettori, in which Machiavelli informed Vettori of having "composed a little work on princedoms." M. Martelli, in "Da Poliziano a Machiavelli: Sull'epigramma 'dell'Occasione' e sull'occasione," *Interpres* 2 (1979): 230–54, has, however, maintained that the work had been revised and readjusted in 1518. In 1981 a widely argued reply appeared: G. Sasso, "Il 'Principe' ebbe due redazioni?" (now in his *Machiavelli e gli antichi*, 1:197–276), which picked up Chabod's hypothesis and noted the possibility that the author, pointing out in his letter the modifications and corrections that he was making ("I am still enlarging and revising it"), had worked on *The Prince* until May 1514. Martelli, however, reiterated his opinion in the Convention of Lausanne in September 1995. The acts of this convention have been published; see *Niccolò Machiavelli politico, storico, letterato, nella relazione Machiavelli e Firenze dalla repubblica al principato*, ed. J.-J. Marchand (Rome: Salerno Editrice, 1996). G. Inglese, in his critical edition of *De principatibus* (Rome: Istituto storico italiano per il Medioevo, 1994), welcomes, however, the arguments of Sasso.

7. N. Bobbio, "Stato," in *Enciclopedia Einaudi* (Turin: Einaudi, 1981), 13:462.

8. See F. Chiappelli, *Nuovi studi sul linguaggio di Machiavelli* (Florence: Le Monnier, 1969), pp. 34–35.

9. *First Decennale*, in *Works*, 3:1446–55.

10. A. Tenenti, "La nozione di 'stato' nell'Italia del Rinascimento," in *Stato: Un'idea, una logica; Dal comune italiano all'assolutismo francese* (Bologna: il Mulino, 1987), pp. 53–97 (the quotations that follow refer respectively to pp. 55, 73, 92, and 96). See, in the same volume, "Archeologia medievale della parola 'Stato,' " pp. 15–52.

11. Chabod, *Scritti sul Rinascimento*, p. 633.

12. The *Concordanza della Commedia di Dante Alighieri*, ed. L. Lovera, with the collaboration of R. Bettarini and A. Mazzarello (Turin: Einaudi, 1975), p. 2311, records six instances with such a meaning. In Petrarch the use of the term already tends to be articulated, as in the "Triumph of Chastity," vv. 136–38: "Then came Virginia, and her father arm'd / With sword and with affection and with wrath / Who changed her state and changed the state of Rome"; *The Triumphs of Petrarch* (Chicago: University of Chicago Press, 1962).

13. In *Memorie di famiglia* by Guicciardini we read: "Our house [here meaning both 'family' and 'lineage'] was for a long time, around 80 years, in a poor condition and, as one commonly says, good citizens. Afterward it rose both in wealth and in status to the point of becoming, above all for the standard of living, one of the foremost families of the city, which it still remains today," in F. Guicciardini, *Ricordi, diari, memorie*, ed. M. Spinella (Rome: Editori Riuniti, 1981), p. 34.

14. Thus, in the preface to the *Dialogo del reggimento di Firenze* of 1525–1526 (quoted from the edition edited and translated by Alison Brown, *Dialogue on the Government of Florence* [Cambridge: Cambridge University Press, 1994]).

15. Jean-Louis Fournel traces a leading profile of the problem in, "Qu'est-ce qu'un homme d'État? Réflexions sur l'écriture autobiographique de Francesco Guicciardini," speech to conference in Verona, 20–22 May 2004, "Vite parallele: Memoria, autobiografia, coscienza di sé e dell'altro."

16. Berridge, ed., *Ricordi*, p. 46.

17. Ibid.

18. *A Discourse on Remodeling the Government of Florence*, in *Works*, 1:110.

19. *The Prince*, chap. 9, in *Works*, 1:39.

20. *History*, in *Works*, 3:1124.

21. The hypothesis is an early one by Tommasini, *La vita e gli scritti di Machiavelli*, 2:518.

22. See the full passage in H. Baron, *The Crisis of the Early Italian Renaissance: Civic Humanism and Republican Liberty in an Age of Classicism and Tyranny* (Princeton: Princeton University Press, 1966), p. 419n21. Baron notes (p. 428) how in 1439 Bruni himself gave a different evaluation, but judged it unnecessary to "ask here whether this change . . . was justified in the light of the first years of the Medicean Principate." We cannot dismiss that to Machiavelli, a celebration that its own author, Bruni, had in the end retracted may have seemed inopportune.

23. On this, see chapter 20 above.

24. E. Garin, *Machiavelli fra politica e storia* (Turin: Einaudi, 1993), p. 11 (the emphasis is mine).

25. Machiavelli had already noted this in the "Ritracto di cose di Francia," in *Opere*, 1:56–57.

26. F. Chabod, *Storia dell'idea d'Europa*, ed. E. Sestan and A. Saitta (Bari: Laterza, 1961), pp. 49–51.

27. Montaigne's observation is a pregnant one (*Essays* 1.26, in *Complete Works of Montaigne*, trans. Donald M Frame [London: Hamish Hamilton, 1957]); it attributes, however, to Plutarch the following observation: "The inhabitants of Asia served one single man because they could not pronounce one single syllable, which is 'No.' "

28. Procacci, *Machiavelli nella cultura europea*, pp. 171ff.

29. Tocqueville stated that Machiavelli's observations were still valid in his own time, even though he held the inveterate prejudices against "his horrible work *The Prince*."

30. A. Gramsci, *Prison Notebooks*, vol. 2, ed. and trans. Joseph A. Buttigieg (New York: Columbia University Press, 2011), pp. 168–69.

31. Chiappelli, *Nuovi studi sul linguaggio di Machiavelli*, p. 35.

32. D. Quaglioni, "Machiavelli e la lingua della giurisprudenza," in *Langues et écritures de la République et de la guerre*, pp. 180–81. Translation from "Prooemium," in *Imperatoris iustiniani institunionum*, vol. 2, trans. John Baron Moyle (Oxford: Clarendon Press, 1883), p. 1.

33. Here Vivanti is subjecting Machiavelli's use of the word *ordine* to an analysis similar to that conducted for *stato* earlier in the appendix. While *stato* in many of its meanings translates directly into English as "state," *ordine* can have a variety of translations, which makes some of the nuances of Vivanti's discussion of the Italian word difficult to render precisely in English.—Trans.

34. Ibid. Of Quaglioni, also see *La giustizia nel Medioevo e nella prima età moderna* (Bologna: il Mulino, 2004), esp. pp. 110–15. C. Ginzburg shows that Machiavelli may have profited in his early education from the legal works owned by his father; see "Machiavelli, l'eccezione e la regola," *Quaderni storici* 112 (2003): 197ff.

35. "Keep the treasury rich, the individual poor" (2.19, in *Works*, 2:378) as one of the principles suggested by "ancient ways." Cfr. G. Sasso, *Niccolò Machiavelli*, vol. 1, *Il pensiero politico* (Bologna: il Mulino, 1993), pp. 536ff.

36. The positive judgment in the revolts of the Roman republic, in opposition to the condemnation pronounced upon these by such a great part of Italian literature, appears peculiar to Machiavelli's thoughts. An antecedent of such an opinion, however, has been identified by G. Pedullà, "La ricomparsa di Dionigi: Niccolò Machiavelli tra Roma e la Grecia," *Storica* 10 (2004): 28, in *The Roman Antiquities of Dionysius of Halicarnassus*, available in Latin translation at the start of the sixteenth century.

37. F. Guicciardini, "Considerazioni intorno ai Discorsi del Machiavelli," in *Discorsi sopra la prima deca di Tito Livio*, by N. Machiavelli, ed. C. Vivanti (Turin: Einaudi, 2000), p. 350.

38. See G. B. Busini, *Lettere . . . a Benedetto Varchi sopra l'assedio di Firenze*, ed. G. Milanesi (Florence: Le Monnier, 1860), pp. 84–85. See also G. Sasso, "Il 'celebrato sogno' di Machiavelli," pp. 211–300. The account of the dream is also in *Opere*, 1:cxxxvi.

39. Filippo Strozzi to Vettori, Rome, 28 January 1531; see "Documenti inediti spettanti alla vita politica e letteraria di Filippo Strozzi," appendix to G.-B. Niccolini's *Filippo Strozzi: Tragedia* (Florence: Le Monnier, 1847), p. 183.

40. See G. Gentile, "L'etica di Machiavelli," in *Studi sul Rinascimento* (Florence: Sansoni, 1936), p. 141. The comparison regarding Machiavelli's prince, builder of a new state, with the artist who creates his own work is debatable. We should nevertheless bear it in mind because from this Burckhardtian vision, Gentile derives his comment on the creative force of the prince, "a force conceived conceptually, outside history and therefore fighting always with the ghost of fortune. . . . And it is necessary to attach the greatest weight to this abstraction—characteristic of the individualism of the Renaissance—to understand Machiavellism fully" (Gentile, "Religione e virtù in Machiavelli," in *Studi sul Rinascimento*, p. 133). I doubt that this comment is valid for *The Prince*; it does not take into account many pages of the *Discourses*.

INDEX